MOBILIZING MONEY

This book examines the origins of modern corporate finance systems during the rapid industrialization period leading up to World War I. The study leads to three sets of conclusions. First, modern financial systems are rooted in the past, are idiosyncratic to specific countries, and are highly path-dependent. Therefore, to understand current financial institutions, we must take stock of the forces at play in the near and distant past: political and regulatory intervention, natural resource endowments, educational institutions, and social and religious beliefs. Second, financial institutions and markets do not create economic growth without significant first steps in industrial development and supporting institutions. The finance-growth relationship also varies over time, as financial and economic developments influence one another and create a feedback mechanism. Third, and most important from the modern-policy standpoint, there is no one-size-fits-all solution to financial system design and industrial development. Having specific types of financial institutions is far less important than developing a strong, stable, and legally protected financial system with a rich diversity of institutions and vibrant markets that can adapt to changing needs.

Caroline Fohlin has served as research professor of economics at Johns Hopkins University, Baltimore, Maryland, since 2005. She previously taught at the California Institute of Technology from 1994 to 2004. Professor Fohlin's research has appeared in journals such as the *Journal of Finance*, *Journal of Economic History*, *Review of Finance*, *Business History*, *Cliometrica*, *Explorations in Economic History*, and the *Economic History Review*. She is the author of *Finance Capitalism and Germany's Rise to Industrial Power* (Cambridge University Press, 2007) and is a research associate at the Center for Japan-U.S. Business and Economic Studies at the Stern School of Business, New York University. Professor Fohlin gave the Bundesbank Lectures in Banking and Finance at the University of Freiburg in 2007 and received the DAAD Prize for Distinguished Scholarship in German and European Studies in 2005.

Japan-U.S. Center UFJ Bank (formerly Sanwa) Monographs on International Financial Markets

The UFJ Bank (formerly Sanwa Bank) has established the UFJ Bank Research Endowment Fund on International Financial Markets at the Center for Japan-U.S. Business and Economic Studies of the Stern School of Business, New York University, to support research on international financial markets. One part of this endowment is used to offer an award for writing a monograph in this field. The award is made annually on a competitive basis by the selection committee, and the winning published titles and proposals are listed below.

1991, Richard C. Marston, University of Pennsylvania. *International Financial Integration: A Study of Interest Differentials Between the Major Industrial Countries*

1992, Willem H. Buiter, University of Cambridge, Giancarlo Corsetti, University of Bologna, and Paolo A. Pesenti, Federal Reserve Bank of New York. *Financial Markets and European Monetary Cooperation: The Lessons of the 1992–1993 Exchange Rate Mechanism Crisis*

1993, Lance E. Davis, California Institute of Technology, and the late Robert E. Gallman, University of North Carolina, Chapel Hill. *Evolving Financial Markets and International Capital Flows: Britain, the Americas, and Australia, 1865–1914*

1994, Piet Sercu, University of Leuven, and Raman Uppal, London Business School. *Exchange Rate Volatility, Trade, and Capital Flows under Alternative Exchange Rate Regimes*

1995, Robert P. Flood, International Monetary Fund, and Peter M. Garber, Brown University. *Speculative Attacks on Fixed Exchange Rates*

1996, Maurice Obstfeld, University of California, Berkeley, and Alan M. Taylor, University of California, Davis. *Global Capital Markets: Integration, Crisis, and Growth*

1997, Pravin Krishna, Johns Hopkins University. *Trade Blocs: Economics and Politics*

1998, Kose John, New York University. *Corporate Governance and Agency Problems: Theory and Empirical Evidence*

(*continued after index*)

Mobilizing Money

*How the World's Richest Nations Financed
Industrial Growth*

CAROLINE FOHLIN
Johns Hopkins University

CAMBRIDGE
UNIVERSITY PRESS

CAMBRIDGE
UNIVERSITY PRESS

32 Avenue of the Americas, New York NY 10013-2473, USA

Cambridge University Press is part of the University of Cambridge.

It furthers the University's mission by disseminating knowledge in the pursuit of education, learning, and research at the highest international levels of excellence.

www.cambridge.org
Information on this title: www.cambridge.org/9780521810210

First published 2012
Reprinted 2014

A catalog record for this publication is available from the British Library.

Library of Congress Cataloging in Publication data
Fohlin, Caroline, 1966–
Mobilizing money : how the world's richest nations financed industrial growth / Caroline Fohlin.
    p. cm. – (Japan-US Center UFJ Bank monographs on international financial markets)
Includes bibliographical references and index.
ISBN 978-0-521-81021-0
1. Banks and banking – History.   2. Financial institutions – History.   3. Investments – History.   I. Title.
HG1551.F64   2012
332.1–dc22   2011015308

ISBN 978-0-521-81021-0 Hardback

To Benjamin, Helen, and Theodore
and to John, again, as always

Contents

Figures and Tables   *page* x

Acknowledgments   xiii

1. Introduction   1

PART I   FIVE SUCCESS STORIES

2. Creating Corporate Finance Systems   15

3. Organizing Commercial Banking   48

4. Governing Corporations   84

5. Financing Industrial Investment   112

PART II   THE BIGGER PICTURE

6. Classifying Financial Systems   139

7. What Shapes Financial Structure?   166

8. Does Financial Structure Drive Industrial Growth?   191

9. What Is Important for Long-Term Growth?   222

References   231

Index   257

Figures and Tables

FIGURES

3.1. Ratio of deposits to capital and reserves   *page* 67
3.2. Cash-deposit ratios   73
3.3a. Return on assets, 1880–1925   78
3.3b. Return on equity, 1880–1913   79
8.1. GDP per capita growth, 1870–1900 and 1900–1913   194
8.2. GDP per capita, 1850 and 1913   195
8.3. Log GDP per capita in 1870 versus growth rate for 1870–1994   196
8.4. Log GDP per capita in 1900 versus growth rate for 1900–1994   197

TABLES

6.1. Banking system characteristics, nineteenth and twentieth
      centuries   152
6.2. Persistence of banking system characteristics during the
      twentieth century   157
A6.1. International comparisons of financial system
      structure, circa 1990   165
7.1a. Economic factors in financial development   180
7.1b. Economic roots of modern financial system structure   182
7.2a. Political factors in banking structure and market orientation   184
7.2b. Political factors in modern financial system structure   185
7.3. Legal tradition, banking structure, financial development,
      and GDP growth   186
8.1. Growth rates of real per-capita GDP   193
8.2. Financial institution assets as a percentage of GNP   198

8.3. Cross-country growth regressions: 1880–1900 and 1900–1913   212
8.4. Pooled cross-country growth regressions, 1850–1913   214
8.5. Economic factors in financial development, 1900–1913   215
8.6. Estimated annual growth rates, Germany and Italy, 1895–1913   217
8.7. Bank assets and economic growth, 1895–1913   219

Acknowledgments

I would first like to thank Ryuzo Sato, Rama V. Ramachandran, and the UFJ (formerly Sanwa) Bank Prize committee for selecting this project for the prize and for their patience in awaiting its fruition.

This book has grown out of research that I undertook over several years and has therefore benefited from the insights and constructive critiques of many colleagues, numerous seminar and conference participants, discussants and referees, as well as a steady flow of research assistants and students. I thank each and every one of them without implicating them for any remaining errors. I do want to highlight the contributions of Marco Casari, Silvio Contessi, Johanna Francis, and Damien Kempf, who provided excellent research assistance; of Will Wolfe, Jessica Ziparo, and Sara Nelson, who helped indefatigably with the task of creating the index; and of Angelo Riva, who read much of the manuscript and offered detailed comments.

I am very grateful to The National Science Foundation (NSF) for funding since 1997 most of the research that has gone into this book, and thank, in particular, Dan Newlon for his advice and the anonymous grant reviewers who have helped shape my research program. I also thank the Social Science Research Council, the Center for German and European Studies (the University of California, Berkeley), the Economic History Association, the American Academy in Berlin (Berlin Prize Fellowship), the Fulbright Foundation, the German Marshall Fund of the United States, the Alexander von Humboldt Stiftung (TransCoop Fellowship), California Institute of Technology, the University of Freiburg (Bundesbank Lectureship), and Johns Hopkins University for various forms of fellowship and grant funding over the years.

My thanks, once again, go to Scott Parris of Cambridge University Press for his expert guidance through the publishing process.

On a personal note, I would like to thank my three wonderful children, Benjamin, Helen, and Theodore, for their love and patience and for providing endless distractions. And most of all, my immeasurable gratitude goes to John, my greatest supporter, who every single day makes it possible.

1

Introduction

Financial systems arise to intermediate between capital owners seeking productive investments and entrepreneurs with profit-making ideas but with insufficient funding. Why they emerge at particular points in time, and why they are organized as they are, remains to be understood in its entirety. From a theoretical standpoint, we have a number of explanations for the endogenous evolution of institutions to bridge the gap between the supply and demand for investment capital.[1] Beyond this simple brokerage function, financial intermediaries also change the nature of assets between borrower and lender; hence, the notion of qualitative asset transformation, or QAT. For the institutions of interest in this book, QAT typically means the alteration of the maturity or liquidity of assets – allowing investors to take part in large-scale, illiquid, and possibly high-risk and extended industrial investment with either a relatively low-risk, high-liquidity, short-maturity (even on-demand) depository account or a moderately risky yet relatively liquid – that is, tradable – equity position in the bank itself. This sort of QAT is effective, in large part, because the intermediary can invest in a wider range of projects than is feasible for the individual and thereby diversifies away some portion of the risk inherent in any one project.

The very fact that brokerage functions are necessary – because suppliers of capital may often be unacquainted with the full range of investment opportunities – raises another potential way that financial intermediaries alter assets: risk profile. In addition to diversifying away the natural risk of industrial investments, banks may also mitigate the problems that can arise when investors have poor information about the quality of investments or their true returns. Banks are well suited to serve this function by screening

[1] See Freixas and Rochet (1998) for a technical treatment of financial intermediation theory.

1

entrepreneurs before investing and monitoring the progress and performance of projects after investing. In all of these cases, financial intermediaries provide a key service to wealth holders and entrepreneurs, and the premium on their stock or the interest they earn on lending (net of their payments for deposits) constitutes their payment for this service.

Entrepreneurs, of course, can fund their projects in a number of ways, such as using internal cash flows, borrowing from either associates or intermediaries, or selling off ownership stakes in the venture. These options – and their maturity and liquidity profiles – parallel the offerings of a bank, where deposits to a bank represent borrowing by that bank. In a world of imperfect information, and where conflicts of interest can arise, the choice of financing type matters to entrepreneurs.[2] Indeed, in the worst case, these problems can prevent investors from providing funds altogether or cause entrepreneurs to use only internal funds. In deciding between debt and equity, or between bank lending and securitized debt, firms and investors face certain trade-offs. Equity can appreciate unbounded, and stakeholders therefore care much more about the firm's choices of projects and efforts to increase equity values. Because debt returns are limited to a contracted payoff, investors need only be convinced that the firm will perform sufficiently well to pay back the debt, and that they will repay. Clearly, then, debt and equity holders' interests, particularly risk tolerance, often diverge. The choice between bonds and bank debt hinges on similar, if milder, issues of information. Bank debt is thought to be subject to tighter control and monitoring and therefore represents the presumed first step in the pecking order of external funding.

Intermediaries may therefore facilitate transactions, allowing external finance, by providing efficient monitoring services, credibly transmitting information, or resolving conflicts of interest among contracting parties.[3] Such observations may also imply that the efficiency of financial intermediaries and their impact on the real economy may depend partly on their structure and practices – in particular, the range of services provided within one institution, the type of financing used to fund bank operations,

---

[2] Modigliani and Miller's (1958) well-known proposition that firms cannot alter the total value of their securities by varying the mix between debt and equity depends, of course, on assumptions of perfect information and markets. Many doubt the extent to which the real world fits these ideal assumptions.

[3] Jensen and Meckling (1976) is the classic article on problems arising from the separation of ownership from control of firms. Theoretical models comparing the costs of debt and equity finance include Myers and Majluf (1984), Diamond (1984), Gale and Hellwig (1985), and Townsend (1979). See Harris and Raviv (1991) and Hellwig (1991, 1997) for reviews of this and related literature.

and the extent and intimacy of relationships built up between banks and their clients.

Financial institutions and markets comprise the building blocks of financial systems. For the past century, economists have debated the relative advantages and disadvantages of different systems of finance and governance, many taking strong views. The universal banks are thought to have mobilized the financial resources that made industrialization possible for continental Europe – especially in Germany and Italy. The original statutes of one such bank in Germany, for example, empowered the bank "to bring about or participate in the promotion of new companies, the amalgamation or consolidation of different companies, and the transformation of industrial undertakings into joint stock forms."[4] As Chandler explains, "[T]hese banks provided initial capital for new industrial ventures and helped guide them through their early years of growth…. They supplied much of what today would be called venture capital."[5]

The view that, until very recently, heavily favored the universal banks gathered steam in the mid-twentieth century as countries with these systems rebuilt themselves in the wake of World War II. Surrounded by this apparent success, authors adopted many of their views from the late-nineteenth- and early-twentieth-century literature on industrialization. Among the contemporary observers of the rapid growth of pre–World War I Germany was Werner Sombart, who proclaimed, "Doubtless, a good portion of the increase in economic life in Germany is attributable to this interest of the banks and bankers in productive, economic activities. The banks have become the direct promoters of the spirit of enterprise, the pacemakers for industry and trade."[6] This sentiment was widely shared by his contemporaries and finds continued support among modern economists and historians – many of which use the German case to illustrate the great benefits of universal-relationship banking.

INSTITUTIONAL DESIGN AND FINANCIAL SYSTEM STRUCTURE

The theoretical literature places heavy emphasis on the costs of information asymmetry and the need to equalize it. These considerations lead naturally

---

[4] The clause referred to was Article III K of charter for the Bank für Handel und Industrie in Darmstadt. Translated and quoted by Whale (1930), p. 12.

[5] Chandler (1990), p. 417–419.

[6] Sombart (1909), p. 203, my translation. For a thorough bibliography of contemporary literature, primarily in German, see Riesser (1910 [German original], 1911 [English translation]). Whale's (1930) bibliography is a useful supplement and covers later works.

to the hypothesis that universal banking – combining as it does the range of financing options needed by any one firm – benefits from economies of scope: mostly from the reusability of firm- and market-specific information across time and products, but also from the reputation spillovers among branches of financial services.[7] Universal banking can arguably lead to, or even require, the formation of long-term relationships between banks and firms because these relationships theoretically enforce the repeated inter-action that allows information cost savings. Even aside from their role in promoting and sustaining efficient universality of services, banking rela-tionships might enhance banks' access to firm-specific information and thereby improve the accuracy of screening, monitoring of projects, and enforcement of repayment obligations. These information improvements may lessen the risk of investing in individual ventures and reduce the need for rationing of credit. Relationship building may also permit firms to take a longer-term view of their investment projects and possibly undertake investments that yield higher returns but over a longer horizon.[8] Similarly, information-yielding relationships can work as a certification device, enhancing a firm's appeal in equity markets and reducing the cost associ-ated with adverse selection – that is, the problem that outsiders assume that insiders will only issue new equity when it is overvalued.

The theoretical literature indicates that financial intermediaries generally increase both the quantity and the quality of investment in the economy. More specifically, there is theoretical support for the argument that univer-sal and relationship banking further raises the quantity of funds provided to industry and may also increase both the quality of projects undertaken and the long-term returns to investment. These benefits come with potential or hypothetical costs, such as systemic fragility, unwarranted concentra-tion, excessive conservatism, and conflicts of interest (such as underwriting securities for poor-quality debtor firms). In other words, it is far from clear, even theoretically, what the net impact of financial structure might be at either the firm or economy-wide level.

The structure of financial intermediaries, particularly commercial banks, may influence real variables, because different institutions may handle their tasks with varying degrees of efficiency. Theoretical differences in growth effects may be inferred from some other recent work. Relative to

---

[7] See Greenbaum, Kanatas, and Venezia (1989) on theoretical economies of scope resulting from information reusability.

[8] Stein (1989), Dewatripont and Maskin (1995), and von Thadden (1995) offer models in which relationships prevent premature liquidation of projects that need a longer gestation period, but which eventually produce higher long-run returns.

specialized, arms-length systems, for example, universal and relationship banking may be better suited to perform the growth-enhancing functions described by King and Levine (1993) or Thakor (1996). Recent conceptions echo views put forth much earlier, largely in view of the German experience. Lavington (1921), for example, stressed screening, monitoring, risk management, venture capital activities, and economies of scale and scope:

An organization of this kind, intermediate between the sources of enterprise and the sources of capital, must evidently possess machinery for investigating business ventures, financial strength adequate to sustain the heavy risks to which it is exposed and the reputation and business connexions necessary for the efficient sale of securities to the public. An organization such as the Deutsche Bank possesses these qualities to a high degree.... It is easy to see that, with able management and machinery of this kind, the risks of industrial banking are greatly reduced; business ventures in need of capital can be thoroughly investigated and the development of the more pioneering enterprises may be promoted with a reasonable prospect of success.[9]

In this line of reasoning, universal banks' combination of investment and commercial services promotes long-term relationships with corporate clients and thereby raises efficiency of financial transactions. Efficiency gains hinge not just on the reusability of information but on its quality as well. Thus, close, long-term relationships between banks and industrial firms are seen as central to the banks' acquisition and transfer of useful information – not just financial, but also strategic and entrepreneurial. Moreover, the banks are thought to have gained significant say in the use of funds and thus the types of investments made by firms. Such involvement and oversight is argued to have reduced banks' uncertainty about borrowers, mitigated risks of moral hazard or simple bad judgment, and facilitated long-term lending. The conventional view of the advantages of universal banking hinges on economies of scope that stem in large part from the perceived cradle-to-grave relationships between banks and firms. This view is evident from the earliest commentaries from bankers themselves: Jeidels (1905) argued that it was "in the interest of the security, profitability, and longevity of a credit institution to provide for all of the credit needs of a firm, from its formation to its liquidation."[10]

Formalized relationships between banks and firms – placement of bank representatives on firms' boards – are closely associated with universal banking functions in the literature. Gerschenkron, among others, claimed

---

[9] Lavington (1921), p. 210.
[10] Jeidels (1905), p. 63, author's translation. See also Gerschenkron (1962) and, for a modern restatement, Mayer (1988).

that "the German banks, and with them the Austrian and Italian banks, established the closest possible relations with industrial enterprises."[11] Gerschenkron echoed Jeidels, saying that "through development of the institution of the supervisory boards to the position of most powerful organs within corporate organizations, the banks acquired a formidable degree of ascendancy over industrial enterprises, which extended far beyond the sphere of financial control into that of entrepreneurial and managerial decisions."[12] Thus, bank seats on supervisory boards are traditionally thought to have permitted not just oversight, but also direct control, over firms' operations and decisions. Chandler (1991) notes, "The representatives of the German Großbanken participated to a greater extent in the top-level decision-making of new industrial companies than did representatives of financial institutions in the United States and Britain." He goes on to report that "the banks often had a significant say (particularly in the early years of a company's history) in investment decisions, in the selection of top and even middle managers, in establishing administrative procedures, and in reviewing the internal financial management of the enterprises that they had helped to finance."

Together, a system of universality and relationship formation is seen as more efficient than one of arms-length and specialized banking because it lowers the costs of finance and promotes industrial investment.[13] Even at the economy-wide level, universal banks are credited with promoting efficient allocation of the economy's investment portfolio, particularly historically, and in comparison with Britain.[14]

Banks versus Markets

Some of the existing literature focuses on the difference between banks and stock markets in the allocation of investment capital rather than the real effects of various types of banking institutions.[15] Although most of the

[11] Gerschenkron (1962), p. 14. Jeidels (1905), Riesser (1910), Schumpeter (1930), Wallich (1905), Whale (1930), Tilly (1994b), Chandler (1990), and most others writing on the subject also emphasize this point.
[12] Gerschenkron (1962).
[13] Economies of scope is a modern interpretation of the traditional accounts. Calomiris (1995), for example, advances such an argument and has argued that German companies faced lower costs of issuing new equity compared with their American counterparts. Tilly (1994a) produces similar figures for Germany.
[14] Tilly (1986) and Kennedy and Britton (1985), for example.
[15] Often, banking structure is conflated both with corporate governance issues and with financial market activity, probably because of the perception that universal, relationship-based

literature offers no comparison of the relative benefits of different types of financial systems, Greenwood and Smith (1997) find that, with sufficient risk aversion on the part of the investing public, equity markets produce stronger growth than do banks. In a series of papers, Boyd and Smith (1995, 1996, 1997) introduce the changing roles of debt and equity in the development process and argue that, although stock markets should develop after a period of intermediary dominance, both debt and equity remain viable and complementary sources of finance. Moreover, Greenwood and Smith (1997) show theoretically that growth rates obtained in economies with either banks or equity markets exceed those of economies without financial intermediaries.

Another line of research highlights the trade-offs between banks and financial markets in the revelation and transmission of information necessary for making optimal real decisions; the desirability of one system over another depends on the context. Allen (1992) reasons that, because markets aggregate information from a wide range of disparate sources, whereas banks depend primarily on their own assessments, markets dominate banks when technologies are new, complex, or rapidly evolving. Banks prevail when technologies are clearly understandable and optimal investment decisions are easy to make. Also, as Thakor (1996) argues, bank-dominated systems exacerbate effort aversion and overinvestment, whereas market-based systems lead to excessive reliance on borrower reputation as well as greater asset-substitution moral hazard.[16] Furthermore, the analyses of von Thadden (1995) and Dewatripont and Maskin (1990) suggest that banks tend to prolong low-quality projects for too long, whereas markets often liquidate good projects prematurely. All of these problems can lead to suboptimal investment decisions and lower real economic growth.

The Variety of Perspectives on Financial System Design

The existing literature combines a number of different approaches to the issue of financial system design. Many older studies, as exemplified by Gerschenkron's work, treat universal banks as a second-best substitute for missing markets. Recent research on modern institutions, on the other hand, conceives of the debate as a battle of competing systems arrayed on an even

banks dominate the financial systems in which they operate, and that financial markets dominate in systems in which financial intermediaries are specialized. See Helmut Dietl (1998) and Jonathan Story and Ingo Walter (1997).

[16] Thakor bases his argument on the predictions of Rajan (1992), Wilson (1994), and Diamond (1991).

playing field. The results to follow in this volume indicate that several countries maintained at least partially specialized, arms-length systems even in the absence of prohibitions on universal or relationship banking: British law has always permitted commercial banks to engage in universal and relationship banking, but the banks generally remained specialized. Until recently, the "battle of the systems" literature has represented universal, relationship banking as a superior solution to asymmetric-information problems. Traditionally, German banks were thought to have engaged in all of the activities seen as central to the promotion of economic growth, and to have executed these functions more effectively and efficiently than the British banks. In echoing the common perception that the British banks and securities markets heavily favored short-term and gilt-edged instruments, Kennedy (1987) attributes the lack of long-term lending and venture capital to the "informational weaknesses" of the British system. Much of what is seen as the decline of the British economy has been blamed on the failure of financial institutions. British industry is thought to have been constrained by a lack of capital; the banks, it is argued, held back necessary financing from industry. Many have chastised the British banks for avoiding engagement with domestic industry and leaving firms to find financing from other sources. The banks' involvement in foreign and imperial ventures is claimed to have drained away funds from domestic industry; firms' resultant recourse to securities markets is argued to have advanced investors' short-term profit motives at the expense of long-term growth.[17] Kennedy concludes that, "What was unique in Britain was not the existence of imperfect sharing of risk and control among those with a stake in corporate ventures but rather the unusually slow development of recognition of the extent of the problem and of effective means to rectify it."[18]

In other words, this strand of the literature interprets the British and American resistance to universality as, respectively, entrepreneurial and regulatory failure. The substitute-for-markets literature would see this persistence of specialization as a sign and natural upshot of the continued availability of the preferred market institutions. This divergence in perspectives is worth keeping in mind in analyzing the differences among financial systems as well as the factors that produce these divergent designs.

These perspectives on financial system differences may also be understood within the more recent literatures on varieties-of-capitalism (VOC)

---

[17] For a review of the literature on British banking and industrial development, see Michael Collins (1991, 1998). Also see Forrest Capie and Collins (1992). For a critical appraisal of the British banking system, see George Edwards (1987).

[18] Kennedy (1987), p. 127.

and law-and-finance that have primarily concerned political scientists and sociologists (in the first case) and legal scholars and economists (in the second case). The VOC literature differentiates between liberal and coordinated market economies, whereas the law-and-finance literature divides the world into common and civil (or statue) law tradition.[19] Both literatures would see each country as a member of or at least leaning toward one category or the other, and both paradigms suggest natural implications for financial system structure and economic development. Indeed, the two approaches may conceivably be merged, to the extent that the poles of one tend to match up with the poles of the other. Indeed, common-law countries appear to align with the "liberal" pole and statute law countries migrate to the "coordinated" pole. Even though the extremes are too extreme, it may prove useful to carve up the world in this manner, because doing so allows us to attempt quantitative analysis of the impact of institutional design. However, simple categorization is too blunt an instrument to fully explore the complexity and diversity of financial systems and to reveal the more nuanced story of their effects that I argue for in this book.

PLAN OF THE BOOK

The book is divided into two principal parts. The first part explores the key issues of interest for understanding financial development and growth, providing detailed comparisons across five exemplar countries: Germany, Italy, Japan, the United States, and the United Kingdom. The first of these chapters examines the patterns of industrialization and the emergence of banking institutions and capital markets primarily during the second half of the nineteenth century up to the start of World War I.[20] Because Japan developed later than the other countries, the analysis of Japanese development necessarily extends into the 1930s. Chapter 3 delves deeper into the industrial organization of each country's banking sector, the development of banking services, and the competitiveness and profitability of the banking industry. The final two chapters in this part investigate corporate governance relationships and the role of banking relationships in corporate financing.

---

[19] See La Porta, López-de-Silanes, Schleifer, and Vishny (1998) on the law-and-finance approach. Both hypotheses have been debated extensively in their respective literatures, with a consensus view similar to mine: Categorizing systems is useful for some exercises but misses crucial institutional detail much of the time.

[20] Even though the interwar period is very interesting, and a topic certainly in need of a unifying treatment, that period of upheaval and crisis would take us well outside the scope of this book, which is largely about the financing of long-run industrial growth.

This systematic comparative approach reveals that even though Germany and Italy did develop classic universal banking and relationship-oriented financial systems largely as described in the historical literature, their development varied in substantial ways from the standard views. Particularly in the case of Germany, many central features of the universal banking system developed late or not at all in the industrialization period. The Italian system appears more similar to the traditional conception on the surface. And yet the impact of the system on firms and on economic growth appears quite mild and even neutral in both cases. Japan, because of its dramatic cultural and technological differences with continental Europe, expands on the German and Italian cases and provides a richer view of universal-relationship systems and the paths systems take over time. Similarly, the United States and the United Kingdom, related in legal tradition at their core, differed remarkably in the implementation of those legal paradigms and the shape of their financial systems. In some cases, the UK institutions look and behave more like those in continental Europe than those in their former colonies.

These case studies reveal the variety and complexity of financial systems and hint at the difficulty of trying to categorize systems by type. Building on this idea, the second part of the book sets out to establish broader patterns in financial system design and economic growth. We would like to understand both the underlying causes of financial system structure – "why do certain kinds of financial institutions appear in some places but not others?" – and the possible consequences of systemic variation – "do certain kinds of institutions make the economy grow faster?" Older theories dictated that banks had to develop faster, and needed to provide more services, in countries that were undergoing rapid industrialization during the end of the nineteenth century. The most- and least-developed economies of the time, respectively, did not need or could not support such large-scale, industrial banks. Newer work, such as the VOC and law-and-finance literature, has brought political and legal factors to the fore, hypothesizing specific relationships between banking structure and state centralization and between financial development and legal tradition.

Chapter 6 begins the second part by laying out a framework for distinguishing among financial system types and then classifying all available countries into those categories.[21] Such a sorting exercise generalizes the more fine-grained portraits of the five country cases and confirms the findings of the in-depth studies: Few banking systems fit the extreme paradigms

---

[21] All countries for which pre–World War I data are provided in Maddison (1995).

of universal-relationship or specialized-arm's length banking; the vast majority fall somewhere in between. In addition, even though connections do emerge among various designs of banking institutions, engagement in formal relationships, and prevalence of stock markets, there are few hard-and-fast rules. In general, actual institutions and systems are very difficult to categorize neatly. The long-term view of financial system evolution adds further complications and demonstrates how institutions change over time. In the end, however, the chapter points out that, despite several cases of temporary upheaval and recent widespread movement toward conglomeration in banking, broadly viewed, financial system structure has remained remarkably stable over the long run.

The second stage of the analysis, in Chapter 7, uses this categorization scheme to identify the political and economic characteristics that unify countries under a given financial paradigm. This exercise reveals a number of consistent patterns. For example, economic factors in the late nineteenth century provide relatively strong explanatory power for financial system development, market orientation, and banking structure at the eve of World War I and in the present day. Banking specialization and market orientation appear strongly associated with legal tradition, although it seems more likely that the three characteristics are jointly determined or that the legal system variable simply proxies for a close or historical tie to England, the exporter of many political and economic institutions. Finally, political structure relates significantly to market orientation but not to banking system design or legal tradition.

The penultimate chapter, Chapter 8, takes up the question of consequences: Does the financial system structure or legal tradition matter to aggregate real development? Whereas it is clear that financial systems could vary in their real effects, it is not yet clear what kind of system offers the greatest net benefit to the real economy – either historically or at present. Perhaps tellingly, authors such as Levine (2002) find no statistical relationship between the emphasis on banks relative to markets and real economic growth in the 1990s. The analysis in Chapter 8 therefore offers a much longer-term view than the extant literature – stretching back to the origins of modern growth in the mid-nineteenth century. Such an extended period of time allows a much more robust analysis of potential effects of institutions at their inception. The results demonstrate that, even though certain systems have prevailed for even extended periods of time, no one system dominates over the past 150 or more years.

The findings in this book lead to three sets of conclusions about financial system design and industrial development. First, modern financial systems are rooted in the past, are idiosyncratic to specific countries, and are highly path-dependent. Therefore, to understand the current structure of financial institutions, we must take stock of the forces at play in both the near and distant past: political and regulatory intervention, as well as natural resource endowments, educational institutions, and social and religious beliefs. To be sure, legal, political, and societal contexts play important roles in shaping institutions, but these idiosyncrasies make it difficult to pinpoint consistent relationships among economic, political, legal, and financial variables.

Second, financial institutions and markets do not create economic growth without significant first steps in industrial development and supporting institutions. Financiers create new institutions and markets in response to perceived needs. Finance may then enhance growth once economic development is sufficient to benefit from external finance. The finance-growth relationship varies over time, as financial and economic developments influence one another, creating a feedback mechanism.

Third, and most important, at least from the modern policy standpoint, there is no one-size-fits-all solution to financial system design and industrial development. Certain kinds of financial institutions or systems do perform particular functions better than others, but economies differ in their needs, and those needs vary over time. Moreover, individual financial institutions – even of a particular type, such as commercial banks – often differ more within a given country than they differ among countries. Therefore, nobody can specify a type of system that will always and everywhere promote the highest growth. Much more important than creating specific types of financial institutions, policy makers should aim to develop a strong, stable, and legally protected financial system with a rich diversity of institutions and vibrant markets that can adapt to changing needs.

PART I

FIVE SUCCESS STORIES

2

Creating Corporate Finance Systems

By early in the nineteenth century, wealth sufficient to fund industrialization existed in many parts of the world; the primary challenge was mobilizing those funds and channeling them to the most productive uses. This process required collection of idle funds from investors and then distributing them to entrepreneurs to invest in industrial undertakings. The continuous repetition of this process, in large part through the financial system, greatly expanded and redistributed the supply of financial capital. This "virtuous" cycle increased the share of the economy's resources directed to industrial development and drove economic growth.

As the drivers of capital mobilization, financial institutions play a key role in theories of economic growth and industrial development. But questions persist about how banks play their part in matching savers and entrepreneurs and whether particular types of financial systems achieve greater success than others. At the same time, much remains to be learned about how financial systems form and why they take the various shapes they do. This chapter begins the process of addressing these questions, following the development of five important corporate financial systems in their early development: the United Kingdom, Germany, Italy, Japan, and the United States. While other types of institutions naturally contributed to the financing of industrialization by funneling capital toward industrial enterprise, the analysis here focuses on the components of financial systems that directly financed industry – commercial banks and securities markets. Subsequent chapters consider related questions of the organization of commercial banking industries, the scope of services provided within individual banks, the development of relationship banking practices – active involvement in corporate governance of firms and equity stakes in industrial companies – and their consequences for industrial firms and economic growth.

INDUSTRIALIZATION AND THE CREATION
OF THE MODERN FINANCIAL SYSTEM

The United Kingdom is often seen as the birthplace of the first industrial revolution; its beginnings can be dated to the mid-eighteenth century. The country's infrastructure system was upgraded early on, largely out of private financing by early industrialists and notably with the formation of the Bank of England, then a private institution, in 1694. Entrepreneurs set to mechanizing the production of cotton textiles and pottery, moving work into progressively more advanced workshops and then factories. By the end of the eighteenth century, the United Kingdom had developed the locomotive, based on steam and coal power, thus opening up a whole new range of industries.

By some accounts, even as late as 1907, the textile, coal mining, iron and steel, and engineering sectors produced half of Britain's net industrial output, the first three of which accounted for more than 70 percent of export earnings.[1] Together, the four top industries employed a quarter of the working population. Industrial firms, such as those in coal mining, often remained small and private, commonly in the legal form of a partnership or private limited company.[2] As industrialization progressed and began to filter wealth farther down the ranks of the population, the service sector grew, as did a range of new consumer industries such as soap, footwear, bicycles, and food processing.[3]

As British firms grew in scale and scope, particularly in heavy industry, small firms, with craft-style, workshop-based production, continued to proliferate throughout the nineteenth century.[4] Indeed, the largest 100 firms in 1880 accounted for less than 10 percent of the market.[5] As that century progressed, however, concentration quickened, even in lighter industries, such as tobacco and brewing. In the latter case, for example, the top 200 brewers produced more than half of total UK output in 1881, but nearly three-quarters by 1913.[6] By no means was this a highly concentrated industry, but the rate of change was marked.

As the United States and continental Europe started on their paths of industrialization, the United Kingdom began to face increased competition

---

[1]   Kirby (1981), p. 3. See Allen and Gale (2000) on the role of high wages and cheap energy in stimulating the industrial revolution in Great Britain.
[2]   Kirby (1981), p. 15.
[3]   Ibid., p. 23.
[4]   Hannah (1976), p. 10
[5]   Ibid., p. 13.
[6]   Watson (1996), p. 63.

from abroad. Cotton textiles remained one of the largest industries into the late nineteenth century, but newer products and processes took over as the industrial leaders – motor vehicles and other manufactured consumer goods. In this regard, the United Kingdom differed somewhat from such countries as the United States and Germany, where large-scale, capital-intensive heavy industry seemingly played a more central role to industrialization.[7] This apparent concentration in smaller-scale, lighter industry led to much debate and discussion over the "decline" of British industry and its relative failure compared to the United States, Germany, and others.[8] Detractors pointed out that the five largest firms in Britain in 1919 were small in comparison with the largest American companies.[9] However true, most scholars now agree that these figures are misleading and should not be viewed as symptomatic of a general economic failure. British industry was, at the end of the nineteenth century, slowing down from its peak growth and growing more slowly than the more recently industrializing economies of the time. The economy may even have been too heavily focused on a narrow range of staple industries and lagging in new technologies and products. The British economy was hardly in decline or failure.[10] Indeed, with the spread of industrialization through the world, "the falling British share of world markets was no index of 'failure,'" as D. N. McCloskey explains, but rather "was an index of maturity."[11]

Given the early industrialization and commercial expansion in England, it comes as little surprise that the banking system developed early there as well. The exigencies of the French Wars in the seventeenth and eighteenth centuries increased demand for capital and credit and spurred the development of financial innovations. Country banks emerged and created

---

[7] Some have argued that the UK economy remained heavily populated by smaller-scale, lighter industry. The cotton industry is a typical example – the average firm had 150 workers, almost all were family-owned and had only a handful of partners. See Botticelli (1997).

[8] The themes of "economic decline" and industrial "failure" were stressed by economic historians of the 1960s, in particular D. H. Aldcroft (1964) and D. S. Landes (1965). D. N. McCloskey, quickly followed by others, strongly reacted against this pessimistic interpretation of late-nineteenth-century British economy in a series of studies starting in 1970. Dintenfass (1999) provides a good summary of these debates.

[9] These were J. & P. Coats (textiles), Lever Bros. (food and soap), Imperial Tobacco, Vickers (armaments and ships), and Guinness (brewing). The largest of these J. & P. Coats, had capital of £45 million (Botticelli, 1997).

[10] See, for instance, *The Cambridge Economic History of Britain since 1970, volume 2: 1860–1939* (2nd ed., 1994) and *The British Industrial Decline* (1999).

[11] McCloskey, 1999, p. 40. Same conclusion in Greasley and Oxley (1999), p. 82: "Faster growth in France, and other European countries, in the twentieth century, arose from a process of convergence rather than from Britain's decline."

something of a nationwide banking system even by 1750. These banks contributed to and partly resulted from industrialization in the provinces. Indeed many of the country banks were founded by industrialists and merchants. By the end of the eighteenth century, there were 400 country banks in existence, and by 1810, the number had risen to almost 800. Savings rates reached double digits in Britain by 1865. Willing to hold a particularly diverse range of securities, British savers poured capital into the British financial system.

Despite its characterization as a market-oriented economy, it is often argued that formal markets provided little of the financing of domestic UK industry. Early industrial financing came mainly from families and other insiders and also from banks. Many industrial firms remained small and often family-controlled, and they used little outside capital, particularly via equity issues to the general public on formal markets. At least one study concludes that "it seems that small and medium-size firms seeking external capital were able, in fact, to raise funds from a miscellany of small-scale, locally based-suppliers rather than from the formal capital markets."[12] Some notable evidence to the contrary has also appeared for the brewing industry: that capital subscribed via the new issue market dominated the industry circa 1900, with public offerings providing close to 75 percent of the total capital invested in brewing.[13] It is worth emphasizing, as most scholars do, the shortage of hard evidence on these questions. Thus, some debate continues, but Britain's system clearly cannot be accurately described as truly market-oriented – at least not for most of the nineteenth century.[14]

English banks took primarily private company form in the first decades of the nineteenth century. The growing scale of industrial operations in the mid-nineteenth century prompted growth in the banks' scale and a desire for a joint-stock company form. Incorporated banks appeared in two waves: 1820s–1830s and the 1860s–1870s. The first burst of incorporations resulted primarily from slackening of banking regulations, particularly the Banking Act of 1826, which broke the Bank of England's monopoly on joint-stock banking in England and Wales (since 1707) and permitted the establishment of banking partnerships outside a 65-mile radius of London.[15] As the joint-stock banks grew in number, they edged out and ultimately took over the private banks. By the end of the century, the larger joint-stock banks had taken over many of the country's banks and converted them into their

---

[12] Collins (1998), p. 17. Michie (1990) makes similar points.
[13] Watson (1996), p. 63.
[14] See Capie and Collins (1992).
[15] Joint-stock banking was permitted in Scotland and in Ireland after 1821.

own branches. In the second half of the nineteenth century, the British commercial banks accounted for 50 percent to 60 percent of aggregate UK financial system assets.[16] Total assets of financial institutions as a share of gross national product also grew substantially in Britain over the period.

Industrialization spread from the United Kingdom to the European continent over the early nineteenth century. As in most of continental Europe, agriculture and proto-industry led the German economy for the first half of the century, but by the 1840s and 1850s, the population began its shift from agrarian into industrial sectors. Steam power propelled the textile industry and then the railroads. Steel revolutionized heavy industry starting in the 1850s. New technologies and industries brought a spate of new firms in both railroads and in related lines of business. Economic development demanded financial development, and banking and insurance companies began to appear across the country. Capital also flowed into Germany through international trade and stimulated the private banking activities of merchant families. Most financial intermediaries opted to remain private rather than subject themselves to the governments' tight control over banks of issue. Barred from issuing notes, these private bankers issued acceptance credits (like IOUs) instead, and in so doing still increased the circulation of financial capital in the economy. The private banks of the early to mid-nineteenth century also provided crucial maturity transformation and securitization by converting short-term loans into long-term securities. In these formative years, private bankers in most of the German regions attended primarily to government finance, but those in the Rhineland seem to have taken much greater interest in financing industry. Thus, most private external financing of industry in the first half of the nineteenth century flowed through local banks.[17] By the mid-nineteenth century, the sheer size of investments for railroads and associated heavy industry required new financing techniques and may well have inspired the combination of short- and long-term finance

[16] These figures, based on Goldsmith (1969), could actually be higher, because they almost certainly undercount private banking assets in Britain after 1891. Goldsmith used Sheppard's (subsequently published in 1971) figures from *The Economist*, which were not comprehensive. Thus, unless total financial assets are also underestimated, the ratio of commercial banks to total financial institutions in Britain should be higher, especially for 1880. Capie and Webber's aggregate UK bank deposit series is 38 percent higher than Sheppard's. Goldsmith's sources for private banks in the earlier years are unclear and therefore difficult to judge. See Capie and Webber (1985).

[17] See Heyn (1981 [1969]) on private banking and industrialization in Frankfurt am Main. See also Tilly (1965, 1966) and Neuberger (1977), pp. 57–61, giving the example of the private banking firm Gebrüder Bethmann. Loewenstein (1912) provides some details on the private bankers in Württemberg.

that would ultimately become full-fledged universal banking.[18] By the late 1840s, private bankers and others began creating joint-stock commercial investment banks (credit banks or universal banks), and the institution had firmly established itself by the mid-1860s.[19]

Germany united under the Second Empire in 1871, following a string of military engagements culminating with the Franco-Prussian war. The country unified its currency in 1873 and created a national central bank (the Reichsbank) on January 1, 1876. Joint-stock companies appeared in rapid succession – particularly during waves in the early 1870s and again in the 1890s.[20] The numbers exceeded 5,000 by the late 1890s. At the same time, the large, multifunction universal banks evolved into their full-fledged form.[21] Having given up their right to issue notes in exchange for minimal government regulation, the universal banks developed alternative sources of funding – primarily equity capital.[22] Their high capital ratios freed them to participate in less liquid investment opportunities, such as unsecured, long-term lending and securities issues.[23]

The German universal banks distinguished themselves from other financial institutions primarily by their combination of credit and off-balance-sheet operations. But the joint-stock banks came in many sizes and shapes: Capitalization, assets, clientele, and activities varied considerably from one bank to the next. As a rule, the large universal banks served corporate firms and large private enterprises. Small business had little access to the universal banks, particularly the larger, urban ones; but many small joint-stock banks and private banks did supply credit to such customers. The most famous of the banks were true universal banks and held hundreds of millions of marks worth of assets in the early years of the twentieth century. But in 1908, there were still eighty joint-stock credit banks with less than

---

[18] See Fremdling (1975, 1983) on the contribution of the railroads.

[19] According to Riesser (1911), p. 892, fourteen credit banks, with capital ranging from 600,000 to 42,936,000 marks, were founded between 1848 and 1856.

[20] See Fohlin (2005) for the longer-run picture of corporate formation and ownership in Germany. The government paved the way for the foundation booms, having loosened restrictions on the founding of joint-stock companies throughout the 1860s and 1870s.

[21] See Fohlin (2007a).

[22] The Bank Act of 1875 authorized certain banks to issue currency and also regulated their activities. See Lotz (1976 [1888]) on the development of German note-issuing banks and for a critical analysis of the Bank Act of 1875 that regulated such banks.

[23] See Verdier (2002) for a more detailed argument linking liquidity and universal bank development and later chapters for an international comparison of political, economic, and legal factors in financial system development. Such high capital ratios seem like an old-fashioned concept in light of capitalization ratios of the early 2000s.

100,000 marks of share capital, many of which had previously operated as credit cooperatives (*Genossenschaften*).[24]

Despite their perceived dominance in the financial system and in the political arena, the joint-stock credit banks accounted for considerably less than half of the assets of German financial institutions throughout the later industrialization period. Savings banks (*Sparkassen*) made up the next largest group of institutions and rivaled the size of the universal banking sector in total assets. The clientele of the two types of banks differed significantly, of course. The savings banks served mainly working-class customers, with a focus on earning interest. Municipalities created, regulated, and guaranteed the savings banks, and these institutions lent conservatively and on a small scale.[25] Cooperative credit societies (*Creditgenossenschaften*) also served private clients, primarily small-business owners, farmers, and laborers – those whose credit needs and creditworthiness made them undesirable customers to a large bank.[26] Two other sets of institutions, the joint-stock mortgage banks (*Hypothekenbanken*) and the agricultural credit unions (*Landschaften*), also provided basic lending services and raised funds via interest-bearing mortgage bonds known as *Pfandbriefe*. In addition to the private institutions, provincial governments created their own institutions, *Landesbanken*, to provide central banking-like facilities to the savings banks at a regional level.[27]

Despite the long-standing picture of Germany as the exemplar of bank-led industrial development, the archetypal universal banking system emerged late and to a limited extent during industrialization. Indeed, the sector blossomed along with the final push of industrialization in the 1890s and early twentieth century – not clearly providing a causal role in overall economic growth of the time.[28] Up until the second wave of industrialization, the German financial system consisted primarily of private bankers. They dominated the German financial system of the mid-nineteenth century; their assets far surpassed those of other banks in the

---

[24] For more on the small joint-stock banks and provision of credit to small business, see Lansburgh (1909) and Schönitz (1912).

[25] For a picture of the clientele of savings banks, see Statistisches Amt der Stadt Frankfurt a.M. (1903, 1906). See Schönitz (1912) on the provision of credit by savings banks to small- and medium-size businesses.

[26] The cooperatives were regulated by the *Genossenschaftsgesetze* of 1889 and 1896. See Schönitz (1912) for comprehensive details on the *Genossenschaften*. For an interesting modern analysis of the functions of the credit cooperatives, see Guinnane (1993).

[27] Whale (1930), p. 3.

[28] Fohlin (2007a) and Chapter 8 of this book.

1860s.[29] In 1860, institutions dealing mostly with commercial business, the incorporated mixed banks, barely appeared on the financial radar, accounting for less than 10 percent of financial institution assets and only 4 percent of GNP. The banking industry underwent significant organizational change over the course of the nineteenth and early twentieth centuries, however, and by 1913, joint-stock banks took over the vast majority of the commercial banking business.

Net of central bank assets, aggregate bank assets grew fastest after 1900 and slowest between 1860 and 1880.[30] The joint-stock universal banks' real assets, of which the largest banks maintained a nearly constant share, increased more than sixfold between 1883 and 1913, with total real bank assets growing at around 6.8 percent per annum. Even controlling for population growth, in the thirty years leading up to World War I, real bank assets per capita more than quadrupled, growing from less than 100 (1913) marks per capita to approximately 450 (real) marks per capita.

Notably, in the second half of the nineteenth century, the German commercial banks amounted to only half as much of aggregate financial system assets as their British counterparts (50 to 60 percent for the United Kingdom). By the broader measure of total financial institutions assets as a share of gross national product, Britain's financial sector exceeded Germany's during much of the nineteenth century. But Germany's system grew more rapidly than Britain's over the late nineteenth century and overtook the British by 1900 (114 percent of GNP versus 93 percent). By World War I, German financial institution assets far outweighed British financial institution assets, compared to each country's GDP (158 percent in Germany versus 103 percent in the United Kingdom).[31]

Not long after Germany began to industrialize, Italy, too, embarked on the industrialization path. Industrial production grew robustly during the Giolitti Era, particularly 1896–1913, but economic historians agree that, in international comparison, Italy's "takeoff" was disappointing – nothing like the German boom.[32] Gerschenkron (1955) argued that Italy's industrialization suffered primarily from the state's tariff policy – a system that propped up old, declining industries rather than promoting emerging entrepreneurs in chemicals and engineering.

---

[29] The figures, based on Goldsmith's data, should be viewed as rough, because the sources are difficult to follow or judge for accuracy. See also Deutsche Bundesbank (1976).

[30] Based on Goldsmith's (1969) estimates of banking assets.

[31] It is worth noting, however, that the pattern reversed after World War II; by 1963, Britain once again led Germany by a substantial margin.

[32] See Federico and Toniolo (1992) for an in-depth discussion of various indices of industrial production. See also Cohen (1977) for a survey of major industrial sectors.

Even more than in the German case, Italy's financial system remained relatively unsophisticated and disjointed for the first half of the nineteenth century. Savings banks grew rapidly in the 1820s and thereafter, and banks of issue were established mid-century. Before the unification of the Kingdom of Italy in 1861, however, multiple monetary systems persisted in individual states, provinces, and even towns. Tuscany alone had twenty-four currencies.[33] By 1865, Italy had joined the Latin Monetary Union under a bimetallic standard, but currency union came much later.[34]

Universal banking emerged later and more slowly in Italy than it had in Germany, and with the possible exception of Credito Mobiliare (1863), banking remained specialized until quite late in the century. Just as it had in Germany, joint-stock banking flourished in the early 1870s. The number of firms grew eightfold, and capital quintupled between 1869 and 1873. Within another six years, however, and again in close parallel with Germany, more than a third of these banks disappeared, and their capital fell 66 percent.[35] The crisis of 1893–1894 again brought down many banks, this time including one of the banks of issue and the two largest deposit banks. The crisis prompted the establishment of the Banca d'Italia – mostly a national bank of issue at this point, rather than a true central bank, by some accounts – and spurred the importation of German-style universal banking.[36] The first of these banks (Banca Commerciale Italiana, or Comit) was created in 1894 by a consortium of the largest German banks augmented with Austrian and Swiss capital. The second, both in chronology and stature (Credito Italiano, or Credit), was founded the following year in a similar manner, albeit with more substantial participation by Italian capitalists and managers. These two institutions drew from the clientele and management of their predecessor institutions, and they instantly became the most significant commercial banks in Italy.

Gerschenkron attributed great importance to the rise of German universal banking in Italy: "It is possible to surmise that the upsurge of 1896–1908 was largely rendered possible by the importation of the great economic innovation of German banking in its most developed and mature form."[37] Jon Cohen concurred with Gerschenkron and argued that the importation

---

[33] Clough (1964), p. 21. He also gives an overview of the development of various financial institutions from the beginning of the nineteenth century. See also Zamagni (1993) and Cohen (1977).

[34] See Sannucci (1989) for a detailed account of the evolution of the Italian monetary system.

[35] See Clough (1964), pp. 119–120.

[36] See Bonelli (1971, 1982) on the Banca d'Italia and the 1907 Crisis.

[37] Gerschenkron (1955), p. 374.

of German-style universal banking "profoundly affected the industrial growth of the nation."[38] By now, Italian scholars have severely diluted or even discarded most of Gerschenkron's points on Italian industrialization.[39] An in-depth study has demonstrated a far more limited role of these banks in the pre–World War I period.[40] Still others have suggested that the financial system had a distorting effect on the economy as a whole.[41]

The Italian industrial banking sector expanded markedly after 1895, with total bank assets growing 6.5 to 7.2 percent per annum. Perhaps not surprising, given the later introduction of universal banking in Italy, the largest four of the Italian universal banks grew more than twice as fast as the equivalent group in Germany.[42] Bank assets also expanded markedly relative to population (6.2 percent per annum). Despite their rapid growth, the sector remained rather small, particularly compared to Germany: In 1913, bank assets hit 4.5 million marks per capita in Germany; they were just over 500,000 marks per capita in Italy. Real bank assets as a share of capital formation shows a similar size gap between the German and Italian banking sectors.

Japan lagged behind Germany and even Italy in its industrial development over the first two-thirds of the nineteenth century. The belated realization of Europe and America's growing power pushed Japan into the industrial revolution midstream. The Meiji Restoration, ending the Tokugawa period in 1867–1868, marked a turning point not just in Japan's political history but its economic and financial history as well. In making its concerted effort at economic development in the nineteenth century, Japan looked to Europe and the United Sates, consciously emulating their paths to modernization. The Meiji government rapidly replaced the feudal system of the Tokugawa period with western-style political and economic institutions, opening the country to international markets and economic forces in the process. Still, Western Europe's head start in industrialization meant that a wide technological gap had opened up between Japan and the leading industrial nations of the time. The government played a particularly central role in establishing modern manufacturing and transportation industries

---

[38] Cohen (1977), p. 85.

[39] For example, Barone (1972), Fenoaltea (1973, 1983), Lanaro (1979), Toniolo (1977, 1990). All of these studies are considered in Federico and Toniolo (1992).

[40] Most significantly, on Comit, see Confalonieri (1974, 1982). See also Fohlin (1994, 1998a) on the role of Comit in corporate governance and investment.

[41] See Cohen (1977), pp. 139–143, for a summary of his findings.

[42] See Fohlin (1999b). The four largest Italian universal banks were Banca Commerciale Italiana (Comit), Credito Italiano (Credit), Banco di Roma (BDR), and Società Bancaria Italiana (SBI).

in Japan, and acquired most of the railroad lines between 1905 and 1907. By 1913, it owned nearly seven-eights of the railway network.[43]

Japan's weak industrial base created little or no pressure to modernize the financial system for much of the nineteenth century. But financial development benefited as industry had from the new political agenda of rapid renewal and advancement. Around the mid-1880s, Japan entered into a period of sustained economic growth and financial development; by World War I, Japan had created a modern financial and economic system. Per-capita wealth continued to lag behind that of the United States and Europe into the interwar years, but Japan continued its industrialization push and its attempt to close the gap. As in Germany, the creation of a national railroad network tested the limits of the existing financial structure, demanding new institutions and instruments to finance their enormous capital requirements.

Organized financial institutions of the European type appeared in Japan only in the last quarter of the nineteenth century: As of the mid-1870s, only a handful of private and national (later "ordinary") banks existed. In one of its institutional adoption programs, the Meiji government introduced a U.S.-style national banking system. National banks, organized as joint-stock companies with limited liability, were granted the right to issue notes. The banking population exploded soon after the amendment of the National Bank Act in 1876. With the creation of the Bank of Japan in 1886, and its assumption of a note-issuing monopoly, the national banks converted their operations more completely to those of ordinary commercial banks found elsewhere in the industrialized world.

A range of other banks and financial institutions appeared in this period as well.[44] Private commercial banks, without issue privileges, constituted the most important segment for industrial business finance. The first of these, the Bank of the House of Mitsui, was organized in 1876, and many more followed in its wake – more than 200 less than a decade later. Premodern lenders still played an important role in financing agriculture and small business well into the twentieth century, but by the start of World War I, Japan had created western-style modern financial institutions, with broad coverage over most of the country, if not entirely complete national networks.

As in the German and Italian cases, the Japanese commercial banks served certain sectors of the economy and left other sectors to a range of

---

[43] See Goldsmith (1983).
[44] See Goldsmith (1983) for a thorough overview of Japanese financial system development in this period.

additional financial institutions and insurance companies. The Yokohama Specie Bank, for example, was set up by the government in 1880. In contrast to the commercial banks, the Yokohama Specie Bank was a truly Japanese institution, a response to the Japanese-specific needs relating to international trade.[45] The government also established and provided implicit guarantees for long-term credit or mortgage banks starting in 1897 with the foundation of the Hypothec (Kangyo) Bank. European forerunners once again served as a model, but the divergent needs of the Japanese economy demanded greater provision of long-term credit to industry and agriculture through these institutions, rather than the European norm of residential mortgage finance. As elsewhere, Japan created a parallel system of savings banks, in many respects a replica of the British postal saving system.[46] Private savings banks expanded rapidly as well – both in number and assets – in the early years of the twentieth century, primarily through a combination of demand and time deposits. Like savings banks in the United States and Europe, Japanese banks pursued the goal of modest capital growth for working-class customers; they invested conservatively and maintained substantial liquidity through both cash and government securities.

The Japanese banking sector expanded rapidly after 1885, with total bank assets growing around 10 percent per year from 1886 to 1913.[47] Assets expanded from 388 million yen in 1885 to 5.5 billion in 1913 – a nearly fourteenfold increase.[48] Despite the rapid growth, the sector remained rather small compared to its counterparts in Germany and Italy.

Meanwhile, on the other side of the Pacific, the United States had created one of the fastest-growing economies in the world during the nineteenth century. Industrialization progressed, as it did in many parts of northwestern Europe, gradually out of agriculture and into craft production and textiles, on to mechanization and factory systems, railroads, and the full array of late-nineteenth- and early-twentieth-century industries. Population growth, along with particularly bountiful natural resources, fueled American economic growth, which in turn shaped a variety of emerging economic, political, and legal institutions. As in all other countries studied here, banking and financial markets played a prominent role in financing industrialization efforts in the United States.

---

[45] The yen was introduced in 1871, using both metallic and paper money. But the metallic standard was based on silver, which was rapidly losing its position vis-à-vis gold in the international monetary system.

[46] For more details, see Goldsmith (1983).

[47] See tables 3–12 in Hoshi and Kashyap (2001).

[48] See tables 3–11 in Hoshi and Kashyap (2001).

Banks began to develop in the United States in the late eighteenth century, typically propelled by state pressure for financial resources; the commercial banking sector grew rapidly between 1790 and 1835.[49] While the United States would become known for its highly restrictive banking regulation for much of the twentieth century, the regulatory stance remained decidedly hands-off in the antebellum era. States held significant power over bank regulation, but many of them imposed little or no hurdle to creating banks – or to closing them. The liberal approach had its shortcomings: Severe banking panics hit in 1837 and 1857, and between 1838 and 1863, one in seven of the so-called free banks failed, often due to insufficient collateral and many bad loans.[50] One early observer described American banking history prior to 1840 as ranging "from recklessness ... to downright swindling."[51]

The crisis of the mid-nineteenth century brought calls for reform and resulted in new restrictions on lending practices and on branching. The National Bank Act of 1863 created the National Banking System, and most banks switched to federal charters. State banking persisted, though, and commercial banks could take either a state or a federal charter.[52] Banking panics continued to crop up even after the National Bank Acts of 1863 and 1865.

As in the other cases here, a variety of institutions emerged over the late nineteenth century to serve different clienteles and segments of the economy. As with the German joint-stock and private banks, American private banks avoided state chartering, and in doing so, they agreed not to issue bank notes. More than 1,100 private banks formed by 1860, compared with almost 1,600 state-chartered banks.[53] Savings banks also appeared in step with many other countries at the time, providing similar services and likewise offering a safer alternative to commercial banks. Two proto-central banks appeared early on (in 1791 and 1816), but both dissolved after their charters expired.

True central banking of the modern type arrived only in 1913 – quite a bit later than in much of Europe and Japan. It also differed in its structure and operations. The Federal Reserve's design reflected the national suspicion of centralized power, with the unusual arrangement of an overarching Board

[49] Sylla (2001).
[50] Klebaner (1990, p. 50) gives the failures at 104 of 709.
[51] Walker (1876) as cited in Klebaner (1990, p. 50). He also indicates that the cumulative depreciation of currency during bank suspensions "aggregated $95 million by 1841, $72 million of which had occurred from 1837 to 1841."
[52] See Sylla (1999).
[53] Klebaner (1990), p. 54.

of Governors but twelve regional banks that fed back into the national level organization. The regulatory power and financial heft we associate with the Fed of recent years, however, really emerged in the post–World War II era.

Corporate finance in the United States developed rapidly over the period of industrialization between the mid-nineteenth century and the early twentieth century. Among the range of institutions that emerged, commercial banks took first place. Even though U.S. commercial banking assets lagged a bit behind the levels in Germany and the United Kingdom before World War I, they did grow rapidly: on the order of sevenfold between 1880 and 1912.[54] Commercial banking assets grew almost twice as fast as the economy as whole during that time, and most especially between 1880 and 1900.

Specialization of financial services came much later in the United States than it did in the United Kingdom, and ostensibly different types of intermediaries often overlapped in the services they provided. Trusts, for example, blurred the boundaries between banking and trustee services and could certainly be considered universal banks in many cases. These intermediaries operated outside of banking regulations and combined traditional trustee services with commercial lending, interest-bearing checking accounts, and investment banking. Indeed, in 1901, one such institution, the Knickerbocker Trust Company, proclaimed that "the trust company of today, combining as it does every function of financial business, might well be called the department store of finance."[55] This description sounds nearly identical to the "supermarket of finance" metaphor often applied to universal banks, particularly those in Germany. Still, not all commercial banks or trust companies, probably a small proportion, provided the full range of corporate and investment banking services. A subset of them did, and among these, only a small group financed the largest corporations of the turn of the twentieth century. In this heterogeneity of size and scope, however, the U.S. commercial banking sector mirrored the Japanese, Italian, and German "universal" banking sectors.

THE ROLE OF SECURITIES MARKETS

By the late nineteenth century, securities markets had emerged in essentially all industrialized economies. As with banking institutions, size, activity, and performance of financial markets varied significantly between countries. In contrast to banking, far less is known about the historical

---

[54] Based on Goldsmith's data.
[55] Knickerbocker Trust Company (1901), p. 11, as cited in Klebaner (1990), p. 73.

development of financial markets and their legal and political bases. The country case studies therefore must investigate the extent to which the various governments dictated rules of incorporation, exchange listing, financial accounting, securities trading, and transactions taxes.[56] The historical finance literature has only recently started to take up questions of market structure, efficiency, and rationality, and the data collection process is still in its infancy. To the extent permitted within these data constraints, the country studies also investigate the quantitative patterns of development.

Differences in financial system design or market microstructure are thought to influence the workings of securities markets. The abundant literature on universal-relationship banking suggests that banks become actively involved with firms listed on the stock exchanges and possibly altered pricing. If so, we might expect that markets within systems of this sort might perform differently from those operating without bank influence; potentially even to such an extent that bank relationships weakened the normal link between asset risk and returns. For this sort of manipulation to show up in broad-based statistical measures, the banks would have needed to consistently influence prices over many decades and to do so contrary to firms' fundamentals. In addition, the many banks, hypothetically representing each of the many stocks listed on the exchanges, would have needed to act in concert in their lobbying of official brokers. Moreover, to attribute this influence to a systematic outcome of a particular type of financial system – as opposed to an anomalous feature of a particular country's system – the pattern would need to appear (more or less) in all countries with the same institutional arrangements. It is more likely that a small number of banks, perhaps those most involved in the securities business, wielded the greatest power in the marketplace and led to some alteration of prices on a periodic basis. In that case, the overall effect on the market would be considerably smaller, though far more plausible.

Arguments about the interventions of banks in price setting are difficult to assess and are problematic to compare internationally. The main point in this sort of analysis is to determine whether or not the various markets yield the normal trade-off between risk and return and whether other firm characteristics enter asset pricing as they appear to do in highly developed markets of the more recent past. Given these limitations, the subsequent discussion sets rather modest goals for assessing the securities markets in the five cases.

We begin with the United Kingdom, where capital markets began to take shape in the mid-seventeenth century. The London Stock Exchange was

---

[56] On rules of incorporation, see Guinnane, Harris, Lamoreaux, and Rosenthal (2007).

officially founded in 1773 and, like many markets up to the mid-nineteenth century, listed primarily debt securities, particularly government-issued or -backed. With governments (foreign and domestic) amounting to more than three-quarters of the market, and railroads taking up another 20 percent, hardly any industrial shares gained listing as of 1853.[57] As the national debt declined after 1850, more and more alternative issues – foreign debt, municipal bonds, domestic railroads – made their way onto the London market. Yet by the early 1870s, government securities still accounted for significantly more than half of all securities quoted on the London Stock Exchange, railroads accounted for nearly one-third, and commercial and industrial securities accounted for just 1.4 percent (plus 5 percent in financial services). Over the next four decades, the government's share declined and the railroads' share increase; by 1913, however, the proportion of commercial and industrial securities was still less than 10 percent.[58] The London exchange did expand substantially over the late nineteenth and early twentieth centuries; between 1885 and 1907, the number of listed companies increased by a factor of ten.[59] Transport, utilities, and communications constituted approximately 70 percent of new issues in the half-century before World War I; manufacturing firms issued only 4 percent.[60] The London exchange erected few barriers to firms wishing to list shares, and even small companies could gain entry to the market.[61] On the eve of the twentieth century, the capitalization of the London Stock Exchange stood in the range of $4.3 billion dollars, or about 46 percent of the country's GDP.[62]

Nearly 150,000 companies registered as joint-stock companies in the fifty years following 1863; of these, only a small fraction issued and listed shares on any British exchange.[63] In terms of size and volume, the London market took first place among UK exchanges; yet for industrial financing, especially initial funding of new firms, the provincial exchanges played a more significant role than did London. The provincial exchanges attracted their clientele

---

[57] Michie (1990), pp. 98 and 104.
[58] Collins (1991). Michie (1990, pp. 98 and 104) gives similar figures.
[59] Capie and Collins (1992).
[60] Edelstein (2004), p. 195.
[61] To this lack of entry barrier Michie (1986) attributes much of the absence of impulse for size among British firms. See also Davis and Gallman (2001), who argue that the unique microstructure of the London exchange accounts for its ability to maintain the lion's share of listings internationally up until World War I.
[62] Dimson, Marsh, and Staunton (2002), p. 23, quoted in Musacchio (2010), p. 43, who himself provides new estimates of market capitalization, broken down by origin (foreign, empire, and domestic) and type (stock versus bond).
[63] Michie (1990), p. 93. He gives the figure of 147,932 enterprises registering.

by locating near the centers of industry, primarily northern English and Scottish cities: Manchester and Liverpool both founded exchanges in 1836; Glasgow and Edinburgh did so in 1844; and Leeds, Bristol, Birmingham, and Leicester founded their markets in 1845.[64] Like regional exchanges in other countries during the same period, the regional stock exchanges usually focused on the industries of the surrounding area, concentrating similar securities in places where the greatest knowledge and information could be transmitted and aggregated.

The multiplicity of exchanges (at least eighteen outside of London) survived throughout this era due in large part to the easy policies of the London exchange. Imposing no minimum commissions on trades, and only loosely enforcing rules on membership, allowed intermarket dealing to flourish, which in turn helped integrate national markets.[65] As the trend continued, particularly as communications technology permitted faster transmission of London prices, members of the London Stock Exchange began to object to the competition for their business and began to respond with ever more restrictive rules on who could trade and for what commission.[66]

In the exchanges more broadly, a range of industries – breweries, cycle manufacturers, automobile companies – issued shares on the market, particularly in the upturn starting in the mid-1890s. In certain industries, such as brewing, the stock exchanges offered an important means of financing for firms seeking to expand rapidly in the face of intensifying competition over the 1880s and 1890s.[67] Many new issues came from the conversion of preexisting companies – often very large ones – from private concerns into publicly traded ones. At the same time, however, many companies raised financing via debentures, not only because investors apparently preferred their relative security, but also because companies often wished to maintain family control.

Stock markets also played a major role in corporate finance in so-called bank-based systems, yet the traditional emphasis on the universal banks in Germany's industrialization experience has, until recently, pushed the securities markets well into the background. Newer work demonstrates, on the contrary, that Germany's pre–World War I financial system made extensive use of market-based finance and that those markets functioned at a

---

[64] Michie (1990), p. 93.
[65] Michie (1999), p. 111. See also Davis and Neal (2006).
[66] Michie (1999), p. 111. He argues that these new rules raised trading costs and dealing times.
[67] Cottrell, (1980), pp. 168–171, Watson (1996), pp. 62–67. Cottrell (1980), p. 178, notes that new issues dropped off between 1901 and 1912.

high level, even by contemporary American standards. Securities exchanges emerged in many parts of Germany from at least the seventeenth century, often stemming from early commodity-trading institutions.[68] Frankfurt and Hamburg, the old commercial centers, maintained the country's leading stock exchanges for the first half of the century, but Berlin took over the lead position after the unification in 1871. The growing numbers of joint-stock companies rapidly expanded the listing of industrial securities, particularly after the loosening of company law at the national level in 1870.

German securities exchanges often developed under the auspices of local businessmen, through chambers of commerce or similar trade organizations, and they generally governed the securities exchanges at least for the first half of the nineteenth century. Private bankers played a major role in the early exchanges, and, as they began to develop after mid-century, the universal banks participated actively in exchange governance as well. The crisis that ended the unification boom in the early 1870s spurred much criticism and demands for government intervention and regulatory reform.

During the early 1880s, the government obliged and issued new regulation to govern the founding and governance of corporations, to impose taxes on the issuing and trading of securities on the exchanges, and to set rules for the appointment and behavior of official brokers, as well as restrictions on the types of transactions taking place on the exchanges. The new laws aimed to make the securities exchanges, and the firms listed on them, safer for investors. To the extent that the regulations threw up roadblocks that hindered some firms' access to markets and delayed or prevented their going public, the laws may have pushed more financing into the hands of universal banks.

The 1896 Stock exchange law – a response to the Baring financial crisis of the early 1890s – added hurdles to listing and prohibited most futures contracting. Traditionally, observers have viewed this law as the crucial turning point in the growth of the German securities markets. The law did specify a range of prescriptions for protecting shareholders, but as the earlier laws had done, they also provided new reasons for firms to turn to universal banks for more of their financing and for investors to work through the banks to borrow cash for trading and to simulate futures contracting. The increasing taxation on listings and trading should have further compounded these influences, as they increased the costs associated with

---

[68] See Fohlin (2002b) for much more detail on the regulation and taxation of the German securities markets and its possible impact on the financial system more broadly. See also Burhop and Gelman (2008).

securities markets relative to banks. Tax hikes also provided a new economy of scale in trading within banks because the large banks could net out more positions among their brokerage customers and place only the small remainder on the markets, at least until the tax loophole closed with the 1908 amendment to the stock exchange law.

As hypothetically appealing as the arguments are about the negative effects of regulation on the markets, the empirical evidence remains contrary or only weakly supportive for the most part. Indeed, the markets seem to have continued to prosper throughout the period, and the banks grew and concentrated in line with industry and the rest of the economy at the time. Moreover, detailed scrutiny indicates that the growth and concentration of the universal banking sector bears little relationship to the imposition of new regulations on corporations and securities markets. To the extent that any of the laws mattered, it seems that the tax hikes took the greatest toll on markets.[69]

The performance of the German markets remains understudied, but the available evidence suggests that the Berlin market functioned fairly efficiently by modern measures, such as autocorrelation of returns.[70] Moreover, stock risk (measured as the covariance between the stock's return and that of the market) related positively with returns.[71] Market-to-book ratios related negatively to stock returns – the opposite of the effect seen in most of recent U.S. experience – whereas size and earnings effects were weak.

Recent historical research on Germany has also moved beyond basic market efficiency to investigate market quality and price discovery. Transactions costs or liquidity in the Berlin market, as measured by effective spreads, fell between 1880 and 1900, particularly in the latter part of that period.[72] The results bolster the argument that the German financial system supported highly functioning securities markets within its universal banking framework. Moreover, the findings also support the idea of symbiosis – not just coexistence – between the banks and the markets.

A similar pattern of stock market development appeared in Italy. And, as in the German case, the stock markets have taken a backseat to the universal

---

[69] See Fohlin (2002b and 2007a, Chapter 7). Burhop and Gelman (2008) later underscored these points using analysis of autocorrelation of returns to demonstrate that market efficiency continued despite the tax increases and the 1896 law.

[70] Burhop and Gelman (2008) for the period between 1892 and 1913.

[71] Fohlin and Reinhold (2010).

[72] Computation of effective spreads requires long series of high-frequency data. See Madhavan (2000) for a technical survey on the empirical estimation of transaction costs. See Gehrig and Fohlin (2006) on estimating spreads for Berlin.

banks in the story of Italian industrialization as well. In Italy, however, the reputation is perhaps better deserved. The lack of deep and liquid markets in Italy, in contrast to the German case, seemingly did constrain the financing options of industrial firms.[73] The early history of the Milan Stock Exchange parallels the German case, though the Milan exchange was founded quite a bit later than the earliest German bourses, in 1808, and showed little vitality during its first forty years.[74] Similar to its German counterparts, the Italian exchanges originally developed within the Chamber of Commerce, and those bodies selected the stock exchange agents.[75] In both countries, the most important bankers and traders of the localities used their influence in the Chamber of Commerce to shape the functioning of the stock exchange. By some accounts, these bankers also influenced the selection of stock exchange agents themselves, due to the requirement that candidates gain backing from multiple bankers.[76] Like many German exchanges, the Milan Stock Exchange traded a range of securities and commodities for most of the nineteenth century and only became specialized later on.[77]

The Italian stock exchanges developed rapidly, though not uniformly, after the unification in 1861. As in both Germany and the United Kingdom, Italy instituted provisions for incorporation by the 1860s. In 1865, the first Italian Commercial Code established the public corporation (Società per Azioni, s.p.a.), along with three other company forms.[78] The national law derived from the 1842 Sardinian Commercial Code, itself an inheritance from the Napoleonic Code.[79] In contrast to the United Kingdom and German laws, however, the Italian law required governmental authorization of SAs at first.[80] The revised Code of Commerce of 1882 – more than a decade after Germany's similar legal shift – liberalized public incorporation and transferred control from the government to shareholders. As it had elsewhere, the new legal framework permitted the broader adoption of corporate forms that spurred the expansion of publicly traded equity capital; in other words, the basis for a modern stock exchange.[81]

---

[73] Baia Curioni (1995), p. 7.
[74] Ibid., pp. 48 and 49.
[75] Ibid., p. 63.
[76] Ibid., pp. 66–67. Approximately 60 percent of stock exchange intermediaries had worked previously for some bank.
[77] Baia Curioni (1995) p.74.
[78] Unlimited Partnership (*Società in Nome Collettivo*, s.n.c.), Limited Partnership (*Società in Accomandita Semplice*, s.a.s.), and Partnership Limited by Shares (*Società in Accomandita per Azioni*, s.a.p.a.). For details, see Augello and Guidi (2002).
[79] See Kuhn (1912) for an international comparison of early corporate law.
[80] Augello and Guidi (2002).
[81] Ibid.

The boom years of 1870 to 1873 had similar effects on the Italian stock exchanges as it had done in Germany.[82] The Milan and Genoa stock exchanges grew rapidly. For most of the 1860s, the exchanges had dealt in a handful of securities, and only two equities traded in Milan.[83] Yet by 1873, Genoa was trading 3 billion lire, and Milan traded 1.5 billion lire; the number of listed corporations grew apace.[84] Additional exchanges opened as well, albeit on a very small scale: Cuneo in 1871, Chieti in 1872, and Messina in 1873. Sixteen stock markets operated around the country by the 1870s, most of them also functioning primarily at a highly localized level.[85] As in Germany, and elsewhere, the regional markets tended to specialize by type of security or industrial sector.[86]

Even though the exchanges expanded, some have argued that organizational and institutional problems prevented them from reaching their greatest potential growth.[87] For example, the commercial code of 1865 caused some complications to the appointment of market intermediaries.[88] The code law strengthened the monopoly position of the official stockbrokers, enumerating relatively strict criteria for candidates to be nominated as official stockbrokers and confirming that only official stockbrokers, intermediaries in commodities, and merchants can enter the exchange. At the same time, the law eliminated the cap on the numbers of official brokers and stated that "intermediation is a free profession."[89] By decentralizing both the selection and nomination of the brokers to the chamber of commerce, the ambiguity of the new law generated conflicts that the chambers of commerce solved on the basis of local power relationships. In Genoa, for example, the national rules were not enforced, given the dominance of the bankers over the official stockbrokers; in Milan, by contrast, merchants supporting free intermediation battled with the official stockbrokers.[90] Still,

---

[82] Baia Curioni (1995), p. 101.

[83] In 1867, Strade Ferrate Meridionali was listed, instead of Strade Ferrate Lombardo Venete; Baia Curioni (1995), p. 102.

[84] Baia Curioni (1995), p.103 gives the numbers as twenty shares (thirteen of which were banks) and thirteen different bonds in Milan. See Riva (2005, p. 31, and figure 14, p. 549), indicating numbers more than thirty-five in Genoa, compared to twenty-five in Milan.

[85] See Tronci (1891), cited in Toniolo, Conti, and Vecchi (2003), p. 446.

[86] Volpi (2002), p.16.

[87] Baia Curioni (1995).

[88] Riva (2009).

[89] The law extended to Italy the 1854 Sardinian suppression of the limits on numbers of official brokers.

[90] After two years of conflict, the 1867 Milan Stock Exchange internal rules stated that free brokers could enter the exchange. In response, the stockbrokers' committee (the body in charge of stock exchange monitoring) resigned, and the stockbrokers refused to vote for a new one. Then, according to press reports of the time "disorder and anarchy" reigned

at the end of the 1870s, there were 354 official agents, as opposed to 639 unofficial ones.[91]

Despite their small size relative to the leading markets elsewhere, the stock exchanges nonetheless helped finance the modernization of Italian infrastructure, particularly railways, and led to a growth in securitized finance. With the growth of securities, new windows for speculation opened up, and this opportunity led financial institutions to introduce new credit instruments, such as the report loans and margin purchases (*anticipazioni su titoli*), imported from Germany.[92]

The stock exchanges faced numerous problems. The government began taxing forward contracts in 1874, with the view that taxes along with the official brokers' monopoly would control speculation and make transactions more serious and safe. The 1873 crisis led to a drop in trading activity and an outflow of traders.[93] A significant number of companies formed for the sole purpose of selling shares and then disappearing.[94] All told, in 1876, the top seven exchanges still only dealt in eighty-one bonds of various types and sixty-seven shares – nowhere near the numbers in the United Kingdom and Germany.[95] Private bonds and shares, particularly in transport, banking, and textiles, gained in importance between 1875 and 1888, as public debt dropped off.[96]

As it had in Germany and elsewhere, the crisis of the mid-1870s raised calls for radical reforms. The resulting Commercial Code of 1882 effectively ended the monopoly of stock exchange agents, converting them from public officers to private traders "with dual capacity," that is, allowing them to trade on their own account. The brokers now faced competition and free entry, even if the law maintained the profession of official stockbroker.[97] By substantially reducing the number and extent of national rules, the legal reforms transferred regulatory powers to local authorities. Barriers

at the Milan Exchange. Responding to the resulting upheaval of the market, the banker-dominated chamber of commerce changed the internal rules in 1869: Access to exchange was denied to unofficial brokers.

[91]　Volpi, p. 40.

[92]　These financial innovations constituted one of the early experiences of technology transfer through international commerce in modern post-unification Italy. See Mattoo, Aaditya, Marcelo Olarreaga, and Kamal Saggi (2004), "Mode of foreign entry, technology transfer, and FDI policy," *Journal of Development Economics*, forthcoming.

[93]　Riva (2005). Baia Curioni (1995), p. 115.

[94]　Volpi, p. 15.

[95]　Baia Curioni (1995), p. 142.

[96]　Ibid., p. 138.

[97]　See extensive discussion in Riva (2005) as well as Baia Curioni (1995), p. 122, and Volpi, p. 40.

to entry into the official side of the trading profession – such as examinations and payment of a solvency-guarantee deposit – then varied from market to market, as did privileges and responsibilities, as well as handling of illegal behavior.[98] Thus, despite political and monetary unification, as well as advancements in information and communications technology (though only Genoa and Turin installed telegraph connections early on), the Italian securities markets only integrated in the late 1880s.[99] Even by 1888, except for 5 percent Rendita, very few securities traded regularly. Seven securities produced almost two-thirds (64 percent) of the quoted prices, and twelve securities were not traded at all.[100]

The market began to demonstrate generalized instability through more pronounced expansions and contractions.[101] The financial crisis between 1889 and 1894, which had led to a profound change in the Italian banking system, also hit the stock exchanges. Banks attempted to divest their securities holdings to generate liquidity.[102] The subsequent crisis of Banca Generale and Credito Mobiliare stopped most market activities, and prices fell by 80 percent between 1891 and 1894. The exchanges grew even more concentrated in fewer securities, mostly in the transport sector.[103]

The Italian stock markets began to rebound in 1894 (as in Germany as well).[104] Along with the foundation of Comit, events seemed to signal the development of a modern securities industry in Italy and a turning point in the development of Italy's corporate financial system more broadly.[105] There is considerable debate over the reasons for the turnaround and over the impact of institutional and technological developments – such as clearinghouses and major investments in telegraph connections – taking place in the wake of the crisis. By some accounts, the new telegraphic connections spurred competition among exchanges, as well as greater integration of markets within Italy and with Paris and Berlin.[106] Notably, as a result of heavy lobbying, Milan managed to secure a position at the center of the

---

[98] Riva (2005), Baia Curioni (1995), and Toniolo et al. (2003), p. 455.

[99] Toniolo et al. (2003) find that the prices of Italian *consols* converged across six markets in 1887.

[100] Baia Curioni (1995), p. 150.

[101] DeMattia.

[102] Confalonieri "Banca ed Industria," cited in Baia Curioni (1995), p. 150.

[103] Baia Curioni (1995), p. 153.

[104] Ibid., p. 164.

[105] Riva (2004) argues that not all of Italy's markets were as progress-oriented as Milan; in Genoa, for example, traders and bankers thwarted the development of a public and transparent organization.

[106] Baia Curioni (1995), p. 165.

new telegraphic network, so that all the Italian exchanges connected directly with Milan but not with each other. Thus, if a Genoa operator wished to send a telegram to the Rome Exchange, he had to send it to Milan, and the Milan operator would redirect the telegram to Rome – often, it was claimed, with errors and delay. Milan thusly obtained a disproportionately strong competitive advantage through these communications improvements. Some have argued that improved communications also improved regulatory oversight, furthering the uniformity of regulations.[107]

More recent research suggests that telegraphic connections perhaps facilitated information flows about prices and volumes of Italian *rentes* trading on the exchanges but did not improve regulatory oversight. Archival evidence indicates increasing power of local authorities on the exchanges and ongoing instability of the Genoa exchange throughout the period.[108] Moreover, even if regulatory oversight improved, it did not prevent the 1907 crisis; indeed, the 1907 crisis arguably underscored the lack of government monitoring of financial activity.[109]

Along similar lines, newer research argues that from 1894 on, precisely because of increasing local power on stock exchange design, Milan and Genoa diverged in their microstructure. For example, Milan established open outcry trading in a pit in 1895; Genoa did so only in 1912. Regulatory oversight by local bodies was strong in Milan, whereas it remained very weak in Genoa. Milan imposed many membership criteria for official stockbrokers, and bankers became increasingly powerful there. Meanwhile, Genoa relaxed their membership criteria. As a result, in 1906, approximately 1,200 brokers operated in the Genoa stock exchange, compared with 160 in the Milan stock exchange. The heterogeneity between the two main Italian markets created major problems for the central regulators.[110]

These intermarket differences aside, expansionary fiscal and monetary policies during the Giolitti era expanded the exchanges through both an increase of public debt (in 1896) and a subsequent increase in share

---

[107] Toniolo et al. (2003) and Baia Curioni (1995), p. 167. In contrast to the 1882 Code, which allowed for extensive local regulatory power. See Baia Curioni's study, along the lines of Garbade and Silber (1978), pp. 211–216. The data on Rendita in Toniolo et al. (2003) suggests that the 1887 drop in price dispersion exceeded that of 1894 quite considerably.

[108] See Riva (2005, 2009). Riva finds that Genoa officials were generally uncooperative: The clearing house of Genoa was founded in the same year of the Milan one, but Genoa operators started to use the clearing house in 1899 and organized in a very different and opaque way, compared to Milan's clearing house.

[109] See Bonelli (1971, 1982).

[110] Riva (2005, 2009).

issuance.[111] The transport, banking, and textile sectors remained dominant, but new issues appeared in the food and electric sectors as well. After a downturn in the first years of the twentieth century, both primary and secondary market activity accelerated again in 1903, as it did in a number of other countries. New issues grew as well, and by 1905, Milan listed 137 securities – more than double the listings three years earlier, but still far smaller than its German counterpart. Equities increased from 15 to 23 percent of volume, and activity expanded in steel and rails.[112]

Serious liquidity problems began in Genoa in May 1907, and the crisis peaked that summer and early fall, as it did in many markets around the world at the same time. Up to this point, the Genoa exchange led the other markets. The crisis and the regulators' reactions hit and destabilized the Genoa Exchange. As in Germany and elsewhere, financial activity began to shift toward a dominant locale, and market power began to centralize within the Milan Stock Exchange. Arguably, the complete lack of cooperation of Genoa with the central power (and Genoa's instability during the crisis of 1907), in contrast with the strong cooperation and stability of Milan, fueled the shift in Italy.[113] Regardless of the motivation, the Milan exchange replaced Genoa as the leading market by the beginning of the twentieth century. In contrast to most leading markets, the malaise dragged on in Italy. Markets had recovered in Germany and elsewhere by 1909, but Italian markets continued to conduct little business and floated very few new issues of shares.

Between 1908 and 1912, the government attempted to unify regulation of the exchanges, but reform only became official with the passage of the new stock exchange law, Act no. 272, in 1913.[114] The law transferred control from the local chambers of commerce to direct involvement of the national government and eliminated the dual capacity of the official brokers.[115] The new law imposed Milanese microstructure and rules on all Italian stock exchanges, as well as a common schedule time for sessions with the declared goal of centralizing the activity in Milan. Under regulators' pressures, Genoa adopted the same rules as Milan for admission of official stockbrokers and

---

[111] Baia Curioni (1995), p. 168.
[112] Ibid., p. 248.
[113] Riva (2005).
[114] See Baia Curioni (1995), p. 287 for details. This time, the Milan Chamber of Commerce summoned a meeting of all bankers and stock exchange agents hoping to come to an agreement.
[115] Baia Curioni (1995), p. 304. See Riva (2005) on the radical divergence in microstructure – rules and procedures – between Milan and Genoa in the 1890s.

for its clearinghouse operations. Given that Genoa had maintained its market share by offering a different type of basically unregulated trading, the 1913 law spelled the end of the Genoa stock exchange.

Debate also remains over the role of the universal banks and the impact of the regulatory changes. By some arguments, the regulations strengthened the power of big banks at the expense of the exchange agents. Yet, the opposing view holds that the banks already held that power much earlier.[116] As in Germany, the universal banks had worked closely – if often as a competitor – with the securities markets since their inception and funneled capital into the market through their brokerage and underwriting activities. The Italian banks, more than the German ones, invested on their own account and in a few cases held long-term stakes in industrial firms – particularly after 1898. The banks financed speculation through report loan contracts, allowing traders or brokers to purchase securities on margin.[117] They also managed client portfolios and influenced investor's choices and expectations.[118]

In contrast to the earlier German regulation, the Italian law failed to stipulate the removal of the large, universal banks from direct involvement in exchange business (such as the price-setting process).[119] The new regulations thus arguably expanded the banks' traditional role as dominant players, creating potential conflicts of interest and, by some accounts, hindering the markets in their ability to channel capital most effectively to industrial enterprise.[120] At the same time, the 1913 law stipulated the creation of trading pits in all Italian stock exchanges, and only official stockbrokers could enter the pit and participate in price discovery. From this standpoint, the banks were restricted from the price-setting process even if they were by far the largest clients of the official brokers. The analysis is so far incomplete,

---

[116] Riva argues that throughout the nineteenth century, the banks' role in the rule-making process created problems for the Genoa stock exchange, which in turn led to the 1907 crisis. Nevertheless, Riva underscores the 1913 uniformity of market microstructures and the subsequent shift of financial activity toward Milan as the device the government employed to improve regulatory oversight.

[117] Baia Curioni (1995), p. 179.

[118] Investment banking activity for COMIT has been documented extensively by Confalonieri, page 179. Confalonieri identifies a change in the practice of reporting for COMIT in 1898–1899, with a clear change of direction from Rendita 5% to shares (Vol. III, pp. 147–152). For an analysis of report loans for COMIT, pp. 186–187. Baia Curioni (1995) provides extensive details on these and subsequent developments (p. 182). Fohlin (1998a) examines the stock holdings of the top two universal banks and the bank relationships that resulted.

[119] Volpi, pp. 53–54 and B.C., p. 299.

[120] According to Baia Curioni (1995), these conflicts lasted for a large part of the twentieth century (p. 305).

but studies have shown that the intervention of universal banks possibly increased the liquidity of the securities in which they were directly interested but had no influence on pricing.[121]

As in both Italy and Germany, modern-style securities markets emerged in Japan by the last quarter of the nineteenth century. Though some of Japan's markets lacked the centuries-old tradition of several European securities markets – the first two being founded only in 1878 – they did have similar predecessors in commodities markets. Because the exchanges used practices developed from these early domestic commodities markets, they were, in character, more Japanese than foreign as many of the banking institutions were. Unlike the German and Italian markets, and more similar to the London market, Japanese stock exchanges tended to take on joint-stock company form, rather than remaining private and issuing memberships, and their own shares constituted some of the most actively traded securities in the market.[122] Stock markets also spread quickly in Japan: By 1898, there were forty-six of them in cities across the country.

Similar to the German experience, the Japanese government intervened in the markets fairly early on, though arguably with less success. The 1874 Stock Exchange Act attempted to apply rules essentially borrowed from the London Stock Exchange to the informal markets, but market participants rejected the strictures.[123] A new attempt at regulation came in the form of the 1878 Stock Exchange Act that regulated transactions and, rather than imposing new rules, to some extent formalized long-standing practices from commodities markets (such as futures contracts).[124] Twelve years later, the government enacted the Commercial Code, regulating corporate form as well as the issuance of securities, particularly bonds. The rules initially required owners' names to be inscribed on bonds – similar to the Anglo-American method – but an 1899 amendment permitted bearer bonds in the interest of facilitating ownership transfers – as in Germany. Japanese firms issued substantial amounts of bonds in the pre–World War I era, most of which were issued without collateral. In the decade leading up to World War I, corporate bond issues exceeded 10 million yen, compared with a total paid-in capital of about 1 billion yen.[125]

---

[121] Baia Curioni (1995), p. 184. The causal connection remains unclear, particularly in light of Comit's involvement with the largest firms in the steel and mechanical sector.

[122] Tamaki (1995), p. 108.

[123] Hoshi and Kashyap (2001), p. 25.

[124] See Hoshi and Kashyap (2001) on the regulatory changes at this time.

[125] See Hoshi and Kashyap (2001). Hamao, Hoshi, and Okazaki (2009) argue that listing requirements at the Tokyo exchange discouraged new firms from listing there until the 1910s, at which point liberalization encouraged a boom in listings. Notably,

Over the 1890s and first decade of the 1900s, more than two-thirds of the Japanese stock exchanges disappeared. As their numbers diminished, however, activity at the remaining thirteen exchanges increased. Few companies listed shares on the exchanges until very late in the 1890s, but these sorts of listings began to take off in the years leading up to World War I, reaching more than 200 in 1910. Market capitalization increased more than three and a half times between 1897 and 1911, and more than doubled again in the next eight years. In this development, as well, the government and financial institutions played an important role, supporting trading via discount facilities at the Bank of Japan.[126] The Tokyo market took an increasing share of business in this period and by World War I had risen to its dominant position that would endure thereafter.

The stock exchanges grew in significance, particularly for corporate firms, during World War I and through the 1920s. Share listings in Tokyo rose from the mid-hundreds before World War I to more than 1,000 by 1927; capitalization of the Tokyo market doubled as well.[127] By one estimate, between 1914 and 1931, more than 40 percent of new corporate funding came from the stock market – just slightly more than funding from bank borrowing.[128] A different study puts the estimates of new stock issues in the 1920s and early 1930s between one-third and essentially all of total net business financing.[129]

We lack comprehensive studies of the performance of the Japanese markets; such analysis depends on large-scale, high-frequency, firm-level data gathering, which is absent for all but one or two markets in the pre–World War I era. Thus, we can say that the Japanese stock exchanges appear to have developed in similar fashion to those of other industrializing countries of the early twentieth century, but stronger statements about their efficiency await further research.

As they had in the other four countries studied here, early securities markets appeared in the United States starting in the eighteenth century. The New York Stock Exchange came into being with an agreement among brokers in 1792. Markets opened in many cities around the country during the

---

however, similar patterns appear in other countries as well, such as Germany and the United States.

[126] See Tamaki (1995), p. 109.

[127] See Hoshi and Kashyap (2001), p. 39 for additional figures.

[128] Goldsmith (1983), p. 102, who notes that the figure may include a substantial amount of paid-in capital that replaced unincorporated equity. Even so, the point is the increasing use of publicly traded shares.

[129] See Hoshi and Kashyap (2001) based on Matsumoto's figures on the financing patterns of a sample of listed firms.

nineteenth century, but by the early 1860s, with New York's rise to prominence in corporate finance and banking, the NYSE became the country's premier market. Stock markets played a similar role in the United States as they did in other rapidly industrializing countries over the last half of the nineteenth century, primarily helping raise funds for financial companies (banks and insurance), railroads, and an increasing range of industrial firms as the twentieth century began.

Parallel to many other countries in the mid-nineteenth century, financial institution securities and government issues dominated the markets early on. Railroads followed soon after, and by the late nineteenth century, they were trading larger and larger amounts of funds. Railroad securities were treated much like municipalities, as an investor was investing in the area surrounding the railroad, not necessarily the company itself.[130] Listings on the New York Stock exchange grew rapidly – just as they did in most other countries – as incorporation spread to more and more firms and industries from the 1870s and particularly in the 1890s and early 1900s.

The move into trading in new industries progressed slowly over the last decades of the nineteenth century, as the NYSE imposed stringent listing requirements, often rejecting mining and petroleum companies, for example, due to their perceived risk. Once companies gained acceptance at a market elsewhere, the NYSE allowed them to list.[131] It was the end of the nineteenth century before industrial issues grew to take up a substantial portion of listings and trading at the exchange, and even then, railroads continued as the largest market segment. Corporate reporting regulation remained week quite late in the United States. In 1895, the NYSE suggested that all companies trading on the market should send their shareholders an annual report on their finances; the practice became mandatory four years later.

Size and capitalization barriers offered firms greater incentives to create large corporations. Being quoted enhanced the value of a company, providing additional and cheaper sources of capital. Moreover, listed companies could absorb other smaller companies by swapping its quoted stock for the other's unquoted stock.[132]

The NYSE operated under the oversight of the Governing Committee, with significant decision-making power distributed among permanent committees responsible for particular areas of exchange operations.[133]

[130] See Baskin (1988), pp. 208–209.
[131] Michie (1986), p. 185.
[132] Ibid., p. 186.
[133] See Michie (1986) for a thorough survey.

The exchange granted memberships, raising the fee from $3,000 in 1862 to $10,000 in 1866. As of 1868, the exchange fixed the number of seats at 1,060 (1,100 in 1879) and allowed their purchase and sale. After that point, joining the NYSE meant paying the membership fee and also buying the seat of an existing member. The seats themselves thus became a valuable commodity, with prices following the market: $4,000 to $4,500 in 1870 and $64,000 to $94,000 in 1910. The governing body had the power to discipline members with expulsion or fines and could take a member's seat as punishment or repayment of debts.[134] The courts upheld these tough sanctions, finding no restraint of trade in the fining and expulsion of members, or in the restriction of trading to members alone.[135]

Brokers and jobbers divided exchange operations between them, with the former performing transactions for clients on commission and the latter performing market making functions. Jobbers developed rapidly after 1865 and gradually gained specializations in certain securities or industries.[136] Membership demand soon came up against the constraints on new member admissions, and more established brokers began operating away from the exchange, thus eventually creating competition for the NYSE. Even though the NYSE merged with its main rival, the Open Board, in 1869, competition persisted. The Consolidated Stock Exchange, with 2,403 members, presented the most significant challenge, as did the unorganized "curb" market.[137] By 1908, the three exchanges contained 424 million shares of stock, with close to half being traded on the NYSE.[138]

Technological innovation over the second half of the nineteenth century drastically altered the functioning of the securities markets, speeding communications and reducing the costs of moving information.[139] The Atlantic cable was built in 1866, the stock ticker was introduced in 1867, and the telephone appeared in 1878. Before the stock ticker came into operation, providing instant transmission of prices, quotes were recorded by hand and carried back to the office of a firm. These technologies led to a continuous market on the NYSE in 1871 and opened up trading to all regions of the country – and elsewhere. The advances also facilitated off-exchange trading at official NYSE prices, meaning further competition for the main exchange.

[134] See Mulherin et al. (1991), pp. 597–598.
[135] Ibid., pp. 598–602.
[136] See Michie (1986), p. 183.
[137] Brown et al. (2008) argue that the Consolidated provided a useful check on the market power of the NYSE and its specialists.
[138] Michie (1986), pp. 175–176.
[139] See Mulherin et al. (1991) and Michie (1986) on technological change in the markets.

The New York Stock Exchange also closely regulated commission rates. At 1/8 of 1 percent, the official commission encouraged additional outside dealing. The much lower commission on trades within member firms (1/32 down to 1/50) prompted the growth of brokerage firms that could net out substantial amounts of trading at the deep discounts – quite like the practices of many of the largest Berlin banks operating in the Berlin stock exchange around the same time.[140] High commissions also invited outside competition. The Consolidated Stock Exchange charged a commission rate of 1/16, drawing nonmembers into dealing off the NYSE. The Consolidated took this competition one step further in 1885, when it began trading NYSE-listed stocks at the NYSE official quotes. This free-riding on the price discovery mechanism of the larger exchange enhanced the Consolidated exchange's attractiveness, adding to the draw of its lower commissions, and thereby siphoning off additional NYSE business.[141] This new access to NYSE quotes permitted by tickers and telephones also brought competition from exchanges across the country, whose brokers canceled out each other's commissions via "joint-account arbitrage."[142]

The NYSE attempted to deal with its competition, first by requiring members affiliated with both exchanges to withdraw membership from the Consolidated Stock Exchange (1886), then by creating its own Unlisted Trading Department to trade in shares previously relegated to the lesser Consolidated exchange.[143] The NYSE also attempted to remove tickers from both the Consolidated Stock Exchange and outside brokers, and it later forbade phone links to the Consolidated Stock Exchange. Neither measure proved effective in preventing the dissemination of NYSE price quotes to outside traders.[144] The NYSE also took measures to defend against joint-account arbitrage. They first banned the practice in 1881, allowed it to continue in 1883, and then reinstated the prohibition in 1894. In 1896, dealing in differences between domestic exchanges was banned, and in 1898, the exchange banned the transmission of continuous price quotes.[145] These measures were difficult to enforce, yet they still limited transactions between the NYSE and other domestic exchanges and created price differentials. These attempts to curb competition also hampered the NYSE's ability to

---

[140] Michie (1986), pp. 177–178; Fohlin (2007a).
[141] See Mulherin et al. (1991), p. 608.
[142] See Michie (1986), p. 179.
[143] Mulherin et al. (1991), p. 609.
[144] See Michie (1986), p. 178. For a detailed description of the legal battle for exchanges to control their quotes, see Mulherin et al. (1991).
[145] Michie (1986), p.179.

operate as efficiently or with the greatest breadth and liquidity as possible. But they simultaneously prevented the competition from doing so as well.

Overall, then, the NYSE constrained its own growth and efficiency through its restrictive regulations. In doing so, it stimulated the development of alternatives in the form of large, national, diversified brokerage firms, as well as other markets able to circumvent the NYSE. It is difficult to quantify, based on available evidence, the impact of NYSE rules and regulations, or how they played into the broader effectiveness of the American financial system during industrialization. Considerable research efforts are underway on a number of fronts, but the results so far remain provisional. Based on what we do know so far, it appears that the NYSE was smaller than the Berlin market, listing a few hundred shares, compared to Berlin's thousands. The NYSE possibly also had higher trading costs – at least those captured in modern spread measures – at the start of the twentieth century.[146]

CONCLUSIONS

Each of the countries examined here began the process of large-scale industrialization at some point in the nineteenth century – early on in the case of the United Kingdom, mid-century for Germany and the United States, and toward the end for Italy and Japan. Over the same period, all of these countries created diversified financial systems that comprised a variety of institutions to provide intermediation for virtually all segments of society. Savings banks and credit cooperatives took care of the least wealthy and small business; commercial banks and trust companies catered to larger business and wealthy individuals; and investment banks, universal banks, and investment banking arms of commercial banks all served the needs of firms wishing to incorporate and gain access to securities markets. The systems that emerged did differ, often markedly, but all gathered resources from investors, grew rapidly, and mobilized enormous amounts of capital toward productive ends.

Mostly in the 1850s to 1870s, all of these countries enacted some sort of regulation, often a series of laws, to formalize, standardize, and liberalize incorporation and liability, thus laying the groundwork for modern corporate financial systems. By the 1870s or 1880s, corporations in all five countries became a crucial mode of allowing companies to expand and to finance an unprecedented scale of operations. The progression accelerated in the last years of the nineteenth century and into the twentieth, demanding

---

[146] See Fohlin and Gehrig (2010) and Gehrig and Fohlin (2006).

ever more development of the corporate financial sector and of the securities markets. This new system of corporate firms began to loosen the ties of families to the firms they started, creating the need for new modes of governing these growing firms. The next chapter takes up the question of how corporate governance systems evolved in these five countries, and what part financial institutions played.

3

Organizing Commercial Banking

Banks form the core of a modern financial system: mobilizing capital, facilitating payments, and allocating resources to productive activity. How banks are designed may affect how they perform these key functions and may also relate to the organization of the banking industry as a whole. These structural characteristics may also tie into the cost of banking services as well as into banks' ability to mobilize resources and to influence the economy overall. This chapter examines the industrial organization of banking, the development of banks' services, and the performance of the banking industry during the late nineteenth and early twentieth centuries. The comparison across all five countries sheds new light on the influence of the banking scope on bank scale, competition, and performance. The results often run contrary to assumptions born out of more recent experience, particularly that of the United States.

INDUSTRIAL ORGANIZATION OF BANKING

In the realm of commercial and investment banking, it is often assumed that universal banks – those that combine services – are large compared to specialized commercial banks. These sorts of assumptions hinge on the idea that minimum efficient scale ought to be larger for a universal bank, or the notion that universality offers greater opportunities for a bank to grow. Although we cannot say for sure what the minimum efficient scale is for specialized versus universal banks, particularly in the historical context, we can investigate the empirical relationship between bank size and scope of services. The average size of individual banks depends heavily on the use or avoidance of branching networks, and branching in turn influences the number of separate banking firms. Growth of branching networks suggests expansion of the banking industry and improvements in

48

capital mobilization. Deposits to the banking system may grow without branching, of course, because it is possible for institutions in other areas to collect funds regionally and make deposits with larger banks in their base cities. But branching by a single institution may facilitate the flow of information and enable more efficient interregional transfers while diversifying short-term liabilities and possibly safeguarding against systemic instability. Geographical diversification therefore permits lower reserve ratios, which in turn pushes more capital into productive uses.

Branching activity tends to increase concentration in the banking industry, because branches of a single institution substitute closely for a new unit banking institution. From an empirical standpoint, branching commonly proceeds most rapidly via mergers of existing institutions; typically, larger banks in larger cities take over smaller banks in outlying areas. Whether or not increasing concentration alters bank behavior is less obvious. In a unit banking system, low-density areas may support only one bank and may therefore face monopoly pricing. Prohibitions on branching prevent existing banks from opening up business in the monopolized market, and other barriers to entry (such as needing a strong reputation) may likewise restrict entry of new firms to the market. Liberalization of branching restrictions may permit the replacement of these small, local monopolies with a more competitive – though more concentrated – regional system of banks. Studying the size and shape of banking industries within a variety of national financial systems offers counterexamples to some common notions of the links between the scope of services (universality) on the one hand and bank scale, branching, and concentration on the other.

England developed one of the world's earliest full-fledged banking industries. The banking system blossomed in the second half of the eighteenth century. In 1750, there were only 12 private banks outside of London in England and Wales; in 1790, there were 280.[1] The first joint-stock banks tended to be localized and grew slowly for the first half of the century, being opposed both by the private country bankers and by the Bank of England (a privately owned institution at the time). By 1837, 114 such banks had formed. Soon after the lifting of the limitation on London joint-stock banks in 1833, the first London-based joint-stock deposit bank appeared in the form of the London and Westminster Bank (1834). By 1857, ten metropolitan banks had been established. Joint-stock banks failed at high rates until banking legislation was liberalized and branching spread. The ranks of joint-stock banks increased little on net from the 1830s to the 1860s, but the banks

---

[1] Cottrell (1991), p. 1139.

grew in size and importance: Deposits in the London banks increased ten-fold from 1840 to 1857. The introduction of limited liability in 1856 marked another turning point in UK banking. Not surprisingly, the twenty-four new joint-stock banks formed between 1860 and 1874 all took this form.[2]

Private banks proliferated in the United Kingdom in the early industrial period, and the industry grew almost continuously over the nineteenth and early twentieth centuries. By 1825, 650 banks had appeared in England and Wales. Twenty-five years later, with the onset of a merger movement, their numbers had dropped by half (327 banks remained). Joint-stock banks began to take over private banks, so that their numbers were roughly equal in 1900, but by 1913, there were forty-one joint-stock banks compared to twenty-nine private banks.[3]

Branching developed early in England as well, starting mostly from the 1850s. By 1865, 2,417 branches had been set up in England, Scotland, Ireland, and the Channel Islands; the figure increased to 3,886 twenty years later.[4] In 1890, the banks averaged thirty branches, and this figure grew to forty-five in 1900 and ninety-three by 1910. Branching varied considerably among banks, of course: Of the 43 joint-stock banks with 5,797 branches in 1913, just 3 had more than 500 branches.[5] Branching in the United Kingdom, as in other countries, often progressed through the takeover of smaller banks, but it also expanded by opening branches in underbanked areas.[6] As a result, the commercial branch network in the United Kingdom covered the country much earlier than in most other countries. On average, a UK bank branch served 8,000 people in 1890 and only 5,500 by 1910, making the United Kingdom more densely branched than other developed economies at the time. The UK deposit banks were also the largest financial institutions by any standard of the time.

Bank amalgamation, and consequent increases in concentration, began early in the United Kingdom as well: 122 mergers between 1825 and 1843, 93 of which involved the absorption of private banks by joint-stock ones. After the 1870s, once most of the smaller private banks had disappeared, amalgamation began to involve more and more mergers of joint-stock banks. From this merger wave, a small number of large regional banks and nationally networked banks emerged.[7] Not surprisingly, it was the largest

2   Anderson and Cottrell (1974).
3   Collins (1994), p. 275.
4   Anderson and Cottrell (1974), p. 326.
5   Nevin and Davis (1970), pp. 81–82.
6   Nevin and Davis (1970), pp. 73–74. See also Sayers (1957), p. 264.
7   Anderson and Cottrell (1974).

members of the commercial banking sector that built the most significant nationwide branching networks during the pre–World War I period
and thereby contributed to the nationwide increases in banking industry
concentration. The top five English banks held approximately one-fifth of
total bank assets in 1890 and held more than a third (36 percent) by 1910.[8]
By the end of World War I, the concentration movement had created the
"Big Five" – Barclays, Lloyds, the Midland, the National Provincial, and the
Westminster – which not only held 80 percent of English deposits, but also
counted among the largest banks in the world.[9] The Midland Bank was then
the largest commercial bank in the world, holding £350 million in deposits
and operating 1,300 offices.[10] At the same time, the extensive branching of
UK banks also stabilized the industry early on: No banking panics or serious financial crises erupted after 1866.[11]

Despite its common roots, the American commercial banking sector
followed an entirely different course from those in England and almost all
other industrialized countries of the late nineteenth and early twentieth
centuries.[12] Whereas major concentration movements reduced most countries' commercial banking industries to a few very large banks with widespread, often nationally networked, branches, the United States built up a
very large number of small banks, mostly with no branches, as well as a
wealth of nonbank financial institutions providing substantially identical
services. The oddity of the U.S. banking industry structure stems from a
combination of factors, mostly politically based and deeply rooted, that led
to a myriad of regulations on the creation and operation of financial institutions and a split between national and state law. The often countervail-
ing goals of promoting competition among banks while ensuring systemic
stability set the stage for a regulatory regime that guaranteed neither.[13]
Instability, in turn, promoted a sense of mistrust of banking institutions,
which then furthered the political pressure to regulate.

Banks appeared early and often in the United States. Chartering and
incorporation began shortly after independence; they numbered in the low

[8] Measures using total assets and total share capital yield similar results. See Fohlin (2006).
[9] Collins (1994), p. 282.
[10] Cottrell (1991), p. 1147.
[11] Capie (2001).
[12] For in-depth discussions of U.S. banking regulation and structure, see the excellent books
     by White (1983) and Klebaner (1990). Barnett (1911) is also a rich resource on pre–World
     War I commercial banks (particularly state banks) and trusts.
[13] In addition to White (1983) and Klebaner (1990), see Calomiris (2000), particularly on
     banking panics and systemic instability (including articles coauthored with White and
     with Gorton).

hundreds by 1820, the upper hundreds by 1840, and into the thousands by 1860. By the late nineteenth and early twentieth century, tens of thousands of them populated the U.S. states.[14] In 1900, commercial banks numbered 12,427 (3,731 national and 8,696 nonnational); by 1920, the number jumped to 30,909.[15] In 1890, there were roughly 6,300 people per banking office, and by 1910, the number had declined to 3,700. Relative to other advanced economies of the time, the U.S. system provided more bank access to the population on average, despite the lack of branching in the United States and despite the limits on bank notes under the National Bank Act until 1875. Counting bank branch offices as well as private banks, there was far more population per banking office in both Germany and the United Kingdom than there was in the United States between 1890 and 1910.[16] Private banks and trust companies added substantially to the numbers of institutions offering commercial banking services. By some accounts, there were some 4,000 to 5,000 private banks from the 1880s through 1910, and trust companies increased more than fifteenfold between 1886 and 1913.[17]

The enormous numbers of American banks naturally hinged on the regulation of banking institutions, particularly those restricting branching. Despite some early branching activity before the Civil War, the practice was essentially – though not literally – prohibited by the National Banking Act of 1864.[18] Many state legislators also frowned on branch banking, stymieing even statewide branching. These widespread limitations on the practice meant there were virtually no bank branches in the United States until the early twentieth century. Up until the very end of the nineteenth century, however, the United States hardly lagged behind most other countries, other than the United Kingdom. On the one hand, it seemed on the surface that unit banking would promote competition and serve customers, but as pressure mounted to consolidate the industry around the turn of the twentieth century, it was the bankers themselves who lobbied for limits on

---

[14] Board of Governors of the Federal Reserve (1959) and U.S. Bureau of the Census (1960). See Barnett (1911), appendix table I (following p. 248), for an augmented series of state banks, based on Homan's Bankers Almanac and Register. Barnett indicates that many banks failed to report to the Comptroller, as required by law, but did send reports to Homan's.

[15] Board of Governors of the Federal Reserve (1959) and U.S. Bureau of the Census (1960).

[16] There were approximately 8,000 people per UK branch in 1890 and only 5,500 per branch by 1910.

[17] White (1983), p. 38, citing Barnett's series (private banks) and p. 39, citing John Fred Bell's Ph.D. dissertation on the commercial banking activities of trust companies.

[18] Section 8 of that act dictated that "usual business shall be transacted at an office or banking house located in the place specified in its organization certificate." See Robertson (1968), as cited in White (1983), p. 14.

branching.[19] Branch banking did start to take root in the early twentieth century, when certain states, notably California, explicitly permitted mostly unfettered intrastate branching. More commonly, state laws allowed for limited branching, often capping the number of branches or their distance from headquarters. Banks increasingly took advantage of their freedom, but the process remained slow up to 1914 and well past that date. Many states restricted even intrastate branching until the 1990s.

Branching restrictions clearly limited the size of American banks in most parts of the country. Compared to banks in Europe and Japan, American banks were small on average, and they even declined in size as more and more of them sprung up in the early years of the twentieth century. Banks averaged $640,000 of assets in 1890, $890,000 in 1900, and $790,000 in 1910 – all in constant (1913) values. International comparisons bring home the importance of unit banking for the structure of the U.S. banking industry. Most notably, German, Japanese, and English banks far exceeded U.S. banks in average size throughout the period, and the gap grew in the decades before World War I.

Branching restrictions explain a good part of the difference in size between U.S. banks and those of other countries, but that is not to say that all American banks were smaller than banks in other countries. In terms of average assets per bank, American commercial banks lagged the UK commercial banks by a far wider margin than they lagged banks in other countries. However, focusing on the average size of U.S. banks obscures the fact that a significant number of American banks grew to a scale well beyond the vast majority of the rest. The largest banks in the biggest (densely populated) and most finance-oriented cities – New York in particular – reached a similar scale as the second-tier German banks. And plenty of universal banks in Germany remained smaller than many American banks.

Because of the very different industry structure in U.S. banking, national-level concentration statistics are not very meaningful as a measure of actual market power. On that level, the American banking industry looks very competitive and unconcentrated. As measured by five- and ten-firm ratios, concentration increased between 1890 and 1900 – from 3.2 to 5.6 percent in 1890 and from 6.5 to 9.8 percent in 1900. Levels stayed almost constant in 1908 but declined again thereafter, to 4.5 and 7 percent by 1913.

At the state level, concentration ratios varied widely; these measures tell a different story. States with some of the largest banks were less concentrated

---

[19] See Calomiris (2000), p. 47, noting the lobbying efforts of the American Bankers' Association.

than some states that had smaller banks. For example, New York had five-firm ratios of 18 percent in 1900 and 1913, whereas Illinois had ratios of 25 percent throughout the same period. At the state level, the U.S. commercial banking sector averaged five-firm ratios of 24 percent in 1900, and actually declined to slightly less than 20 percent on the eve of World War I.[20] State-level ratios also converged somewhat by 1913, with both the lowest ratios increasing and the highest decreasing. This pattern likely resulted from the entry of new banks into rural and less industrialized states.[21]

Even the state-level data may belie important patterns of concentration of power within a select group of institutions. The data for an entire state may mask the concentration within relevant geographical banking markets. In the pre–World War I era, most customers would have sought to deal with a bank within a short travel distance. Transportation costs circumscribed markets to a small area and likely prevented most customers from taking their business to other banks. Whereas a large city like New York or Boston could sustain several banks, many market areas contained too small a population to support more than one bank. In other words, the largest banks could well have held smaller market shares in their relevant market than did the tiniest banks. In Massachusetts circa 1881, for example, Boston had more than sixty banks, fifty-three of which held well more than $1 million in assets, whereas Nantucket – a geographically constrained market to be sure – had one, with assets of slightly more than $300,000.[22] Thus, clearly, size is not inextricably related to market power, and the urban-rural divide played a major role in the banks' competitive positions.

German banks faced similar conditions in the mid-nineteenth century. Very few had begun to branch by that time, despite the absence of restrictions on the practice. German commercial banks still had set up few, if any, branches by the 1870s, when the newly formed Deutsche Bank began building its network. Even up to the turn of the twentieth century, unit banking, or close to it, persisted in Germany.[23] The nine major Berlin banks (great banks) maintained only ten deposit offices in 1885, and in 1890, less than a quarter of publicly traded banks maintained branches at all. These branching banks averaged only two subsidiary offices apiece,

---

[20] See Fohlin (2009) on state-level concentration ratios, based primarily on reports of the Comptroller.

[21] The top five banks in New Mexico, for example, held nearly 60 percent of total statewide banking assets in 1900, but only 30 percent by 1913. See Fohlin (2009).

[22] Based on reports of the Comptroller of the Currency for 1881, so this small island may have had more banks that do not register in official reports.

[23] See Fohlin (2007a) and sources cited there.

and they typically kept their branches within a narrow regional focus. By 1894, the nine largest Berlin banks had opened seventy-three deposit offices. But even by 1900, the joint-stock banks as a whole averaged only one branch apiece. The total number of joint-stock branches quadrupled over the first decade of the twentieth century, yet by 1913, there were still only 230 domestic branches of the 9 Berlin great banks. As branching took hold, population per branch in Germany declined from 45,000 in 1900 to less than 15,000 in 1910 – still far higher than the comparable ratios for the United Kingdom.[24] Partly as a by-product of this branching process – in large part, turning unit banks into branches of another banking firm – joint-stock banks grew in size, reaching average assets of more than 100 million marks (about $23 million) each on the eve of World War I, and nearly 900 million marks ($180 million) in assets each for the great banks.[25] Even as the German banks grew, they remained smaller than the UK banks: On average, the latter owned almost three times the assets of the former between 1890 and 1910.[26] Even by the start of World War I, the German joint-stock banks had not reached the size that the British commercial banks had attained twenty-five years earlier.

Still, within Germany, the rapid accumulation of branches meant that the largest banks grew larger themselves and simultaneously eliminated enormous numbers of the smaller banks. Naturally, the top banks thereby expanded their share of the total banking market. Over the thirty years before World War I, however, concentration of assets actually progressed irregularly and at a modest rate.[27] The top five banks began the period with 37 percent of total joint-stock bank assets, but concentration ratios remained flat in the mid-1880s and declined steadily between 1896 and 1901 (back down to 37 percent). The ratio declined on net in the latter half of the 1880s and remained around 33 to 34 percent in the early 1890s. By the start of the war, the largest banks held just short of 42 percent of total

---

[24] If private banks are included, using a rough estimate of 1,500 single-office institutions, the figure for population per branch would fall to 9,200 people per office in 1910. Donaubauer (1988) estimates that more than 2,000 private bankers operated in Germany in the 1890s, whereas the Deutsche Bundesbank (1976) estimates around 1,100 for 1913. In addition, Pohl (1982) counts approximately 1,500 such banks at the time of the formation of the German Empire in 1871.

[25] Divide 1913 marks by 5 to get approximate 1913 dollar equivalent.

[26] See Fohlin (2006), and sources cited there.

[27] The measures are five-firm ratios of total assets and total share capital. The joint-stock credit banks are the *Kreditbanken* in the Deutsche Bundesbank (1976) series. Private banks reported little or no data as a group and are therefore only included for total assets and then only included at estimated values.

joint-stock bank assets.[28] By this measure, the English deposit-banking sector remained more concentrated than the German universal banking sector between 1884 and 1913.

To the extent that private bankers competed with the joint-stock banks, banking concentration actually remained considerably lower than these figures indicate, particularly for the period before the incorporated banks began to absorb private banks. In that case, the top five held approximately 16 percent in 1884 and 33 percent in 1913.[29] Certainly, the largest universal banks were not small institutions, but equally sure is the fact that the German commercial (universal) banking industry was not beset by excessive concentration.

Despite the later appearance of German-style joint-stock banks in Italy, branching progressed earlier, and at a somewhat faster rate, in Italy than in Germany. Within its first two years of operations, Comit instituted three branch offices, and the branch networks of the four largest banks reached all areas of the country by World War I. Comit led the Italian universal banks in branching, opening offices in Florence and Genoa in its first year and then in Rome, Turin, Naples, and Messina in the succeeding four years.[30] Comit maintained thirty branches outside of its Milan headquarters by 1906 and fifty-eight on the eve of World War I – 20 percent more than the German leader, Deutsche Bank. Though lagging Comit in branching, Credit (thirty-eight), Banco di Roma (twenty-nine), and SBI (thirty-three) fell in the middle of the range for the German great banks at the start of World War I. The twenty- to forty-year lag in the onset of universal banking in Italy compared to Germany, however, implies a relatively much faster progress of the Italian banks' branching.

The four principal credit banks together held only 2 percent of all bank assets in 1895 (more than half of which were held by Comit), but by 1911, they held 15 percent of the total. Comit and Credit alone held 10 percent of bank-held assets in 1911 (6.2 percent for Comit and 3.8 percent for Credit). Within a decade of the founding of the principal universal banks, the big-four Italian universal banks accounted for a similar proportion of joint-stock

[28] Asset concentration ratios grew faster than share capital-based ratios, meaning that the largest banks increased their assets more through deposits than through share capital, compared with the provincial banks. Thus, the great banks expanded their customer base rapidly at the expense of provincial universal banks.

[29] The data come from Deutsche Bundesbank (1976) for the joint-stock banks and from Goldsmith (1969) for the private banks (using linear interpolation between his estimates for 1880, 1900, and 1913).

[30] See Fohlin (1999a) and sources there, in particular, Confalonieri (1974) on Comit and Bava (1926) on the four largest universal banks.

universal bank assets (50–55 percent) as the nine great banks did in Germany and reached 65 percent before World War I. Probably because of the longer history and more gradual development of universal banking in Germany than in Italy, the provincial German banks retained a greater share of bank assets than their Italian counterparts until after World War I. Thus, relative to Germany, the Italian universal banking sector was more concentrated, with two banks holding by far the most dominant positions.

The Japanese commercial banking sector combined features of the continental European and American systems: a small number of large, well-branched banks and a much larger number of small, unit banks. Some of the Japanese banks opened branches early on and built up networks rapidly. The first of the private banks gained early advantages and virtual monopoly in their markets. Mitsui Bank (1876), for example, had its roots in the retail trade business and therefore had a natural tendency to branch, building thirty branches throughout Japan, largely in the Tokyo and Osaka areas.[31]

The commercial banking sector flourished thereafter, particularly in the 1890s and the early decades of the twentieth century. In the first seven years of the 1890s alone, banking offices (including branches) grew fivefold, to nearly 2,500. Most of the growth in commercial banking came from the private banks; by 1897, the so-called ordinary banks' offices (headquarters plus branches) numbered around 2,000 – an increase of nearly 500 offices over the previous four years.[32] The number of banks continued to expand in the early years of the twentieth century, but with 1,802 ordinary banks operating 1,374 branch offices in 1900, branching remained far from commonplace. The "Big-Five" (Mitsui, Mitsubishi, Yasuda, Sumitomo, and Daiichi banks) had opened up seventy-five offices by 1911, but these were by far the largest networks. At that point, 1,613 "ordinary" banks remained, down from the peak – before the effects of the 1900–1901 crisis – of more than 1,800 banks. These banks operated 1,784 branches, a 30 percent increase from the 1,300 branches in 1900.

Even as the number of banks grew, a small subset of them gained increasing market shares over the 1890s. In 1897, the fifty banks with at least 1 million yen owned 40 percent of the total assets of the ordinary banking

---

[31] See Tamaki (1995) for an in-depth discussion of the industrial organization of early Japanese commercial banking.

[32] See Bank of Japan (1966) Hundred Year Statistics for extensive data on the banking industry. Between 1896 and 1899, the original national banks disappeared. Of the 153 national banks, 122 were reorganized as ordinary banks, 16 were absorbed by other banks, 9 were voluntarily liquidated, and 6 were wound up by the government.

sector.[33] The "Big Five" alone owned more than 20 percent of commercial banking deposits by 1910, and between 1911 and 1919, they more than doubled their share of outstanding capital (from 7 to 16 percent).[34] Still, compared to Germany, Italy, and the United Kingdom – and compared to the United States on a state-by-state basis – banking concentration lagged in Japan. On the other hand, Japanese banks tended to stay geographically concentrated quite late. Similar to the U.S. case, many banks – and typically the largest banks – appeared in the major urban centers, chief among these being Tokyo, whereas outlying areas remained sparsely populated by banks.[35]

These international comparisons tell us something important about the relationship between the scale of bank assets and the scope of bank activities: The latter is not necessarily dependent on the former. Italian and Japanese banks were also universal in many cases but were much smaller than the German universal banks. There were plenty of specialized, American commercial banks that were the same size or larger than universal banks elsewhere. Thus, the minimum efficient scale for universal banking to survive must have been smaller than the scale of many U.S. commercial banks. In other words, size was not the crucial roadblock for at least some American banks to become full-fledged universal banks.[36] Given that the specialized commercial banks in the United Kingdom outpaced the banks in all of these other countries, it is also clear that banks could grow without resorting to broadening their scope. Thus, international comparison demonstrates that universality is not inextricably linked to size, as either cause or effect.

In international perspective, the U.S. banking market was less divergent when considered at the level of banking markets. Concentration levels remained moderately high in many areas of the United States, and other countries surely had some geographical segmentation of banking markets, as well as an urban-rural dichotomy in industrial organization, particularly in the early stages of development considered here. Still, the fact that European and Japanese banks used branching meant that the large banks faced competition with each other in multiple markets, and that could well have mitigated their market power, even in markets where they held large market shares.

[33] Tamaki (1995), p. 80.
[34] Goldsmith (1983), based on Ehrlich (1960) and Shibagaki (1966).
[35] Tamaki (1995), p. 38, indicates that 21 (57% of the total national bank stock) of the 153 banks in 1879 were based in Tokyo. Another 14 (5%) were headquartered in Osaka. Tokyo was home to the largest 15 banks.
[36] Recall, as well, that German private banks are excluded from the German averages. Their inclusion would dramatically reduce the German figures – to about 1.5 million 1913 dollars average assets per bank (compared to just short of 900,000 for the American commercial banks and 43 million 1913 dollars for the British banks).

DEVELOPMENT OF BANKING PRACTICES

The shape of banking industries may dictate the choice of operations and policies by individual banking institutions, and these functions may in turn influence the role of banks in industrial development. The financial organization of banks offers insight into the scope of services offered and the relative importance of various lines of business and creates a finer-grained portrait of institutional development during the formative years of the industry. For example, loans and advances relate primarily to banks' commercial business from the asset side. Interest and commissions on current accounts and loans versus income from securities underwriting and participation – all reported in bank income statements – offers another measure of the relative importance to the universal banks of commercial and investment services.

Much of the investment side of the universal banking business takes place off the balance sheet. Underwriting and brokerage activities do not always result in asset holdings that remain in the portfolio long enough to be booked on an annual balance sheet. To the extent that these services did yield longer-term holdings, they appeared in the banks' balance sheets in the form of securities. Nongovernment securities usually represented issues that the banks were unable to place or investments that the banks kept to earn income or to maintain direct-control rights.[37]

Banks fund their business through some balance of equity shares and deposits, and the choice between these types of funding sources hints at the trade-off between investment and commercial banking. Shares may have been more difficult to place with the public than deposits because equity shares carry a higher degree of risk and uncertainty and may also be sold in denominations larger than the total amount of the average depositor's desired savings. High levels of equity finance might also evidence a lack of access to depositors and a resulting focus on investment banking activities to yield the comparatively higher returns required by equity owners.[38] Thus, deposits may be favored by both bank and investor, but equity still may have proved necessary for banks to operate on a large scale, particularly early in their development.

British commercial banking of the pre–World War I era is commonly seen as highly specialized and narrower in scope than most of their

---

[37] The following chapter investigates securities holdings in depth.
[38] This point is emphasized by Verdier (1997), who suggests that the German banks' universality hinged on such factors.

contemporaries. Commercial banks provided essentially no investment banking services in the pre–World War I period, when specialized investment banks reigned over the securities-issuance business. In the dichotomous world of banking structure, therefore, UK deposit banks historically always fell clearly into the specialized category rather than the universal one. Worth noting, in light of the more recent emphasis on law and politics in understanding financial structure, British commercial banks chose specialization of their own volition: They were always entitled to engage in universal banking practices, but for most of their history, they avoided investment banking activities and long-term equity positions in industrial firms. English banks provided short-term capital through bills of exchange and short-term loans – typically maturing within days or weeks. For these banks, very short-term loans, termed "money at call," consisted primarily of loans to stock brokers for transactions in the London discount market or the London Stock Exchange.[39]

British banks typically lent on the collateral of bills of exchange and marketable securities. The percentage of bills on the banks' balance sheets fell from approximately 35 percent of assets in 1873 to 20 percent in the 1880s and stabilized at 10 percent in the 1900s. Cash and near cash amounted to 15 percent of assets in 1873 but almost 25 percent of assets at the outset of World War I.[40] Banks also offered (relatively) longer-term loans and advances, and they accounted for the largest single component of assets – about half – throughout the thirty years or so leading up to World War I.[41] Loans to industries appeared to have been first granted for trading or working capital purposes, and these made up the majority, although declining proportion, of loans, compared to loans made specifically for capital investment purposes.[42]

The most recent studies of British deposit banks suggests that, contrary to the orthodox view, the British banks did roll over loans to industrial firms and may have also provided credit without full collateral.[43] Banks financed industry primarily with bills and advances. Bills were private-sector bill discounts of three to six months, whereas advances included all

---

[39] See Goodhart (1972) for further descriptions of bank balance sheet items.
[40] Baker and Collins (1999), p. 436.
[41] Ibid., p. 438. On these issues, see also Cottrell (1980), pp. 200–205.
[42] Capie and Collins (1999), pp. 50–51. In 1880–1884, trade and working capital accounted for 74.3% of the number of loans, and in 1910–1914, it was 65.1%. Loans for capital investments ranged from 17.1% in 1880–1884 to 3.1% in 1912–1914.
[43] See Collins (1998), pp. 1–24; Watson (1996); Baker and Collins (1999). Ollerenshaw (1987, pp. 94–101) notes that, in Ireland, the industries' overdrafts could run for decades.

loans to the nonbank private sector.[44] From the 1860s, the banks' greater liquidity led them to offer their industrial customers advances rather than discounting bills.[45]

The primary characteristic of the English banks is their lack of involvement in the investment business. Merchant banks dominated the investment business, taking the lion's share of underwriting and placement of new issues, although they were primarily concerned with overseas business.[46] Similarly, specialized stockbrokers and jobbers handled the trading on the exchanges.[47] The focus on commercial banking is also apparent from the liability side, in the sense that the English banks leaned overwhelmingly toward commercial and personal deposits throughout the period. Although the Companies Act of 1862 required that twice a year statements of account must be displayed (this did not apply to private banks), the majority of banks included current and deposit accounts together; in addition, there was suspicion of some "window dressing" of the accounts (U.S. National Monetary Commission, 1910). The two types differed ostensibly in their notice for withdrawal – that is, their liquidity. Current account credits were immediately accessible, whereas deposit accounts often carried a seven-day withdrawal notice. But because the notice conditions were apparently infrequently enforced, even the personal deposit accounts could pose significant solvency issues for the banks.[48]

Whether cause or effect of their capital structure, the English banks focused on commercial business that could be financed out of relatively short-term liabilities. Still, the English deposit banks did take some part in underwriting, particularly toward the very end of the pre–World War I period. Securities that could be underwritten and placed directly to customers would not have tied up bank assets and could therefore provide an income source without appearing in the balance sheet; a so-called off-balance-sheet operation.

---

[44] Both Cottrell (1980), p. 204, and Goodhart (1972), p. 153 indicate that the most common form of advances was loans in London but overdrafts in the provinces. The latter were popular in part due to their flexibility.

[45] Cottrell (1980), pp. 200–204.

[46] It is not until the aftermath of World War I that they started getting involved in domestic industrial finance and issues (see Diaper, 1990, p. 72).

[47] Brokers acted as intermediaries, bringing buyers into contact with sellers, while jobbers were dealers. According to Michie (1999), brokers represented two-third of the members of the LSE in 1877 and jobbers one-third, but in 1908, the proportion had completely reversed with two-thirds of jobbers (p. 105). A very clear presentation of the respective functions of the brokers and jobbers is to be found in Cassis (1987), pp. 45–47.

[48] Goodhart (1972), p. 171.

Comparing the English commercial banks with their merchant banking counterparts allows some perspective on the divergent institutional
structures. The General Credit and Finance company, for example, held
approximately 15 percent of its assets in the form of securities in 1866, the
majority of which was held as equity shares.[49] Many of these shares were
probably of railway companies, but it is impossible to tell from the given
figures (Cottrell, 1985). Another bank, the International Financial society,
held, in 1872, nearly a quarter of its assets in the form of securities and by
1877 had increased its security holdings to 56 percent of assets.

The American banking system vies with the British system as the prime
example of specialized commercial banking. But a closer look at history
reveals a more complicated story, in which a combination of universal
and specialized banking played important parts in the corporate finance
system that prevailed up to its abrupt end with the Glass-Steagall Act in
1933. Like the uneven industrial development and the diverse composition of industry across the country, the U.S. financial system evolved in a
heterogeneous fashion well into the twentieth century. In New England –
the leading industrial region – banking and financial structure developed
early and, in some respects, resembled that of universal-relationship banking even before such institutions were established in most of continental
Europe.[50] Banks provided most of the external funding for local industries
in antebellum New England, underwriting securities through affiliates and
managing portfolios. Early New England banks substantially funded their
activities through large issues of shares. As industrialization progressed,
banks faced larger and more diversified industrial firms with greater potential financing needs, putting pressure on the banks to grow or somehow
offer large-scale finance.

Government regulation surely shaped the American banking industry,
but public policy had little to say about the scope of banking services in the
pre–World War I era. The Banking Act of 1864 did limit the national banks'
investments to short-term, self-liquidating loans, but also allowed them to
provide other services that were necessary for their operations. This provision left the door open for banks to engage in any finance-related activity
that was not explicitly prohibited.[51]

---

[49] Cottrell (1985), p. 419 reproduces the firm's balance sheet as given in *The Economist* of
   November 1866.
[50] Calomiris and Ramirez (1996) make this argument, explicitly in comparison with the
   German banks. Predecessors appeared in France and Belgium earlier in the nineteenth
   century.
[51] See White (1986) on the national banks' entrance into the securities business.

Although investment banking business at this time was performed by commercial banks, private bankers dominated the investment banking business through World War I.[52] Private investment banks emerged and developed in parallel with the commercial banking sector rather than within the same institutions. The Civil War, with its sudden demand for large-scale financing, spurred the transformation of small investment houses into a true investment banking sector.[53] The enormous financing needs of railroads further bolstered demand for investment banking services over the latter half of the nineteenth century. In the last quarter of the nineteenth century, private investment banking was dominated by the German-Jewish community (Kuhn, Loeb & Co., Goldman, Sachs, and Lehman Brothers, for example) and the so-called Yankee houses – most prominently J. P. Morgan. In both cases, the success of these investment banks hinged on ties to their countries of origin and their ability to funnel capital across the Atlantic.

Commercial banks could not hold stock directly, on their own accounts, but they could do so through affiliates. By the beginning of the twentieth century, commercial banks began to engage in investment banking activities through bond departments and affiliates; these investment-oriented arms of the banks rapidly expanded their services in the subsequent decades, particularly in the 1920s. Investment affiliates competed directly with the private investment houses and turned commercial banks into quasi-universal banks. Reverse processes also blurred the definition of investment bankers, who themselves formed close ties with commercial banks, often owning stock in them or sitting on their boards to ensure their access to short-term loans to cover operations during a flotation of securities. J. P. Morgan stands out as the preeminent example of American universal banking in the pre–World War I era, perhaps acting even more like the stylized view of a German universal banker than the Germans ever did: providing abundant capital to firms with which it had close relationships and monitoring the management of the same.[54]

Trust companies fell outside the purview of banking regulation, and financial historians often overlook the sometimes active participation of the trusts in commercial and investment banking activities.[55] The trust companies blossomed in the absence of restrictions on their size and

---

[52] See Carosso (1970) for an exhaustive treatment of the history of investment banking in the United States.
[53] See Carosso (1970).
[54] De Long (1992). See Carosso (1987) on the Morgans.
[55] See Neal (1971) and White (1986), who bring the issue of the trusts back to the fore, as Barnett (1911) had done as a contemporary observer.

scope, particularly toward the end of the nineteenth and the beginning of
the twentieth centuries; they became perhaps the most universal-like institution in the U.S. financial system before World War I. Having been con-
ceived as something akin to savings banks for the wealthy, the trusts in fact
offered a host of investment and commercial banking services. Because
they served a clientele of substantial resources, they naturally pursued a
higher-risk, higher-return investment strategy than would a responsible
savings bank for the working classes. Trusts often bought industrial securities directly and lent to customers on the collateral of the same. Moreover,
some engaged in underwriting and distributing securities, helping arrange
mergers and acquisitions, and took securities on deposit.[56] In short,
they looked a lot like a universal bank of the same period. The rapidly
expanding lines of trust companies' business pressured the commercial
banks to find ways to compete, and to a significant extent provided the
impetus for the commercial banks' move into securities business. In some
states – notably Massachusetts – the trust-company form virtually sup-
planted the state-chartered bank among new entrants into the commercial
banking market.[57]

Although the American financial system moved in the direction of universality in the first decade or so of the twentieth century, we cannot say
that most U.S. financial institutions were full-blown universal banks, particularly before World War I. The evidence we have in this regard actually
suggests that most commercial banks took little role in investment banking
until after World War I.[58] By one estimate, out of the tens of thousands of
U.S. commercial banks, only ten had created security affiliates and sixty-
two maintained bond departments.[59] As a percentage of American commercial banks, these numbers are tiny. Compared to the other countries
studied here, however, the numbers of quasi-universal banks in the United
States are on a similar order – even more so if the universal-bank-style
trust companies were counted. Because of this organization of American
commercial and investment banking into a variety of institutions in the
pre–World War I era, it is difficult – perhaps impossible, and in any event

---

[56] See Carosso (1970), citing an article in the Commercial and Financial Chronicle of
October, 1900.
[57] Barnett (1911), pp. 234–235.
[58] See White (1986), based on national banks at least. Also complicating the overall picture
of an increasingly universal system, by some accounts (see Lamoreaux, 1991) the earliest participants in quasi-universal banking, the New England Banks, transitioned toward
more specialized commercial banking at the same time.
[59] See White (1986).

not very informative – to provide quantitative comparisons of commercial bank assets. U.S. commercial banks would not have held direct equity stakes in industrial firms, so we would not expect any such holdings in aggregate commercial bank balance sheets. U.S. commercial banks used a combination of debt, equity, and to a much lesser extent, notes to finance their banking activities.[60]

On the European continent, banks combined the branching activities of the English banks with the broader scope of the largest American banks. By the start of World War I, the largest German joint-stock credit banks developed into mature universal banks, combining the regular services of commercial banks (deposit taking, current accounts, bill discounting, acceptances, trade credits) with underwriting and brokerage of securities. But the banks, especially those founded in the first wave, started out their existence with much narrower focus. The banks' product mix changed over the decades, with true universality becoming the norm after some period of industrialization. Some universal banks began life as private, family-based merchant firms, whereas others started out as joint-stock companies heavily focused on investment banking. Universal banks formed as such came later in the nineteenth century and made up the distinct minority, because most nineteenth-century joint-stock banks were the creation of people with a family background in private banking. In addition, despite its reputation for universality of banking functions, Germany had nearly the same number of different types of institutions as England in the pre–World War I era.[61]

German commercial banks operated primarily through their current account business: providing payment facilities, undersigning of commercial paper, bill acceptances, foreign bills of exchange, and several forms of short-term credit. German banks lent on a range of collateral, from nothing at all to bills of exchange and marketable securities. The loans' liquidity and maturity compared closely to those made by the English deposit banks. Even though the prevalence of this short-term lending fluctuated throughout the late nineteenth and early twentieth centuries, the proportion of bank assets held in this form were very similar for English and German banks.

By the late nineteenth century, such commercial business constituted the universal banks' primary sources of income, but it could also provide the point of entry into underwriting and brokerage services for the same firms.

---

[60] The Constitution granted the power of monetary regulation to Congress, thereby transferring power from the states to the federal government.
[61] See Goldsmith (1972).

A number of German universal banks were actively involved in the full range of investment banking and brokerage activities. Typically, the underwriting bank or group of banks took over the full value of a security issue and subsequently sold stakes to the public. These practices placed securities directly into the hands of bankers, sometimes for longer than the bank actually intended. These promotional operations automatically connected the universal banks, especially the largest ones, to the securities exchanges and forced the banks into liquidity provision in the process. This practice of buying up new issues and placing them subsequently put investment banking services more directly onto the banks' balance sheets, particularly in times when the supply of new issues outstripped demand. Still, by the end of the nineteenth century, more than 80 percent of assets in Germany's universal banking sector flowed to commercial lending. Securities – mostly issued by industrial firms – amounted only to 11 percent of total bank assets over the years.

As the investment banking business could tie up bank assets for years, it created a greater need for long-term liabilities. In other words, the nature of the investment banking business in Germany, not just their engagement in it, influenced the difference in banks' capital structure compared to the English banks. The English deposit accounts were also more liquid than the equivalent German accounts, compounding the fact that the English banks used little equity capital to finance their operations and meaning that the English banks' liabilities remained far more liquid overall than those of the German universal banks or even their somewhat more deposit-oriented Italian and Japanese counterparts (Figure 3.1). But with the move toward branching and expansion via deposit taking in continental Europe and Japan, the heavy use of deposits no longer distinguished the British banks so starkly from the universal banks by the start of World War I.[62] Indeed, the German universal banks shifted from nearly all equity financing to majority deposit funding as their branching movement progressed (Figure 3.1). Deposits reached at least 60 percent of liabilities in 1913 and 75 percent during World War I.[63]

Data from individual bank financial reports suggest similar split between commercial and investment banking during this era. Overall, for the principal German commercial/universal banks, the percentage of income stemming from investment banking and brokerage functions hovered in the

---

[62] Moreover, the German universal banks moved actively into private savings deposits after World War I, and even more so after World War II.
[63] See Fohlin (2001b) on the booking of acceptances.

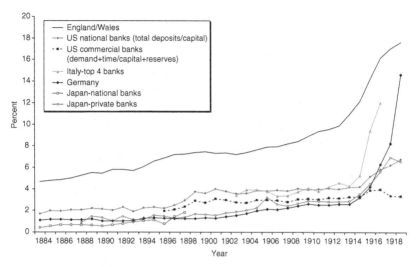

Figure 3.1. Ratio of deposits to capital and reserves.
Sources: Deposit ratios calculated from data in following sources:
Italy: Bava (1926), Credito Italiano (1912), Cotula (1996)
Japan: The Bank of Japan (1996)
United States: All Bank Statistics
United Kingdom: Sheppard (1971) [based on data from *The Economist* magazine]
Germany: Deutsche Bundesbank (1976)

17–21 percent range during the 1880s and 1890s.[64] Still, the emphasis on investment banking ranged widely – from basically nothing to more than 60 percent of total income. The great banks naturally fell into the top half of the distribution, usually around 25 percent of total income.

As in Germany, Italian commercial banks provided a wide range of financial services. Because of their patronage from banks in other countries, particularly the German universal banks, the top two Italian universal banks began life at a relatively more advanced stage rather than beginning in the mid-1890s as the German banks had in the 1850s or even 1870s. Thus, the Credito Italiano report of 1912, for example, lists a diverse array of operations, from exchanging metals and currency, to bills of exchange and letters of credit, to current accounts, to securities transactions. Gerschenkron might have identified this pattern as one "advantage of backwardness."

Unlike their German counterparts, the largest Italian universal banks held an extensive portfolio of securities, amounting to nearly half of assets

---

[64] The data come from Saling's, by way of Fohlin (2007a). The sample comprises all banks listed on the Berlin exchange – approximately fifty to sixty institutions, depending on the year.

on the eve of World War I. The vast majority of these securities appear to have been secondary reserves; very small amounts of their holdings represented long-term equity stakes. Even Comit, the best-known stakeholder bank, averaged less than 4 percent of assets in participation shares between 1895 and 1914. Credit held even smaller total participation stakes, typically around 1 percent of assets and never reaching even 4 percent. Compared to their German counterparts, then, the Italian banks appear to have been somewhat less engaged in the investment side of the business, although the differences may simply reflect the disparate levels of development of securities markets in the two countries.

Still, commercial lending accounts took up a considerably smaller share of assets of the largest Italian banks compared to the equivalent German banks. Over the period, commercial accounts comprised slightly more than half of the big-two's assets, but over the period, both banks decreased their lending accounts from as much as 70 percent of assets down to around 40 percent or less. The two major types of lending – debits to current accounts and report loans – decreased by similar proportions. Both banks filled the gap with large portfolios of securities and substituted portfolio securities in virtually equal measure as they lowered their proportion of loans and advances.

The liability side of the Italian banks' balances augments this story. The Italian universal banks emerged at a time when their German forebears were shifting rapidly into deposit taking. By their very nature – greater security and liquidity – deposits appeal to a broader customer base and encourage faster expansion of assets than do equity shares.[65] Unlike the German universal banks, the principal Italian universal banks used significant deposit financing even from the beginning (Figure 3.1). In fact, the Italian banks used a higher percentage of deposits than the German universal banks had even by the mid-1890s. The two largest Italian universal banks began operations with more than 60 percent deposit financing. Although they lowered their ratios slightly until 1900, they increased them steadily thereafter – reaching around 70 percent by World War I. The smaller commercial banks used even more deposits to finance their business and averaged between 75 and 80 percent deposits over the decade before 1913. The demand component of deposits – those that could be withdrawn most easily – increased in

---

[65] Comit's shares carried nominal values of 500 and 2,500 Lire, and Credit shares had a face value of 500 Lire; most other banks' shares had a face value of 100 Lire. Market value would normally have been higher. And, of course, deposit funding prevents the dilution of control by existing owners.

the first years of the twentieth century, rising to 23 percent of assets on the eve of World War I.

The Japanese banks also started out at a relatively more advanced stage compared to German banks, and they developed their financial services at a relatively rapid pace over the late nineteenth and early twentieth centuries. The Bank Decree of 1890 dictated that "Those who, in their offices open to the public, conduct business of the discounts of securities, or the transactions of exchanges, or the acceptances of deposits, or advances, are the banks – whatever they may designate themselves."[66] Regulations governing ordinary banks allowed the banks to discount bills, give advances on property, and make loans, as well as to trade in securities, gold, and foreign exchange.

The lending business ranked at the top for most ordinary banks, so that loans and advances accounted for the largest share of bank assets. Small, family-owned businesses made up the majority of the banks' clientele, although the banks also provided financing to agriculture as well. Lending, primarily though advances, grew rapidly in the late 1870s and reached 120 to 150 percent of deposits by the 1880s. National banks, while they lasted, operated differently – apparently lending to other intermediaries, who in turn lent funds to ultimate borrowers. Because of the national banks' heavy use of capital over deposits, lending activity exploded in the last half of the 1870s, reaching 428 percent of deposits by 1881.[67] National banks either disappeared or converted to ordinary banks by the end of the 1890s, so that these practices ended up as relatively transient phenomena.

Whether bank lending went to fund anything more than short-term commercial needs is less clear from the records, but from one account (based on 1894 data from a finance ministry official), approximately 40 percent of loans lasted more than one year, although only 20 percent were rolled over at least once.[68] The banks often lent on little or no collateral. The collateral they did take often comprised personal bonds and discounts and, to a lesser extent, securities. Whereas they showed basically no holdings of industrial equities in the 1880s, they did increasingly hold shares over the subsequent three decades and beyond. Government securities made up nearly one-third of assets of national banks in 1885, but these holdings declined rapidly with the transition of national banks to ordinary banks, constituting approximately 6 percent of assets of ordinary banks in 1900

---

[66] The institutions so defined became the "ordinary" banks. See Tamaki (1995), p. 74. See also Moussa and Obata (2009).
[67] For more details, see Tamaki (1995), pp. 32–39.
[68] See Goldsmith (1983), p. 49.

and 1913.[69] Leading up to and following World War I, the banks gradually shifted their asset portfolios from loans into securities, in part due to their move into more and more securities-oriented business.

As in Italy and Germany, equity capital provided the primary source of bank funding in the late nineteenth century. Deposits remained below half of total capital of national banks from 1876 to 1881: Capital increased more than tenfold, whereas deposits grew slightly slower in the same period. By the 1880s, deposits gained in importance, reaching capital levels by the mid-1880s and gaining ground thereafter. Eventually, particularly after the switch to ordinary banking around 1900, deposits became the chief funding source for the commercial banks (Figure 3.1). In this respect, Japanese banks mirrored German banks more than their Italian counterparts, where deposit financing constituted a more significant proportion of funds from the beginning. Still, in dramatically increasing deposit ratios during World War I, the Japanese banks closely replicated the pattern observed in Germany and Italy in the same period. So-called current deposits supplied a declining share of the overall deposit base: about two-fifths between 1885 and 1900 and one-fifth between 1900 and 1913.[70] In contrast to both German and Italian banks, the Japanese banks also used bond funding, substantial enough that financial debentures roughly equaled corporate bonds in the early years of the twentieth century.[71]

This international comparison places the U.S. banks' ratios in clearer perspective. As might be expected of more specialized institutions, the aggregate deposit-capital ratio for the American commercial banks remained higher than that of the German and Japanese universal banks over the 1880s and 1890s, and the gap widened a bit with the spurt of deposit growth at U.S. commercial banks in the last half of the 1890s (Figure 3.1). At the same time, however, U.S. deposit ratios tracked the top four Italian universal banks' ratios very closely for the first decade of the twentieth century. The main difference in the pre–World War I era appears between the UK deposit banks and the banks of the other four countries studied here. Most striking of all, however, is the divergent behavior of the American commercial banks during and soon after World War I. This is the period in which most other banks around the industrialized world found the deposit-banking religion, began to merge feverishly, and fanned out to form national branch networks

---

[69] See the data and discussion in Goldsmith (1983), who notes a significant amount of debate over the figures.

[70] Goldsmith (1983), p. 48.

[71] See Hoshi and Kashyap (2001), p. 43. Bond levels varied substantially from year to year. See also Goldsmith (1983), p. 49.

across their respective countries. Hamstrung by branching restrictions, the American commercial banks now relied more on capital than the universal banks, even the less deposit-oriented Japanese banks.[72]

BANK PERFORMANCE: CAPITAL MOBILIZATION, RISK, COMPETITIVENESS, AND RETURNS

The structure of banking firms and industries can have wide-ranging implications for capital mobilization, systemic risk, competitiveness, and profitability. All of these measures of performance have their own potential to influence the economy more broadly. The basic mechanism of capital mobilization emerges from a simple model of a monetary economy with financial intermediaries and currency holding by the public: The total nominal money stock is a function of the nominal monetary base (currency plus reserves), the ratio of bank deposits to currency, and the cash reserve ratio.[73] The ultimate impact of the banks' activities on the economy depends directly on the amount of funds assembled by the financial system and inversely upon the proportion of the system's assets retained in the form of cash reserves. These variables, in turn, relate at least in part to the funding and lending policies pursued by the institutions involved. Financial intermediaries can raise the deposit-to-currency ratio by encouraging individuals to deposit their savings or buy equity shares in the bank. More directly, they can reduce their reserve ratios by increasing the proportion of funds lent out or otherwise invested in risky assets. These allocations, themselves a natural response to market forces in the banking industry, in turn influence the riskiness of individual banks and the sector as a whole.

Banks determine when and how much to expand liabilities, and simultaneously their own liquidity and maturity risk, through their retention of liquid assets as reserves. Asset and liability ratios therefore offer detailed insight into the banks' methods and performance. Short-term coverage ratios – measuring the extent to which banks cover their short-term liabilities with short-term or liquid assets – gives a broader indication of the maturity transformation taking place and offers an interesting contrast to cash ratios. Profit rates of banks provide additional indication of both the risk taking and the success of those ventures, given that investors will demand a higher return, in general, when they place their capital

---

[72] Of note, the increase in deposits in U.S. banks stemmed from growing interbank deposits – one possible substitute for branching.

[73] See Champ and Freeman (1994) and sources cited there for a straightforward exposition of the theory.

at greater risk. Of course, other factors, such as monopoly rents, play into higher returns, but pressure from potential entrants may have kept at least commercial banking services fairly competitive.[74] Banking profits can be measured by returns on assets (ROA) or on equity. From the perspective of bank shareholders, of course, the latter would be of greater interest. For comparing across banking systems that use highly varying levels of equity financing, however, ROA is more informative.

Financial statements vary considerably among countries, among banks, and even within the same bank. The quality of assets and level of collateral may differ systematically, and some banks may automatically roll over short-term loans for many periods, lengthening the maturity, whereas others do not. Bills could be directly discounted for the banks' own customers or bought on the open market, creating potentially significant differences in risk. Additionally, some banks were more reluctant to rediscount bills or issue bills without collateral, whereas others apparently did so freely. Distinctions of these types are rarely made in the banks' accounts. Yet despite the many potential problems with accounting, financial statements represent a relatively accurate portrayal of the banks' financial positions – particularly at the aggregate level and over the long run. True, banks present as conservative an overall financial picture as possible, but they do so regardless of nationality or time period. Moreover, banks can manipulate their balances only so far, especially over extended periods, and the limits are similar across banks and countries.

As nearly 100 percent deposit-financed banks, English and Welsh banks would naturally be expected to run business a bit differently from capital-funded banks. In particular, with such potential for withdrawals, prudence would dictate greater cash-asset ratios than banks that used share capital as well. And indeed, these specialized commercial banks held increasingly greater shares of cash than their universal counterparts. The cash-asset ratio for English banks as a whole in 1910 approached 10.6 percent, and the London joint-stock banks maintained cash-deposit ratios between 10 and 15 percent of deposits (Figure 3.2).[75] The increasing use of demand deposits added to the need for higher cash ratios, because banks had to be prepared to return depositors' cash on sight rather than planning for withdrawals at the end of the contracted term. In practice, English deposit accounts often carried seven-day withdrawal notice and often permitted withdrawals with less warning.

---

[74] See Fohlin (2006).
[75] Based on Capie and Webber (1985) data.

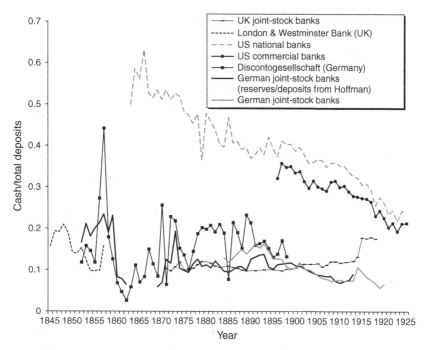

Figure 3.2. Cash-deposit ratios.

Sources: Deposit ratios calculated from data in following sources:
Italy: Bava (1926), Credito Italiano (1912)
Japan: The Bank of Japan (1996)
United States: All Bank Statistics
United Kingdom: Bagehot (1873), Capie and Webber (1985), Sheppard (1971) [based on data from *The Economist* magazine]
Germany: Deutsche Bundesbank (1976) and Hoffman (1965)

Additional reserves in the form of short-term and liquid assets – low-risk (often government-backed) securities, call money, and bills – ranged between 36 percent and 42 percent of total assets for this period. Throughout the period from the 1880s to World War I, the English and Welsh banks' short-term assets ranged consistently between 44 percent and 48 percent, relative to just short-term liabilities. Some argue that the lack of dependable lender of last-resort facilities reinforced the reluctance of English bankers to engage in risky transformation of short-term liabilities into potentially illiquid assets.[76]

It is difficult to disentangle the issues of bank risk taking and maturity transformation; the latter entails the former, although policies of the

---

[76] Ziegler (1993) and Kennedy (1992).

central bank can naturally loosen the link. Wrapped up in the differenti-
ation between universal and specialized banking is the idea that the latter
tends to take a more conservative path; sticking to short-term lending with
significant, marketable collateral and low risk of default. The actual product
mix is rather murky, making it difficult to draw strong conclusions about the
extent of long-term or risky lending, either for the United Kingdom alone
or in comparison with other countries. In addition, there was apparently at
least some perception that the quality of the British loans had declined in
the two decades leading up to World War I.[77]

To assess the broader performance of the banks, including off-balance-
sheet operations, we need to look beyond cash ratios. Banks' aggregate
returns provide one such measure that covers both their commercial activities and their investment services. Specialized commercial banks in a
highly developed financial system like that of the United Kingdom in the
late nineteenth and early twentieth centuries could be expected to yield
modest returns. Banks provided ostensibly low-risk commercial services,
they built expansive networks that promoted competition, and they offered
relatively conservative investment portfolios. Their equity investors earned
an average return on equity of 5.8 percent between 1888 and 1913. From
the 1880s to the early 1900s, there is no discernible trend in UK returns,
and the figures fluctuated considerably over this period.[78]

The vastly different structure of the American commercial banking
industry could well be assumed to have produced an equally divergent set
of performance measures. For one thing, the U.S. banking industry showed
a propensity for instability, far more than the UK or most others at a similar
level of development at the time. Banking crises and failures became more
common place as the nineteenth century progressed: nationwide panics
erupted in 1819, 1837, 1839, 1857, 1861, 1873, 1884, 1890, 1893, 1896, and
1907. Usually, however, only a small percentage of banks actually failed
during the panics. By one estimate, 380 state banks failed between 1892
and 1899, with almost half of them (171) coming in 1893.[79] Comparatively

---

[77] See Weber (1915, p. 141), citing *The Economist*.

[78] These figures are based on Capie's (1988) revised estimates, which cast considerable doubt
on the banks' reported earnings. Based on the banks' own reported returns, average ROE
for the United Kingdom is greater than 10%. ROA figures are as yet unavailable for the
United Kingdom, but given their scant use of equity, the ROA figures would be far lower
than the ROE figures.

[79] See Barnett (1911, p. 189 ff) for state banks (and trusts) in the period to 1909. See Calomiris
(2000), chapter 2 (with Gary Gorton) in particular. More famously, three successive waves
of panics followed the onset of the Great Depression in the 1930s, in which many banks
did fail.

fewer (174) failed in the first decade of the twentieth century, even including the aftermath of the 1907 panic.

The nearly complete absence of branching and the propensity for panics would lead to the expectation of unusually high reserve ratios by the end of the nineteenth century, given that banks obviously faced serious size and diversification constraints and also relied heavily on deposit financing. Cash ranged between one-quarter and one-third of commercial banking assets from the 1860s to World War I – quite a bit higher than all the other banking systems considered here – but the ratio did decline over the period, particularly after 1900. More remarkable is the pattern of cash relative to deposits held in the banks. This ratio started out in the 50 percent range at the beginning of the national banking era (1863) and actually increased to nearly two-thirds in 1866, before dropping off almost steadily for the rest of the period (Figure 3.2).

The overall financial picture of the German universal banks is one of moderation and conservatism in the 1880s through 1913. Cash-liability ratios stayed in the 5 to 6 percent range in the late 1880s and early 1890s, whereas cash-deposit ratios rose over the same period. Aggregate ratios fell as low as 7 percent but rose as high as 22 percent. Both ratios declined after 1893, largely as a result of the marked increase in the universal banks' use of deposits at the turn of the century. By simultaneously holding cash at steady levels while increasing deposits, the ratios naturally fell, and the cash-deposit ratio did so precipitously.[80]

As a group, the universal banks kept their total stocks of short-term or liquid assets (cash, call money, bills, or low-risk securities, often government-issued) between 36 and 42 percent of total assets throughout the period (Figure 3.2). Naturally, compared to short-term liabilities, the ratios reached even higher – 71 percent in 1892, but declined to 50 percent fifteen years later. In line with the underlying theory, cash-deposit ratios demonstrate a strong negative impact on total assets mobilized by the German universal banking system.[81]

In comparing the path of U.S. cash ratios to those in Germany and the United Kingdom, it may seem easy to explain: Unit banking, specialized services, high deposit-capital ratios, and small size all contribute to the need for high cash holdings. However, these factors tell only part of the story.

---

[80] Banks typically practice window dressing, holding more cash at balance sheet time, so it is hard to know just how low cash balances fell throughout the year. The banks' bimonthly balances, published starting in 1909, do show somewhat lower cash reserves than the annual balances. In this practice, of course, the German banks were hardly unique.

[81] See Fohlin (1999a, 2001b).

UK banks were even more specialized and far more deposit-oriented, and German banks remained largely unit banks until very late in the nineteenth century and even into the early twentieth. Perhaps the high cash ratios stem from a relative lack of alternative reserves, for example, if the German banks had greater opportunity on average to hold secondary reserves in the form of high-quality, easily liquidated securities, particularly those of the banks' national government. On the contrary, U.S. commercial banks held ratios of government and other investment securities that were similar to those of Japanese banks and potentially higher than German and UK banks for much of the late nineteenth and early twentieth centuries. Early on, in the 1860s until the early 1880s, U.S. national banks held as much, and often more, assets in the form of securities, compared to cash. These investments then declined compared to cash until the years just before World War I. In other words, taken together, the U.S. banks held extremely large proportions of total liquid assets, not just cash, compared to banks in other countries. So, availability of secondary reserves does not provide the key to the difference in cash holdings. Moreover, these broader measures underscore the issue of capital mobilization. Reserves, whether cash or government securities, crowd out lending to industrial firms or individuals, so that a smaller proportion of resources are multiplied through the economy.[82]

Banks in these other countries did have one feature that the U.S. banks did not: a strong central bank at the top of the system. The role of the central bank in guaranteeing the liquidity of German banks is often touted as a great benefit to that system, a feature that allowed the banks to assume much more risk than they otherwise would. The flip side of this argument would suggest that the absence of such facilities in the U.S. system probably fed into the banks' conservative reserve policies.

Comparison with the United Kingdom tends to undermine the notion that the German banks took risky positions in their reserve policies. The statistical comparison of the English banks to the German universal banks suggests that differences were largely qualitative and possibly hinged on central banking policies.[83] German universal banks' reserve ratios closely resemble those of the UK deposit banks, despite their operational differences. On the

---

[82] Banks could hold bonds under the concept of "evidence of debt." Thus, their nongovernment securities holdings did help mobilize capital. Some might even consider government securities as a form of capital mobilization. Of course, that depends on what the government does with the funds it borrows.

[83] Bills of exchange and current account credits may carry a wide range of risks and degrees of liquidity. In addition, relatively loose accounting practices allowed banks to book illiquid or risky assets under headings that seem to refer to quick assets.

basis of short-term asset/liability ratios, the German universal banks were considerably more liquid than the English banks, particularly earlier in the period. Given that the German central bank (the *Reichsbank*) is usually credited with providing especially dependable "lender of last resort" facilities, particularly compared to the Bank of England, then the German ratios could be considered that much more conservative than the English ones.[84] The gaps among different banking systems' coverage ratios gradually closed around the start of World War I. Whereas some of this narrowing stems from a slight increase in coverage by the British banks in the years leading up to World War I, the more significant change involves the major decline in coverage of the universal banks, the Germans in particular, as they grew and diversified through branching.

Cash holdings also relate to profitability, and the U.S. banks' high cash holdings – that is, low percentage of earning assets – makes their profitability all the more impressive (Figure 3.3). Between 1888 and 1913, ROE for the U.S. averaged 7.4 percent, considerably higher than that of the UK banks. ROE exceeded the risk-free interest rate throughout the period, but the excess return to banks declined significantly through the late 1880s and early 1890s – from the 6 percent range to 1.5 percent at its lowest point – before rebounding dramatically to nearly 10 percent in 1907. ROE tapered off compared to interest rates in the lead-up to World War I. Because the banks used substantial and increasing amounts of deposits as time went by, ROA measures show a less favorable picture of bank profitability, as their returns declined considerably and nearly constantly compared to their total assets. Still, bank returns exceeded those in the United Kingdom and matched pretty closely with risk-adjusted versions found in Germany. Whereas the German universal banks profited handsomely (ROE ranged between 8 and 12 percent over the 1880s to World War I; see Figure 3.3) returns could also reflect greater risk.[85] Subtracting off the prevailing risk-free rate leaves a relatively small premium for the banks, and one that was in line with the U.S. and UK banks of the time. Indeed, there is little sustained difference in return ratios among the United States, United Kingdom, and Germany, particularly in light of interest rate differentials among the countries.

Once again, the Italian case demonstrates the fact that universal banks operated in different ways in different countries. Compared to the German

---

[84] See Warburg (1910) and Weber (1915), especially with regard to bill rediscounting.

[85] See Fohlin (2006). ROA was obviously lower than ROE, but the two ratios got closer as deposits made up a much greater share of total liabilities. Also, due to the changing composition of liabilities, ROA also followed a more stable and more noticeable trend than ROE.

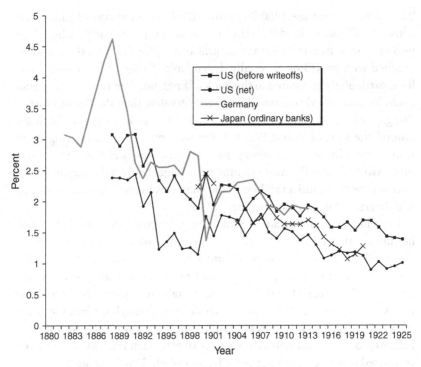

Figure 3.3a. Return on assets, 1880–1925.

banks, the Italian universal banks remained small and more deposit-oriented in the 1890s, but they also engaged less actively in industrial ventures. Whereas the former might have pushed up reserve ratios, the latter would have given the banks less risky investment to cover with cash. For whatever reason, the largest Italian banks kept cash-deposit ratios low compared to those of the German great banks (Figure 3.2). Cash-asset ratios were similar between the two countries, but after 1906, Credit increased its cash/asset ratio markedly and exceeded those of both Comit and the German banks. Thus, although both of the largest Italian banks averaged approximately 6 percent cash-asset ratios between 1895 and 1914, the two institutions followed very different and highly variable paths in achieving that average.

The difference between deposits and loans offers additional evidence on deposit mobilization (as opposed to deposit creation).[86] Again, the Italian universal banks behaved differently from their German counterparts,

---

[86] Because the numbers are aggregated, the results apply to the universal banking system as a whole. Thus, internal drain – the transfer of loaned funds of one bank to deposits in another – causes no problems of interpretation in this context.

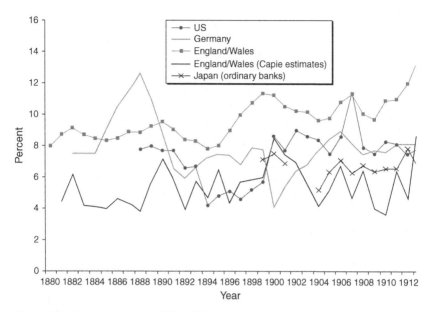

Figure 3.3b. Return on equity, 1880–1913.
Sources: ROA-ROE calculated from data in following sources:
England/Wales: Capie (1988)
Germany: *Saling's Börsenjahrbuch* and *Handbuch der deutschen Aktiengesellschaften*
(various years)
United States: Historical statistics of the United States.
Japan: The Bank of Japan (1996)

with Credit and Comit both maintaining significantly higher short-term liabilities than assets for nearly all of the first twenty years of their existence. In the years leading up to World War I, the deposit surplus of both Comit and Credit amounted to one-third of bank liabilities (and reached as much as 66 percent for Credit during the war). In ratio terms, the top two Italian banks covered deposits with significant volumes of short-term, liquid liabilities, particularly if portfolios are considered in that measure. The ratios increased markedly after the 1907 crisis, going from average of roughly 40 percent to an average of around 65 percent before and after. Still, they held lower ratios than their German counterparts did in the 1890s and early 1900s, although the latter tended to decrease liquidity – from 70 to 50 percent – during the same period.

Taken together, these indicators suggest that the Italian banks engaged quite actively in maturity transformation – changing short-term liabilities (deposits) into longer-term assets – perhaps even more so than the German banks. Although the large portfolios of securities held at the largest Italian banks do raise the possibility of hefty secondary reserves, they were no more conservative than the corresponding behavior of the German banks. These securities holdings may well have represented credit provision to industry, and their increase over the decade before World War I could well evidence a growing role of the Italian banks in the investment side of the business. For Comit, however, securities written off never amounted to more than 1 percent of assets in any given year, suggesting that these portfolio securities added little risk to the bank's financial position. The banks' balance sheets give the overall sense of moderate risk taking, certainly not out of line with even a specialized commercial bank.

Like the German universal banks, the large Italian banks earned a healthy profit for shareholders in the pre–World War I era. Credito Italiano reported dividends of at least 6 percent, and as much as 7.5 percent in every year from its founding until World War I. Return on equity ranged between 5 and 10 percent and averaged 7 percent for both Credit and Comit.[87] Clearly, at least the shareholders of these top Italian universal banks profited significantly – and consistently – from their business. The stability of dividends, and the solid returns on equity, supports the idea that the banks investment programs were deliberate and moderately conservative. Given the extensive use of deposits, however, the banks' ROA remained much lower – typically in the neighborhood of 1.5 percent and never exceeding 2 percent. Comit earned similar returns over the period, as did the Italian "ordinary" banks more generally speaking. Of particular note, the largest two banks actually returned slightly less than the ordinary banks as a group. At this broader level, the Italian banks' figures compare quite unfavorably with those for the German universal banks.

Unlike German and Italian banks, Japanese banks faced government restrictions on their capital structure and reserve policies in the pre–World War I era. At the end of 1872, a National Bank Decree set minimum capital standards for banks, depending on the population size of the city in which the bank maintained its headquarters. Official regulations dictated that banks hold reserves amounting to one-quarter of deposits, primarily in the form of national bonds.[88] Additionally, banks ostensibly needed to hold gold specie amounting to 40 percent of their capital. These rules were intended to ensure that specie reserves would cover two-thirds of the banks' note issues – an extraordinarily high reserve ratio compared to the German

---

[87] Calculated from *Notizie Statistiche* (various years).
[88] See the extensive discussion of banking regulation in Moussa and Obata (2009) and Tamaki (1995).

and Italian banks. The extent to which banks followed these guidelines is less clear, though it appears that private banks took a more cautious approach to their business. At least in terms of lending, they kept greater liquid reserves and lent out a smaller share of their resources than did national banks. Banks overall grew more conservative as the industry matured, particularly in the aftermath of financial crises. Lending rates declined and securities increased as a share of assets.[89]

Profitability declined in step, but not out of line with the German or Italian universal banks. Despite the Japanese banks' relatively underdeveloped securities business in this period, their ROA closely paralleled those of the German banks – ranging around 1.6 or 1.7 percent in the decade before World War I (Figure 3.3). In the late 1890s, their ROA exceeded 2 percent, comparing very favorably to the German banks. Returns on equity averaged around 6 to 7 percent in the first thirteen years of the twentieth century but hit a low of just over 5 percent in 1904. At these rates, the Japanese banks, along with the German and American banks, outperformed the more mature banks in the United Kingdom over the period (Figure 3.3). After World War I, profit rates dropped off, but with an ROA of 1.8 percent in 1935 (and an ROE of 12 percent), their profits compare well with that of postwar banks around the world.[90]

CONCLUSIONS

The development of commercial banking industries in these countries, and likely elsewhere, mirrored the political and economic change of the nineteenth and early twentieth centuries. In Germany, the creation of political empire and the push for national unity coincided with the evolution toward an integrated, national system of depository commercial banks. In Italy and Japan, new political regimes in the later nineteenth century brought new regulatory environments that spurred growth throughout the economy and financial system. As these economies evolved and industrialized, the organization of the banking industries, and of the banks themselves, changed in step. In all of these countries, the largest banks grew larger, and only in the United States did regulatory restrictions prevent the emergence of densely networked, nationwide banks.

---

[89] See Hoshi and Kashyap (2001), table 2.8. Unfortunately, we have little data available on Japanese cash ratios, preventing a direct comparison with the other countries studied in this chapter.

[90] See Hoshi and Kashyap (2001), and sources cited there.

To be sure, the banks in these five countries differed from one another in both form and function. The German and Italian banks took active parts in equity issues, becoming true universal banks in that sense. The Japanese banks, although ostensibly universal, participated little in equity flotations, thereby acting more like the British deposit banks. Yet the British banks remained the most heavily commercial in their lending focus. The U.S. banks are the hardest to encapsulate in brief terms, given the larger expanse of national territory and continued segmentation of banking markets well past World War I. Still, it seems clear that at least some American banks, while specialized on the surface, closely resembled universal banks and likely participated more in industrial securities (particularly equity) issues than did the Japanese universal banks. In all but the British cases, deposits played a limited role in mid-nineteenth-century commercial banking. The UK deposit banks, aptly named, maintained twice the aggregate deposit-capital ratios of the nearest banking system; but, in these ratios, the other four banking systems cannot be distinguished by their breadth of services: The Italian universal banks took deposits in roughly the same proportion as the American commercial banks. All five countries grew their deposit bases throughout the nineteenth century, but it was World War I that brought the most marked increase in that side of the business.

For all the variation in these banking systems, they behaved in remarkably similar ways, particularly outside of the United States. The limits on branching clearly altered American banks' attitudes toward their soundness, not because bank managers were fundamentally more risk-averse than bankers in other countries; rather, they faced greater risks due largely to their lack of diversification. The UK deposit banks and German universal banks, most notably, held nearly identical ratios of cash to deposits, particularly up to the early twentieth century. The U.S. banks decreased their ratios dramatically over time, but they never got as low as the others.

In performance, as well, the banks in these countries look an awful lot alike. As the banks moved increasingly toward deposit financing over the last quarter of the nineteenth and into the twentieth century, profitability (ROA) declined as well. What had been 2–3 percent ROA in the 1880s and early 1890s became 1–2 percent returns by the start of World War I and then falling to around 1 percent or below in the early 1920s. Returns compared to equity fluctuated quite considerably throughout this period, with no clear trends and no apparent distinctions based on the various systems' adherence to universal or specialized banking.

Overall, then, the comparison of these five banking systems dramatizes the wide variety in systems that arose in countries that were, in economic terms, more similar to one another than they were to many other, far less developed economies of the time. Developing their own approaches to the problem of capital mobilization, they created banking institutions that on the surface looked different from each other but that performed in broad terms very similarly.

4

Governing Corporations

Formal relationship building with nonfinancial firms constitutes a hallmark of the canonical universal banking system and a fundamental point of divergence between those systems and that of the Anglo-American, arms-length type. Relationship banking relates to those bank activities that cede to them at least partial control over the decisions and actions of their client firms. In theory, corporate ownership and governance relationships between banks and firms discipline banks and firms to behave in each other's long-term interest. Thus, relationship banking is seen as integral to the operations of universal banks, even though the two characteristics are theoretically and empirically distinct from one another. In most cases, formalized relationship banking combines one or more of three practices: bank-held equity stakes in firms, proxy voting of bank customers' stakes in firms, and representation in the supervisory boards of firms.

EQUITY STAKES AND PROXY-VOTING RIGHTS

One of the most prevalent notions in the literature on relationship banking is the significant use of bank equity stakes in nonfinancial firms and the resulting influence these holdings yield over firms' decisions. Long-term holdings of equities – anything held over the close of an accounting year – will appear in the balance sheets of the banks if they are owned directly by the bank. The size and variety of such holdings offers one way to assess their importance relative to the other activities of the banks. Naturally, we have to contend with reporting problems, and these could vary across countries. Although many reporting laws were weak and vague in the pre–World War I era, banks did book securities holdings if they existed. Using aggregate statistics helps smooth out what is likely to be primarily bank-level variance in practice.

Proxy shareholding provides financial institutions a means of controlling equity stakes without direct ownership of shares. By granting proxy authority to banks, shareholders cede their governance rights but retain their control over cash flows. Smaller shareholders in particular may view the proxy process as a service because they undoubtedly possess little control over company policy on their own but may find that a bank can exert pressure on their behalf. Banks may find proxy voting appealing because they gain the governance power over firms to which they perhaps also lend and yet may avoid the risk inherent in a direct equity stake in the company. Even if the bank does own stakes in some firms, they may find that they also hold even more extensive proxy rights. As a result, they may control firms by proxy but only hold a small stake in that company's cash flow results.

Corporate control practices varied considerably across countries and over time. The five countries studied here demonstrate that these practices do not map directly to the particular type of banking, financial, or legal system in place. The UK system does, however, seem to fit the stylized view of a mostly arms-length banking system. The question of whether British banks should have supported British industry more is the subject of a long debate. In particular, British banks are compared unfavorably with some of their European counterparts, most famously the German universal banks. Although it is true that UK banks did not develop universal banking along the same pattern as German banks and those in a number of other European countries, it does appear that at least some British banks played an active and direct role in industrial finance.[1] Relationship banking characteristics, however, appear quite different for English banks compared to their German and Italian counterparts.

There is little detailed evidence regarding bank securities holdings in Britain, but the British banks are often said to have invested rather conservatively, holding only gilt-edged securities in their portfolios. Goodhart provides details for three English commercial banks (Metropolitan Bank, London and Midland, and Union Bank) and shows that nearly all of the reported investments consisted of British, colonial, or foreign government securities or railway stocks and bonds. Given his warnings about the banks' desire to hide any investments in industrial firms, however, it is impossible to tell for sure what industrial shares the banks may have held under other accounts. For the period between 1883 and 1907, Lance Davis and Robert

---

[1] It is also true that in this, the UK banks were not alone, as the next section of this book details: Banks in other major economies such as France, Netherlands, Norway and Greece all maintained apparently greater distance from domestic industry than did German and Austrian banks. (See also Collins, 1998 [1].)

Huttenback find that the financial community owned around 5 percent of UK share value and averaged 4 percent stakes in those companies.[2] In addition, public companies, some of which may have been banks, held nearly 4 percent of domestic share capital. The proportion of industrial securities reported among banks' assets ranged between 8 and 12 percent. These figures are based on Welsh and English banks, and Scottish and Irish deposit banks held higher levels of investments. Still, it is likely that British banks owned few industrial shares, rather tending to hold debt securities. One recent study found "not a single case of a commercial bank buying any participating equity in an industrial enterprise."[3] More generally, the prevailing orthodoxy of the time kept the banks from providing "investment funds," which would certainly have included equity.[4]

Whereas it is clear that the English banks invested relatively little of their assets in equity stakes of nonfinancial firms, it is less clear that their lack of equity stakes represented unsound or inefficient business practices. For one thing, the companies themselves naturally also had a great deal of say over whether they would issue equity, and to whom to sell it. To the extent that family-owned firms attempted to remain in family control, the firms issued preference shares and debentures. Thus, the pool of available equity was limited. Moreover, as deposit-oriented commercial banks, they would have less opportunity or incentive to hold equity stakes. The German banks provide the typical counterexample to the English banking model, with the idea that they participated more actively and directly in risky, start-up ventures. Similar contrasts could be drawn for the Italian or Japanese banks, given their involvement in investment banking. But the basis for such a hypothesis – that universal banks allowed promising firms to be funded that would not have been otherwise – is certainly weak.[5] In comparing portfolios between the British banks and other countries' universal banks, it is also worth noting that at least the German railroads

---

[2] L. Davis and R. A. Huttenback (1986).
[3] Collins and Baker (2004). Similar statements appear in Baker and Collins (1999), p. 81. Collins (1998, p. 16) states that "In addition to the banks' internal records, a thorough search had been made of published contemporary banking opinion."
[4] Collins (1998, p. 16). The proportions of loans made for capital investment purposes were strikingly low (17.1 percent in 1880–1884 and only 3.1 percent in 1912–1914) See Capie and Collins (1999, pp. 50–51).
[5] R. Tilly (1986), pp. 113–151, points out, in an aside to his main concern about portfolio efficiency, that given that the main clientele of the universal banks appears to have been large, older, publicly traded enterprises, the banks may not have been actively involved in risky, innovative investment in general.

were largely nationalized during the 1870s. Thus, British railroads – a common component of English bank portfolios – may have represented greater risks than did their German counterparts.[6] Perhaps more to the point, however, the tendency to compare the English commercial banks' equity holdings to those of universal banks elsewhere ignores key functional and organizational differences. Given that specialized investment banks covered the underwriting business almost exclusively – the deposit banks issued little or no shares before World War I – the banks had no automatic access to equity stakes. Given their focus on retail deposit markets, English deposit banks were arguably more similar to specialized banks like the German or Japanese savings banks.[7] Likewise, the British investment banks make a more reasonable comparison for universal banks' stake holding practices, and the evidence of British investment banks suggests that they held significantly more equity than their closest German or Italian counterparts and far more than the Japanese. Because of their limited involvement on the equity side of corporate finance, the English deposit banks gained little control over corporate equity. Moreover, the United Kingdom only introduced the practice of proxy voting in the Companies Act of 1948, so the commercial banks had no access to this alternate route to corporate control.[8]

Although closely related to England in legal tradition and banking origins, the U.S. financial system historically falls somewhere in the middle between the strictly specialized UK financial system and the full-fledged universal systems of most of continental Europe and Japan. The takeoff in railroad construction following the Civil War, with its massive capital requirements, created particularly strong demand for investment banking services. As in the United Kingdom and Japan, the railroads remained private corporations and, as a group, soaked up the largest amount of external capital of any industrial sector. In the early and mid-nineteenth century, commercial banks did perform investment banking functions.[9] In the 1880s, however, investment bankers rose in prevalence, taking market share from the commercial banks. As investment banking became increasingly concentrated, a

[6] In contrast to the German experience, Japanese railroads remained about two-thirds private until 1905, when the government began buying them up. By 1913, the government owned seven-eighths of the railroads. See Goldsmith (1983), p. 39.
[7] The German savings banks held as much of the country's total financial assets as the universal banking sector for much of the pre–World War I period.
[8] Amatori and Colli (2007). See Brian Cheffins (2008) on the development of British corporate law over the twentieth century.
[9] Carosso (1970).

small handful of firms dominated the new issues market, with the House of Morgan taking the lead.[10]

In the United States, the investment banks and trust companies, more than the typical commercial bank, owned equity stakes in companies. Because foreign investors tended to invest through a few well-established bankers, those banks gained further control over corporations seeking outside finance.[11] Even though these investment banks clearly did accumulate equity stakes, they often took shares of older firms, not start-up ventures. The pattern appeared most prominently for railroads, in which bankers could buy out control of troubled firms and force reorganizations and mergers.[12] This situation differed markedly from the German case, where railroads became nationalized early on. More broadly, the stakeholding activities of the largest investment banks – most famously J. P. Morgan – contrast rather sharply with those of all the other countries examined here. Indeed, the small number of highly prominent investment bankers likely differed substantially from the lower-ranked bankers in the United States.

Investment bankers used equity stakes to encourage consolidation and discourage competition in certain other industries as well. The most notable example is steel, a highly competitive industry in the 1870s. J. P. Morgan started by merging three companies into Federal Steel and, in 1901, bought out Carnegie Steel Co., to form United States Steel. The use of voting trusts and preferred stock became widespread in the pre–World War I era, and these practices permitted bankers to exert control over a substantial number of corporations.[13] The dissolution of the Standard Oil trust in 1892 reveals an additional example of trustee control over corporations: Nine trustees jointly held more than 50 percent of the trust certificates; John D. Rockefeller alone held more than a quarter, allowing him and his associates to exert majority control in all Standard Oil companies.[14]

Concern grew over the power of the financial sector versus nonfinancial firms. In 1912–1913, the Pujo committee concluded that high concentration

---

[10] See DeLong (1991) for more on J. P. Morgan. He notes: "When questioned by Pujo Investigating Committee Chief Counsel Samuel Untermyer in 1912, Morgan's close associate George F. Baker (President of New York's First National Bank) could not name 'a single [securities] issue of as much as $10 million ... that had been made within ten years without the participation or cooperation' of J. P. Morgan; Kuhn, Loeb; Kidder, Peabody; or Lee, Higginson.

[11] Kotz (1978).

[12] Ibid.

[13] See the discussion in Calomiris and Ramirez (1996).

[14] See Becht and DeLong (2005), p. 30, and references cited there. They provide extensive discussion of corporate control in this period.

in the banking industry that "was created and held together through stock ownership, interlocking directorates, partnership and joint account transactions" was of immediate concern.[15] Attempts to quell the monopolistic trends, particularly the power that was evident in the top levels of the investment banking industry, met with little success in the pre–World War I era. Following the war, in the 1920s, increased issues business did draw in new competition among investment bankers, thus releasing some of their grip on industrial stakes. The growing use of bond financing in the 1920s further weakened investment banks' ability to control firms directly through equity stakeholding.[16] At the same time, however, bankers turned their attention to public utilities. Public utility holding companies allowed a bank's modest investment at the top of the structure to translate into substantial control over lower levels of companies.[17]

The involvement of banks remained significant well after World War I, but that situation changed after 1929. The financial crisis of 1929 and the early 1930s forced many investment banks out of business, drastically reduced the number of securities issued, and quickly altered the role of the large investment banks in corporate ownership. The Glass-Steagall Act of 1933 accelerated and then cemented the lessened status of banks vis-à-vis nonfinancial firms by stipulating the separation of commercial and investment banking. Requiring banks to choose between their commercial activities and their investment services, and dictating that those maintaining investment banking must give up their deposits, the new law clearly divided investment and commercial banks into distinct institutions.[18] Having lost their major source of capital, investment banks ceded considerable control over new corporate issues and therefore their conduits to control over nonfinancial firms.[19] Glass-Steagall also prohibited commercial banks from holding equity in nonfinancial companies on their own account, and subsequent laws (the Public Utility Holding Act of 1935, the Chandler Act of 1938, and the Investment Company Act of 1940) further diminished the equity control of banks over corporations to virtually nonexistent.[20] Further restrictions on banks came with the Bank Holding Act of 1956 that severely restricted the amount of nonfinancial stock that bank holding companies could own.[21]

---

[15] Carosso (1970).
[16] See Kotz (1978) on bond use and Carosso (1970) on regulation.
[17] Kotz (1978).
[18] See Sylla (1999).
[19] Kotz (1978).
[20] Ibid.
[21] Charkham (1994).

After 1930, therefore, the U.S. corporate control system began to look more like the UK system, but the organization of the system and the practices of the banks clearly stemmed not from a natural progression, but rather from active intervention by the government.

In the formative years of industrialization, the U.S. system looked a bit like those of continental Europe, but the extent of direct stakeholding by the top investment banks (primarily J. P. Morgan) seems to have exceeded that found in Germany. German banks did not pursue equity holdings as part of an active policy of direct control of nonfinancial enterprises during the later stages of industrialization up to World War I – and perhaps not even from their outset in the mid-nineteenth century. On the contrary, the banks seem to have avoided holding large proportions of nongovernment securities over the long term. Corporate securities made up a small proportion of universal bank assets, averaging between 7 and 8 percent of (real) assets for the largest Berlin banks, but trending upward toward World War I.[22] For the whole period, the great banks' nongovernment equity holdings never exceeded 11 percent, and many of these stakes arose out of the banks' involvement in underwriting consortia or syndicates. Consortium-related holdings rose during the boom in joint-stock foundings of the late 1890s until just after the stock market crisis of 1900–1901 and in the crisis around 1907–1908. The banks shed securities holdings as the market improved following both crises. Compared to most of the German joint-stock banks, the largest Berlin banks held more of their assets as stakes in nonfinancial firms, probably due to their proximity to the major securities markets and their relatively greater involvement in listed firms. But the emphasis on consortium holdings – stakes that constituted only part of a larger issue shared with a group of banks – further emphasized the nonexclusivity of the great banks' corporate relationships via equity stakes.[23]

The banks' holdings of securities also amounted to a relatively small proportion of total nominal capital of joint-stock companies. Overall, the universal banks never held more than 9 percent of total equity of German AG's, and this figure represents a conservative upper bound on the figure. Surely, for some firms, bank stakes comprised a significant portion of equity, but given the numbers, those cases must have been rare and most likely temporary. Looking at the economy overall, nongovernment securities holdings of the universal banks ranged between 2 and 4 percent of GNP

---

[22] See Fohlin (1997c, 2007a) for details on estimation. The denominators of these series are computed in real terms, given that securities tended to be posted at book values.

[23] Also, see Fohlin (2007a) for a detailed examination of bank-level data that confirms these aggregate patterns.

for the three decades preceding World War I.[24] The German banks' share did increase between 1880 and 1913, but their holdings of nongovernment securities still only amounted to 4 percent of GNP by World War I. The biggest part of the increase came after 1900.

In Germany, proxy shareholding seems to have played a more important role for banks than did direct equity participation.[25] Many banks required customers to turn over proxy control automatically upon opening securities accounts, granting the bank widespread access to control rights of equity stakes they did not own. Banks could acquire voting power in the general assembly of shareholders and directly influence the voting on issues before that body, which could include long-term strategic decisions along with the selection of supervisory board members. Thus, even without any equity ownership, the banks could hypothetically influence and even direct firm management and strategy.

Unfortunately, it is difficult to quantify proxy voting in Germany until quite recently. Companies traditionally issued bearer shares, keeping shareholders largely anonymous. Those with the highest likelihood of turning over uninstructed proxy control to their banks – the small stakeholders – were the most likely to remain anonymous. The little evidence that has been uncovered suggests that shareholder participation was low, so that proxy holder power was high.[26] Given the availability of proxy votes, voting shares at the general meeting in fact required no direct ownership stake at all. And when a majority of the shares were diffusely held, banks needed to gather very few proxies from shareholders to exercise significant influence over the votes at the general meetings.[27] Armed with this level of voting power, a

---

[24] Calculated from Deutsche Bundesbank (1976) and Goldsmith (1972).

[25] See Hüffer (2002), p. 694, and von Falkenhausen (1966), p. 69 on *Stimmrechtsermächtigung*. This form of proxy voting is often referred to as *Bankenstimmrecht* or *Depotstimmrecht*, due to the heavy use of banks as the proxy holder.

[26] See Passow (1922) for evidence indicating how few shareholders turned up at meetings of the largest banks and also listing a number of explanations for the low attendance rate (most of which amount to "rational apathy" among small shareholders). In the most extreme case presented, seventy-one participants at the 1905 general meeting of the Darmstädter Bank represented 4.5% of the company's share capital. Participants therefore voted an average of twenty-two times their average stake.

[27] This statement assumes that shareholders holding significant stakes would have appeared at shareholder meetings. If not, then the small minority of shares represented at meetings does not imply anything about ownership dispersion. Passow (1922) himself bemoans the lack of data on shareholding, proxy voting, and participation at shareholder meetings; thus, the problem appears to be one of few records having been kept, not just destruction of records during World War II (as is the case for many historical archives in Germany). Passow's data came from newspaper articles surrounding the meetings, making it a hit-or-miss proposition to locate additional cases. Franks, Mayer, and Wagner (2006) used

bank would have significant say over the makeup of the firm's supervisory board and therefore firm management.

In Italy, as in Germany, universal banks sometimes took equity stakes in nonfinancial firms. It is difficult to say, however, how actively the Italian banks pursued such equity stakes, or whether they used them as a means of exercising control that they would otherwise not have had.

In the 1860s and 1870s, the two major private banks in Turin, Banca Generale and Credito Mobiliare, led the banking sector in investing in industrial bonds and stocks.[28] As did some of their German contemporaries, these banks explicitly authorized industrial participations in their founding statutes. In the 1870s, both banks created mining firms, which they owned either outright or in a large majority.[29] The ventures fared poorly and discouraged the banks from engaging directly in undiversified industrial pursuits. They continued industrial participation but did so with partners who could undertake the technical management of the enterprise to limit the banks' role to financial supervision. Both banks maintained minority ownership of shares of various companies, especially in construction companies.[30]

When these two banks collapsed during the financial crisis of 1893–1894, their German-backed replacements – Banca Commerciale Italiana and Credito Italiano – renewed and refined the methods of investing in industrial ventures, on the face of it at least, taking on a less risky approach. Often, the universal banks took strategic stakes to build up banking clientele or to deal with existing clients that were underperforming. Banca Commerciale Italiana (with equity amounting to 28 percent of its assets) and Credito Italiano (15 percent), together with Società Bancaria Italiana and Banco di Roma, held 57 percent of the stakes held by private banks.[31] Whereas traditional and older banks (Casse di Risparmio) still avoided direct investments in stocks, the cooperative banks (Istituti di Credito

shareholder lists from new issues offerings that were required to publish a register of all shareholders present at the preceding general meeting to identify proxy voting. They find that between 1890 and 1940, votes cast by individuals declined from 72.1% to 11.1%, and votes cast by banks increased from 13.3% to 41.8% – the latter increase due entirely to proxy voting. Again, the data are sparse, but they do support my arguments about bank proxy voting.

[28] Confalonieri (1974), p. 273.
[29] Banca Generale, Relazione 1872, p. 11, cited in Confalonieri (1974) p. 281.
[30] Confalonieri (1974), p. 294.
[31] Confalonieri (1974), p. 259. Banco di Roma envisioned itself more along the lines of the British merchant banks, with substantial equity stakes and active brokering of such shares (see Sassi, 1986).

Popolare) increased such holdings (especially locally) in an effort to support industrial development.[32]

Banca Commerciale engaged rather consistently in operations of creation of new companies or participation in already existing firms.[33] Although the bank increased its involvement in new issues in the early years of the twentieth century, it invested typically only 5–10 percent of the start-up capital. Based on the bank's archival material, the evidence suggests that Comit did hold stakes in a substantial number of firms, and some of these positions amounted to a significant percentage of the firms' equity. The bank's balance sheet data show very small amounts of assets held in the form of participation shares, but the large portfolio amounts they reported could well have subsumed nonfinancial equity stakes. Issuers desired Banca Commerciale's participation arguably for the positive signal such involvement sent to investors in the new issues market.

The second largest universal bank, Credit, appeared to have significantly less direct governance role in industrial firms. But the farther down the banking food chain we go, the less information there is on banks' business activities or involvement with equity stake holding. It is highly likely, however, that the tight family control over firms, accompanied by less active equity markets, meant that the Italian banks had less access to corporate equity than the Germans had, particularly among smaller, provincial banks. The same can be hypothesized about the availability of proxy-voting rights for banks to hold and exercise. Furthermore, the financial crisis of 1907 deterred the banks from investing in industrial ventures. Thus, in general, the traditional view seems to exaggerate the entrepreneurial or promotional role of Comit and of the Italian universal banks as a group.

Japanese banks, it seems, owned even less equity in industrial firms than their German counterparts did. The lack of equity stakeholding stemmed from a number of characteristics of the Japanese corporate governance and finance system in place at that time. Most of the means by which German and Italian banks ended up with at least small, temporary stakes in industrial firms appeared much later in the Japanese system, if ever. First, and perhaps most importantly, for a large segment of firms – or at least a large proportion of share capital in the Japanese economy – families dominated the ownership structure up until World War II. By creating *zaibatsu*, typically formed as pyramid-style holding companies, families grew and

---

[32] Confalonieri (1974), p. 245.
[33] Confalonieri (1975), p. 108.

diversified their fortunes.[34] At least until the 1920s, families typically owned the holding company (*honsha*) outright as a partnership and owned a variety of other enterprises through the top-level firm. The *zaibatsu* spread their assets over a diverse range of businesses – industrial, financial, and commercial – rather than concentrating on specific industrial sectors.[35] Family control over all levels of the pyramid organization limited the possibility for any outsiders, including banks, to take equity stakes in *zaibatsu*-linked corporations.

Little data has been found for Japanese equity holdings in the nineteenth and early twentieth centuries. What little exists focuses on the *zaibatsu* and suggests that these groups remained relatively independent of banks. For the "old" *zaibatsu*, the families generally owned all member firms up to the early twentieth century; banks held no equity stakes at all.[36] Even when many family members owned shares in the *zaibatsu* holding company, a single family member often controlled the stakes. By contrast, the "new" *zaibatsu* evolved differently, issuing considerable equity to outside shareholders, primarily through public issues on the stock markets.[37] Still, banks did not take equity stakes in these firms either, although in many cases, *zaibatsu* did own a bank within the holding company.[38] As Miwa and Ramseyer (2002b, pp. 137–138) sum up the situation: "Fundamentally, prewar Japanese banks were not institutions that made large, long-term investments in firms. Bankers did search hard for firms willing to borrow, and bank histories recall the frustration they often felt. Yet they primarily saw themselves as specializing in short-term loans and assorted payments functions."

Even financial firms guarded their equity capital and found it difficult to cede control to outsiders. In one of the more remarkable examples, the Mitsui bank (founded in 1876) quickly accumulated 400 managers among its shareholders; the Mitsui family reorganized the bank as a general

---

[34] Morck and Nakamura (2005) argue that the *zaibatsu* structure resembles that of more recent pyramidal groups in Canada, France, Korea, Italy, and Sweden. Korean *chaebol* seem to be the closest modern analogue. They also note the common inclusion of Nissan among listings of *zaibatsu*, despite the fact that, for most of its history, no family owned the majority of Nissan stock.

[35] See Hadley (1970). A few later *zaibatsu*-type organizations (*Shinkō Zaibatsu*) did focus on specific industries, such as chemicals or heavy industry. Hoshi and Kashyap (2001) and Morck and Nakamura (2005) and sources cited therein provide excellent discussions of the *zaibatsu* (as well as the post–World War II *keiretsu*).

[36] See Frankl (1999), p. 1001.

[37] Hirschmeier and Yui (1975), cited in Frankl (1999).

[38] According to Morck and Nakamura (2005), even equity stakes held by competent hired managers and their heirs often proved undesirable, and families often bought them out.

partnership in 1893 and repurchased all of these shares.[39] Likewise, forty distant relatives owned shares in the Thirteenth National Bank, a subsidiary of the Kamoike *zaibatsu* upon its foundation. Only a few years after the Mitsui reorganization, in 1897, the main branch of the Kamoike took the bank private, buying out even the distant relatives.[40] These two examples also underscore the almost reverse position of banks vis-à-vis nonfinancial firms in Japan compared to Germany and Italy in the pre–World War I era: Important Japanese banks were often subsidiaries of large, family-owned holding companies rather than independent, widely held firms with substantial interests, albeit via board memberships and proxy votes, throughout the economy.

We do have a bit more evidence for interwar Japan. At this point, firms began to use more outside finance and to disperse their ownership structures somewhat, but large firms – whether *zaibatsu* or non-*zaibatsu* – still maintained concentrated ownership structures. In 1935, for example, the ten largest shareholders of the largest firms in the mining and manufacturing sectors held more than 40 percent of the total shares of *zaibatsu* on average; the ratio was close to one-third for non-*zaibatsu* firms.[41] Similar patterns emerge for broader samples of companies, regardless of affiliation with a *zaibatsu*.[42]

Banks continued to play only a modest part in corporate equity stakeholding. Banks owned slightly more than 3 percent of shares among large shareholders in 1919.[43] Financial institutions (including banks, trust banks, and insurance companies) held only 6.7 percent of total shares, also regardless of *zaibatsu* affiliation. Strikingly, for *zaibatsu* firms, regular banks and trust banks together owned less than 2 percent of shares. Instead, and seemingly similar to the German case, private investors bought up securities, including industrial stocks.

Given that we have little quantifiable evidence for either Japan or Germany, it is difficult to draw precise comparisons. The German universal banks engaged very little, at least not purposefully, in long-term

---

[39] Morck and Nakamura (2005), p. 15.
[40] This bank became the Sanwa Bank and more recently the UFJ Bank. For more details, see Morck and Nakamura (2005).
[41] See table V in Okazaki (1993). He examines the data for ten large *zaibatsu* firms and ten large non-*zaibatsu* firms. Of note, most of the largest firms in mining and manufacturing were non-*zaibatsu* firms.
[42] See table 4.3 in Okazaki and Okuno (1999). They study a sample of twenty firms made up of the top ten firms in terms of overall assets (1935) in the *zaibatsu* (Mitsui, Mitsubishi, Sumitomo), and non-*zaibatsu* groups.
[43] See Shimura, cited in Miwa and Ramseyer (2002b).

equity stakeholding, so the Japanese banks were not substantially behind in this regard. It seems the Italian banks did a bit more of this than either the German or the Japanese banks, but the more overarching point is the minimal participation in equity shareholding by the universal banks before World War I.

The association of these sorts of banks with equity stakeholding is clearly exaggerated, most probably because of a tendency toward anachronism: The banks in Germany and Japan did, of course, take up substantial and sometimes enduring equity stakes after World War II. More common in the prewar period were transient stakes resulting from underwriting activities. From the little evidence that has been uncovered about the off-balance-sheet activities of the Japanese banks, it appears that they did not typically underwrite equity issues in the pre–World War I era. Thus, this route to substantial temporary equity stakes seems to have been closed to Japanese banks, whereas it was wide open in Germany and Italy.

On the other hand, because banks frequently took equity shares as collateral on loans – around 25 percent of lending in the 1890s through World War I – they did gain potential control over a significant amount of corporate equity in cases of default. Given what we know about the ownership structure of the *zaibatsu*, it seems unlikely that banks could use even this sort of collateral ownership to engage in significant proxy voting – at least not with the objective of gaining voting rights in the firms. More generally, however, the ownership of Japanese firms, especially those outside of *zaibatsu*, tended to become less concentrated in the pre–World War I period.[44]

INTERLOCKING DIRECTORATES

Certain financial institutions, particularly those in Germany, Austria, Italy, Japan, and Sweden, are thought to form close and enduring relationships with industrial firms, formalized via the appointment of bank directors to the firms' boards (interlocking directorates). Interlocking directorates arguably ease information flows and promote investment, a relationship that would have proven particularly useful during industrialization.[45]

---

[44] See Yamaguchi's study of spinning firms described in Miwa and Ramseyer (2002b, p. 141), in which no firms had a majority shareholder, and half of the sampled firms had more than 300 shareholders. Railroads and electrical utilities also sold shares widely at the turn of the twentieth century. Franks, Mayer, and Miyajima (2009, p. 6) present data showing the mean level of ownership among the top three shareholders in 1907 was 29% (median of 20%).

[45] Gerschenkron (1962) is the classic reference here. See also Levine (1998), as a prominent recent example, citing a number of other studies.

Furthermore, by placing individuals on multiple firm boards, banks could create networks of industrial firms with varying investment programs and capital requirements. Thus, financial-industrial networks represent another potential means of capital mobilization if the intervention of the banks promoted information flows among enterprises with excess funds and firms in need of finance. Banks may have provided entrepreneurial advice to firms in their networks; such consultancy services should have yielded competitive advantages to these affiliated companies. Interlocking directorates, therefore, may have improved the efficiency of capital utilization, encouraging resources to go further in individual undertakings.

There is a strong sense, if little solid evidence, that British commercial banks played little role in the governance of domestic firms. Particularly in the nineteenth century, English industrial concerns kept their headquarters close to home, in the provinces, and kept their boards small and protected from outside involvement.[46] Bankers did sit on company boards, but probably not at the frequency with which German and Italian bankers did. In one study, more than half of the bank representatives – those who were not general managers – took no more than two directorship positions. The percentage of bankers and bank directors declined over time, as corporate boards grew without commensurate increases in bank representation: 80 percent of the members of the banking community had seats on no more than four boards at a time.[47] Members of the aristocracy, however, generally held many directorships.[48] Bankers who did take board positions appeared most prominently in the boards of financial institutions and transport companies: insurance companies (49 percent), investments trusts (31 percent), railways (24 percent), colonial banks (19 percent), and navigation companies (12 percent).[49]

Interlocking directorates with industrial companies involved only a small proportion of banks (about 7 percent), although about a quarter of bankers sat on the boards of one or more railway companies.[50] The same men formed the majority of the small group of bankers and bank directors with seats on company boards; Lloyds Bank and the Midland Bank

---

[46] See Cassis (1994) for an extensive discussion of interlocking directorates in the pre–World War I era.
[47] Cassis (1994, p. 150). Post-1880, professional entrepreneurs did not hold more than three directorships in companies. Only 10% held more than three. See Braggion and Moore (2010), pp. 25–26, citing Rubinstein (1981).
[48] See Thompson (1963) p. 307, cited in Braggion and Moore (2010).
[49] Cassis (1994, p. 153).
[50] Ibid., p. 167.

participated most actively.[51] By 1905, twelve of the fifty largest industrial firms had bankers and members of the banking aristocracy on their boards, chief among them the big breweries.[52] A dichotomy persisted between the urban or large-scale business and the smaller, provincial companies. British bankers engaged much more readily in informal relationships with industry than has been previously thought, closely monitoring industry clients and fostering long-term relationships with them.[53] Banks provided significantly more financial support for industry as well, and such lending – much of which was unsecured – increased as a proportion of banks assets shortly after World War I.[54]

The "big" banks often focused their business on particular industries and geographical areas: Midland Bank in cotton, Lloyds in coal, and the National Provincial in iron and steel.[55] It seems clear that the commercial banks provided long-term lending through rolled-over short-term overdrafts, but the total duration of such loans or their distribution among sectors is hard to uncover, thus hindering a quantification of long-term lending relationships with individual firms.[56] Overall, however, the informal approach to bank-firm relationships makes sense within the UK context of deposit rather than investment banking, and the system arguably served industrial clients well.[57]

Notably, whereas bankers did not appear frequently on British firms' boards at this time, Members of Parliament did. Around the turn of the twentieth century, half of all members sat on at least one board of directors, and many sat on multiple boards. On the flip side, more than one-quarter of firms had an MP on their boards. These positions may have proven valuable

---

[51] Ibid., p. 176.
[52] Ibid.
[53] See Collins (1998) and Watson (1995). Collins and Baker (2004) also cite local microeconomic studies showing that banks were "flexible and supportive in their financing of industrial customers."
[54] Watson (1996, p. 68 and note 37) confirms that bankers easily lent to brewers, sometimes without requesting any security. Capie and Collins (1999) estimate that in 1880–1884, 64.6% of the sample loans were granted without any formal security whatsoever. In 1910–1914, it dropped to 27.3% (pp. 42–43). For Collins and Baker, "The greater provision of collateral was associated with changes in company law which led to the much wider adoption by firms in the period of the corporate structure and of limited liability on share-holdings" (1999c, p. 81). Advances of all banks rose from £519 million in 1918 (30% of total assets) to £926 million (42% of total assets) in 1920, many of which, particularly in cotton, steel, and shipbuilding, were unsecured. Ross (1990, p. 56); Cottrell (1992, pp. 55–56).
[55] Kindleberger (1993).
[56] Collins and Baker (2004).
[57] See Collins and Baker (2004). See also Capie and Collins (1999).

to firms by offering them political connections that may have helped gain favorable regulatory outcomes.[58]

In the United States, the role of financial institutions in corporate governance varied quite a bit from institution to institution as well as over time. Close relations emerged between banks – often investment banks – and industry by the 1880s, and bankers took a growing number of positions in directorates and financial committees over the succeeding decades.[59] Railroads probably ranked first among the sectors populated with bank board members, and by some accounts, most of the railroads developed a close relationship with a particular bank, some of which lasted through the 1920s.[60]

J. P. Morgan and Company is typically held out as the prime example of a larger pattern of banking relationships with industry, or in more sinister terms, the means by which bankers exerted control over nonfinancial firms. Though J. P. Morgan was a private bank, it worked closely with the First National Bank of New York and was tied to that bank via equity stakes and board positions, as well as through personal friendships between Morgan and the director of First National, George F. Baker.[61] Morgan and his affiliates exercised control over at least ten of the largest railroad systems, three street railway corporations, United States Steel, General Electric, American Telephone and Telegraph, International Harvester, and Western Union.[62] Morgan partners held seventy-two directorships in forty-seven large corporations, and the First National Bank of New York officers held forty-six directorships in thirty-seven large corporations.[63] In one of the most famous examples of bankers involved in the governance of nonfinancial firms, J. P. Morgan played a decisive role in a merger of Edison General Electric Co. and Thompson-Houston Co. The president of Edison General Electric was forced to retire, and two Morgan partners were placed on the board of the new company. When Morgan gained control over Federal Steel, he personally named its first directors and held veto power over new directors through 1913.[64]

---

[58] Braggion and Moore (2010). They point out that the phenomenon developed in the second half of the nineteenth century as landed gentry faced falling land values and therefore desired to diversify their portfolios, that is, moving out of agriculture and into the newly emerging industries.

[59] Carosso (1970).

[60] Ibid.

[61] Sylla, 1982, p. 49.

[62] Kotz, 1978, p. 36.

[63] Ibid., p. 36.

[64] Kotz (1978).

More broadly, it seems that nearly all partners of investment houses sat on at least one or two boards of companies in which the firm took an interest. Bankers' presence on the boards of corporations became well known by the early twentieth century, and questions arose over possible conflicts of interest.[65] The Armstrong committee began to bring these issues to the fore, particularly the practice of interlocking directorates. The Pujo investigation that followed (1912–1913) found that nearly all principal railroads and large industrial or public service corporations had at least one banker on their boards.[66] The committee's recommendations went largely unheeded at first, but the negative publicity alone prompted some response from the large investment bankers. J. P. Morgan, in particular, had its partners resign from the boards of twenty-seven corporations.[67]

The Clayton Act of 1914 then prohibited interlocking directorates among large banks and trust companies, but attempts to restrict relationships between banks and nonfinancial firms met with minimal success up through World War I. Financing of the war effort tended to encourage the investment banks' involvement in corporate decision making, and the federal government put aside its efforts at restraining such involvement due to more urgent war-related concerns. The postwar boom softened public concern over the issue and relaxed the regulatory stance.[68]

By some accounts, bank positions on corporate boards can be explained by the mutual benefit derived from it, particularly in the case of railroad companies early on, but extending to other sectors later. From the firm's standpoint, the use of board positions is thought to have established credibility for potential investors and thereby facilitated the sale of securities; from the bankers' perspective, the seats allowed them to safeguard their own reputation and potentially tie the firm to future lending from the same bank.[69] By some accounts, financiers also benefited from the information advantage that resulted from the close ties with nonfinancial institutions.[70] At a more direct level, bankers – at least Morgan and possibly a few other investment bankers with their hands on the corporate purse strings – could dictate in a substantial number of cases who would govern corporate firms. These governance decisions included such crucial operations as mergers

---

[65] Carosso (1970).
[66] See Carosso (1970). Bankers were also on the boards of the trust and life insurance organizations that had stakes in these corporations.
[67] Kotz (1978) and Simon (1998).
[68] Calomiris and Ramirez (1996).
[69] Carosso (1970). See Calomiris (2000) as well, for a lengthy and theoretically oriented discussion.
[70] Calomiris and Ramirez (1996). See also Becht and DeLong (2005).

and acquisitions as well as organizing cartelization.[71] These bankers held sway because they owned sufficient direct stakes in the firms or could prevent the firms from accessing needed finance if they rejected the banks' proposals. How widespread or representative these practices were remains something of an open question, but losing this representation did seem to hurt share values, if only due to the loss of cartelization pressure.[72]

To the extent that such dominating behavior happened much at all, it stands in rather sharp contrast to the situation in the other countries examined here. In Germany, interlocking directorates arose to a substantial extent in the last quarter of the nineteenth century and seemed to involve a good deal of give-and-take between bankers and industrialists.[73] As in most countries, prior to the free incorporation movement of the mid-nineteenth century, too few firms maintained formal boards of directors to permit substantial interlocking. The German states liberalized incorporation in the 1860s and early 1870s, but only strengthened requirements for supervisory boards to represent shareholders in 1884.[74] Banks and firms enlarged their boards and expanded formal interaction with each other after this point. [75]

By the time the industrialization process began its last surge in the mid-1890s, directors of the German universal banks appeared regularly – though certainly not ubiquitously – in the supervisory boards of nonfinancial firms. The great banks were actually less involved in corporate boards than might be inferred from the historical literature: Only 12 percent of joint-stock firms received representation from a great bank, and that number is even smaller if attention is constrained to the four largest banks. Moreover, the great banks held relatively few chair or vice-chair positions, amounting to less than 5 percent of share companies and less than 2.5 percent when considering only chairmanships in those firms. Extrapolating to the full population of German industrial firms, these figures indicate that great-bank directors (of which there were dozens) chaired the supervisory boards of fewer than 100 German nonfinancial firms in the last two decades before World War I.

Firms with great bankers on their boards tend to cluster in certain sectors and were often the largest firms in their respective industries. So, the

---

[71] Simon (1998).

[72] Ibid.

[73] Wellhöner (1989) and Feldman (1998).

[74] At the same time, the new law eliminated the 1870 stipulation that supervisory board members must own shares of the firm on whose board they sat.

[75] See Fohlin (1998b). Information on supervisory boards prior to 1895 is very limited and variable. Some firms, particularly in the years before 1884, may have had little more than a chair and vice chair.

banks' relatively small number of positions often translated into substantial proportions of control rights in a few industries. Three sectors stand out: metal working (including machinery and shipbuilding), light rail, and electrotechnicals. In 1910, firms with great bank representation accounted for nearly 70 percent of total assets of joint-stock firms in each of the first two sectors and more than 98 percent in the latter. The bank positions involved a much smaller proportion of the firms in those sectors: only 21 percent of firms in metal working, 18 percent in light rail, and 64 percent in electrotechnicals. This last sector is the most striking because it is the only branch of industry in which the great banks held positions in more than half the firms, representing such an enormous proportion of total assets. Although the prevalence of the great banks in this sector is impressive, it is worth keeping in mind that electrotechnicals accounted for less than 3.5 percent of all industrial joint-stock firms, and 15 percent of the total assets of the same.

The traditional view holds that the great banks dominated most of heavy industry, and the perception is understandable based solely on the appearance of bankers on the boards of some of the largest firms. But even this superficial measure of "domination" suggests a more moderate view of bank involvement. The top nine banks, for example, held supervisory board positions in less than 40 percent of mining sector firms, representing about one-quarter of assets in the sector in 1910. It is therefore safe to say that the banks had substantial interest in the sector, but the facts do not support any kind of bank domination theory.[76]

Formal links between banks and nonfinancial firms are often seen as evidence of "house banking." In the German case before World War I, however, when a firm had at least one bank link, it often had more than one. Firms involved with the largest Berlin banks commonly had three to five bank connections, either directly or indirectly, usually taking up half of all supervisory board positions.[77] Even considering only direct bank representation, firms with banks on their boards averaged two banks in those positions. While certainly not the norm, some firms had as many as six bank directors, sometimes representing as many different banks, sitting on their boards.

The practice of interlocking directorates also extended well beyond the placement of bank directors on company supervisory boards and intertwined

---

[76] The evidence here reinforces doubts raised about the qualitative influence of the great banks over some of the largest German firms of this time. See Wellhöner (1989), in particular.

[77] The term "links" includes directors and supervisory board members of banks sitting concurrently on a firm board.

the boards of many nonfinancial firms. Over half of German share companies had at least one board member (either supervisory or executive) in common with a Berlin-listed nonfinancial firm in 1904. Nearly 22 percent of these "firm-linked" companies had no board interlocks, either direct or indirect, with a bank; and a third had no banker sitting on their supervisory boards. To be sure, the universal banks played a key role in corporate networks, but they were just one part of an overall system of shared corporate governance.

Traditional, and theoretically appealing, explanations of bank affiliations also find little support in the German case. Firm characteristics that help explain bank affiliations vary with the type of bank considered, and many expected correlates of attachment provide no explanatory power at all, regardless of bank type.[78] In particular, investment and profits – both of which are expected to positively predict bank board memberships – provide explanatory power for only one bank type each. Income growth, also considered a positive predictor of board memberships, is actually negatively related to all forms of joint-stock bank representation. Among listed firms, dividend-adjusted stock returns are also statistically insignificant. The insignificance of investment and the negative signs on income growth cast doubt on most theoretical explanations, whereas the results for profitability undermine the consultancy hypotheses most specifically. At least, it is safe to conclude that if universal banks were providing consultancy services, their impact in the areas one would consider most important was small. Age, also expected to relate negatively to attachment, is only significant and negative for firms attached to provincial banks – either with or without a great-bank director also on board. The sign on debt-equity ratios is more difficult to forecast due to conflicting implications of the hypotheses; they are also difficult to interpret, because high levels of debt finance positively predict supervisory board membership by a joint-stock bank but not for private banks alone. Although it is not a general predictor of attachment, debt finance is clearly related in some cases.

Large firms are more likely to have representation by the largest banks and by private banks, but not by the provincial banks. The number of equity shares outstanding is even stronger when the two variables are included simultaneously. Whereas both variables give a sense of firm size, the number of shares also relates to the feasible number of shareholders in the firm and therefore the potential for ownership dispersion. It is not surprising that the largest banks should attract the largest customers, so one would

---

[78] See Fohlin (2007a, table 5.11).

expect that among attached firms, the largest ones affiliate with the great banks and the smaller ones with the provincial banks. It is less clear, however, that size should be closely tied to attachment in general or to the private banks (in most cases much smaller than their joint-stock counterparts) in particular.

These results on size and ownership dispersion suggest a potential role of universal banks in the securities markets. Listed companies are much more likely to have bankers on their boards, indicating that bank board memberships were at least partly related to securities issue and trading.[79] The extensive trading of securities through the banking system likely provided further opportunities for banks to hold firms' shares, directly and by proxy. Bankers not only created their own secondary markets in listed shares but also became fully ensconced in the governing bodies of the stock exchanges. As the gatekeepers of the German capital market, therefore, the universal banks gained easy access to a broad range of securities – particularly those that were listed. Firms could possibly gain from membership in bank networks, if they were able to reap the benefits of network externalities and save on their trading activities.

The connection between stock market listings and board memberships leads naturally to the issue of proxy voting, particularly given that bankers owned so few direct stakes in nonfinancial firms. Bankers must have entered boards by other means, and one important avenue for such bank access is proxy votes – votes entrusted to the bank by the actual owner of the share. Given their involvement with the placement of new issues, their provision of safe deposit services, and their lending secured by stocks, the universal banks would have been the logical parties to take an investor's proxy votes. Indeed, many investors would have seen the banks' proxy voting as a valuable service. If small stakeholders felt less compelled to vote their own shares than did those with large stakes, then small shareholders would have been more likely to deposit their shares with and turn over their voting rights to a universal bank. Closely held firms should experience less proxy voting than widely held firms, so the dispersion of capital ownership should increase the likelihood of universal bank representation.

Because firms were not required to report the identities or holdings of shareholders (in the prewar period) or their proxy holders, only indirect tests are possible. Although it is hardly a perfect measure, the number of shares outstanding relates positively to dispersion: For a given share capital, as the number of shares declines, the value of each share relative to total

---

[79] See Fohlin (2007a) for further elaboration.

capital increases. If shares are indivisible, the number of shares outstanding represents the maximum number of shareholders in a firm.[80] Firms with large numbers of shares could be closely held, but firms with relatively few shares outstanding are more likely to have been closely held.

Further confirmation comes from examining firms that started or ended relationships in the sample period. Firms with growing share capital or those gaining a stock market listing are less likely to drop their bank attachment. Moreover, firms with growing share capital and increasing number of shares issued are more likely to gain a bank attachment. In other words, capital market operations appear as significant factors in decisions about bank relationships – whether to keep an existing relationship or to acquire a bank board member anew. Growing income is also associated with loss of bank attachment, and age is negatively related to losing bank attachment. Thus, firms that eliminated bankers on their boards tended to be young and prosperous. The two effects may be connected, given the slight negative correlation between age and income growth.

In sum, bank affiliation appears to have arisen largely out of the banks' close involvement with securities markets. The combination of commercial, investment, and brokerage services within individual banking institutions may have perpetuated the networking of bank and firm supervisory boards through the practice of depositing equity shares at one's bank and transferring the associated proxy votes to that bank.

The Italian case compares quite closely with the German one. During the late nineteenth and early twentieth centuries, Italian firms were governed by a two-part board, similar in structure to those present in the German system.[81] Universal banking of the German variety arrived late enough in Italy that by that time, interlocking directorates were becoming commonplace. As soon as they began operations, the two largest of the Italian universal banks, those that were founded largely on the basis of German capital, began to form networks of board memberships among industrial firms. Industrialization appeared in Italy a couple of decades later than in Germany as well. Thus, whereas interlocking directorates clearly provided

---

[80] Once again, the lack of evidence on share ownership prevents confirmation or rejection of this assumption.

[81] The *Consiglio d'amminstrazione* comprised the overseers of the firm, much like the German *Aufsichtsrat*. This board met relatively infrequently and took responsibility for the general direction of the firm and the appointment of top management. The top management, in turn, formed the second board and directed day-to-day operations. This board is often referred to as the *Direzione* or *Direzione centrale*, just as the German board of management (the *Vorstand*) is called the *Direktion* in some sources.

minimal stimulus to capital mobilization for the German industrialization, banking networks had the potential to play a more significant role in the Italian experience. Although the general influence of interlocking director-ates may have been small relative to the economy as a whole, the impact on certain industries may have been significant.

Comit clearly outpaced all other banks in the creation of interlocking directorates.[82] Because Comit's practices may have been anomalous among Italian banks, it is important to avoid drawing generalizations about the Italian universal banking system from this one bank. The firms to which Comit sent representatives were in almost all cases the largest firms in their respective sectors. Overall, 18 percent of firms in these sectors received representation from Comit, but attached firms accounted for 40 percent of the share capital in those same sectors. These percentages fall uncan-nily close to those for Germany (23 percent of all firms and 40 percent of economy-wide share capital), though certain sectors are omitted from the Italian figures that are included for Germany. The excluded sectors (other than banks) – insurance, railroads, and automobiles – might be expected to receive more than their share of attention from the main Italian universal bank, so the economy-wide percentages for Italy may be underestimated. Further underestimation may result from the fact that the data cover only Comit. Because Comit apparently placed board representatives at a far greater rate than any other bank, however, adding firms attached to other universal banks would likely increase the percentages by a small amount.[83]

The bias toward large firms pervaded the bank's relationships across industries but was more extreme in some sectors than others. Comit main-tained representation with one-third of the reported firms in the transport sector, but these companies held more than 70 percent of the industry's share capital. In the mining sector, Comit affiliates comprised only 14 percent of firms but 43 percent of the share capital. Equally extreme gaps existed in the chemical and gas, food and beverage, entertainment services (hotels, spas, theaters), and commercial (export) sectors, and more moderate imbalance

---

[82] See Cohen (1977) and *Notizie Statistiche* (1912) for comparisons of interlocking director-ates formed by the two largest banks.

[83] See Cohen (1977). It would be possible to use the reports in *Notizie Statistiche* (1912) to determine which bank executives sat on the boards of other companies. The results would not compare exactly to the measures used here for Comit, because not all bank representa-tives held positions in the bank's executive board. The data on Comit representation were gathered with major help by Francesca Pino-Pongolini, director of the Comit archive, to whom I am very grateful. To the extent that German banks sent representatives to firms and did not simultaneously seat these individuals on the banks' executive boards, the com-parisons between Italy and Germany become more complicated.

prevailed among metal, mechanical engineering, electrical, leather, stoneware, glass, construction, and real estate companies. Indeed, only in the rubber and canal industries do the data show a lack of emphasis on the largest firms; however, this result stems mainly from the small number of firms in those sectors. For example, there were only three rubber companies with share capital over 1 million Lire, and Comit linked itself to the second largest.

Comparing the share of attached firms in each sector with the corresponding percentages in the underlying population reveals that Comit appears to have held a more highly diversified portfolio of firm connections than did Germany's largest banks. Indeed, despite the evident bias toward the largest firms, the sectoral distribution for Comit parallels relatively closely that in the underlying population. Like the German great banks, however, Comit did place greater emphasis on transportation and metals and less on food and beverages. Comit, however, was far more involved with textile and chemical firms than were its Berlin counterparts. Textile companies comprised 18 percent of the population of companies and about the same share of Comit-affiliated firms. Although, relative to its context, Comit had attained equivalent stature as the German great banks, the Italian great bank seems to have pursued a more diversified strategy – perhaps by necessity – in distributing its involvement in the economy.

Much like the German case, traditional theories of bank affiliations have little power in the Italian case. For example, investment in fixed capital does not relate to bank attachment, and measures of revenue and share capital growth, where available, provide either no or negative predictions of bank attachment.[84] The evidence that has been assembled suggests that membership in a universal banking network neither caused nor resulted from rapid expansion of the firms' productive capacity or demand. Indeed, bank-affiliated firms invested less on average relative to their size, and the fastest-growing companies remained independent of bank board membership. Among Italian firms, investment and share capital are much more highly correlated for unattached firms than for attached firms (80 percent versus 49 percent). This may suggest that unattached firms issue new equity to invest in fixed capital, whereas attached firms use other means, but the hypothesis finds only weak support in the evidence on debt-equity ratios of Italian firms. Debt-equity ratios are unrelated to attachment in Italy.

Apparently, firms primarily gained bankers on their boards (at least the largest banks) once they had reached their later stages of growth. The

---

[84] Fohlin (1998a).

finding could simply imply that formal banking networks were not the primary conduit of bank oversight and advice for younger firms, or it might indicate that universal banks failed to foster those firms that contributed most to economic growth. We know from the records of Banco di Roma that the bank maintained conservative standards of financial health for firms it agreed to underwrite, and that the bank generally placed two or more of its representatives on the company's board of directors.[85]

As in Germany, bank-affiliated firms were more often listed on one or more stock exchanges than independent firms. These findings fall in line with expectations. The fact that bank-attached firms were much more likely to have listings on one or more stock exchange, and that attached firms were on average listed on more stock exchanges than unattached firms, may stem from the size of attached firms and not from bank attachment itself. In fact, bank attachment may have resulted from listing in some cases, if the process of obtaining entry onto a bourse required the aid of an intermediary. This scenario seems likely, given Comit's role in underwriting new share issues and based on the bank's archival records that suggest that issuing companies themselves often sought a Comit board member to sit on their boards of directors.[86]

Although the average face value of shares was similar for firms whether or not a banker sat on the board, the average number of shares outstanding was 2.4 times higher for attached firms than for independent firms. It is impossible to determine the relative dispersion of ownership between attached and independent firms, given the lack of source data. Nonetheless, the fact that the relatively large paid-in capitals of attached firms resulted mainly from a high number of shares outstanding, and not from a particularly high share price, may indicate that attached firms were more widely held than independent firms. As in the German case, dispersed ownership might have led to extensive proxy voting by banks and in turn to the placement of bankers in corporate boards. Although the parallels with the German scenario seem plausible, and even likely, they are, nonetheless, still speculation. The currently available data allow little corroboration.

In contrast to the European universal banks, Japanese banks owned and voted few shares of industrial firms during the industrialization period. It therefore comes as little surprise that they also took a much less active part in the governance of corporate firms, particularly in formal board representation. Because capital structure varied depending on a firm's affiliation with

[85] Sassi (1986), p. 14.
[86] Confalonieri (1975), pp. 109–110.

a family corporate group, *zaibatsu* and non-*zaibatsu* firms' governance differed as well. Among *zaibatsu* firms, the holding companies at the top usually retained tight control over equity, and therefore over governance institutions. The *zaibatsu* families did still cede significant management responsibilities to professional, salaried managers. Non-*zaibatsu* firms, by their very nature far more externally oriented and more dispersed in ownership structure, had much greater interplay between ownership and management. Large stockholders usually acted as directors of these companies, and they exerted influence on the management policies of the firms.[87]

So far, the data on board composition of Japanese firms remains meager for the pre–World War II period, particularly before World War I, but the available evidence suggests little involvement of bankers in company boards. Instead, large shareholders dominated boards of non-*zaibatsu* firms, and families wielded significant control over board composition of *zaibatsu*-related firms. In 1935, for example, more than one-fifth of board members of non-*zaibatsu* firms represented ten of the largest shareholders.[88] Top stakeholders controlled much of the boards for *zaibatsu* companies as well; the main difference was the fact that the holding company at the top of the pyramid (the *honsha*) took up an average of 15 percent of seats, whereas the number of directors placed by the ten largest shareholders accounted for only 5.4 percent of the board.[89] Although these numbers certainly leave open the possibility that bankers played a role in corporate boards, the literature makes little mention of bankers in the boards of nonfinancial firms. One exception to this is the finding by Miwa and Ramseyer (2002a, p. 282) that about half of the boards in their sample of Japanese cotton-spinning firms in 1898 included at least one member with a background in the banking field.

The Japanese case parallels the German and Italian universal banking systems in their lack of support for common theories of formalized bank relationships via positions on industrial company boards. In fact, Japanese banks took fewer mandates in corporate boards than their German and Italian counterparts. The notion that banks took positions on company boards in the process of bailing out distressed firms, in particular, finds little support in the prewar Japanese case. Most of these problems arose after World War I, during the recessions of 1920, 1927, and 1930, as well as the 1923 earthquake; and in these cases, the government often stepped

---

[87] Okazaki (1993), p. 178.
[88] Ibid.
[89] Okazaki (1999).

in, via government institutions, to aid insolvent firms.[90] Even when banks were involved in a bailout, they did not generally take over managerial roles in the company. This pattern differs from the German and Italian cases, where the universal banks became more involved in corporate ownership and governance during the interwar years. Part of the contrast with the German and Italian systems must stem from the difference in board structures; German and Italian corporations being governed by two distinct boards, and thereby clearly separating ownership oversight from management functions. This design provided a place for banks to take positions on behalf of depositing shareholders without becoming wrapped up in day-to-day operations of the businesses. And, of course, access to proxy votes gave German banks the means to vote themselves, or their confidantes, into these supervisory positions; an opportunity less available to Japanese banks at the time, given that they (apparently) held less control over proxy-voting rights. In this regard, the Japanese banks looked more like the UK deposit banks, which also had little underwriting activity and therefore no easy conduits to company board positions that were widely available to universal banks.

CONCLUSIONS

Each of the countries studied here developed its own version of corporate governance, and it would be difficult to divide the five countries into only two categories as economists often like to do for simplification purposes. Direct stakeholding in nonfinancial firms over extended periods appears to have arisen in the United States alone, and then it was mainly the private investment banks, though sometimes the securities affiliates of larger commercial banks, that pursued these positions. The German universal banks participated much less in equity stakeholding than the common perception envisions; rather, they acted broadly in accordance with the traditional investment banking business in most other countries of the same era. In other words, in most countries, even those that would ultimately become known as "relationship banking" countries, long-term equity stakes appear not to have constituted the kind of theoretically appealing method of tying banks to the fortunes of their client firms and vice versa, thereby enforcing long-term relationships and a long-term perspective on firm investments.

German, Italian, and Japanese banks played far less formalized role in corporate governance than would be expected from traditional accounts of those systems. By definition, interlocking directorates could be formed

---

[90] See Hoshi and Kashyap (2001) for examples, citing Yamaguchi (1988).

only among firms with formal boards. In many countries, companies had informal and unregulated governance structures for most of the nineteenth century, and such institutions as supervisory and executive boards became formalized and prevalent only quite late in the industrialization process. Thus, at the outset, it is clear that interlocking directorates could only have played a major role in most places after the formative period of industrialization had passed.[91] Interlocking directorates appeared in Germany and Italy and became most prevalent among nonfinancial firms and banks via multiple supervisory board mandates, as well as via the positioning of bank directors in the supervisory boards of nonfinancial firms.

In Germany, and possibly also Italy, bank board positions seem to have resulted from proxy-voting rights stemming from new issues of shares, particularly for more widely held listed companies. In the U.S. case, board memberships could result from direct ownership stakes as well as via other conduits of control. In this regard, Japan provides an interesting counterpoint to the continental European experience, in light of the somewhat delayed onset and later peaking of industrial development in Japan than in Europe. Japan's adoption of practices and regulations from countries that had preceded it in industrial development gave it something of a hybrid system of corporate governance. The more active use of bond financing, along with apparently less dominant banks, meant that banks played little role in corporate governance in the pre–World War I period.

None of the banking systems provided identifiable monitoring of borrowers through networks of interlocking directorates. The evidence suggests that banks provided oversight through informal arrangements in universal banking systems just as they often did in the United Kingdom or Japan. English and Japanese commercial banks therefore could have acted very similarly to universal banks, filling informal monitoring roles and developing long-term relationships with firms, despite their absence from the investment banking business. Indeed, UK banks used lending practices that were surprisingly similar to those on the continent. The UK banks were probably more engaged with industry than the popular view holds, whereas the Japanese banks were probably less so. Overall, the historical literature once again suggests a great deal of variation within each country, more than it spells out clear lines of distinction among countries.

---

[91] Edwards and Ogilvie (1996) estimate the share of joint-stock companies in the capital stock of Germany. Their numbers are based on Hoffman (1965).

5

Financing Industrial Investment

The historical and theoretical literatures offer many hypotheses about the potential advantages of corporate banking systems that provide a wide scope of services and build formal relationships with clients, particularly through bank positions on the boards of nonfinancial firms. From a theoretical perspective, the existence of relationship banking may affect firm financing in myriad ways, from access to and costs of capital to their growth, profitability, and even their survival.

Institutions that facilitate access to information about firms or ameliorate conflicts of interest between investors and entrepreneurs may temper the problems that lead to inefficient financing decisions. In the older historical literature, universal banks are seen as such an institution, the idea being that they resolve problems of moral hazard (improper or suboptimal use of funds) on the part of firms and conflicts of interest between equity holders and debt holders. It is also plausible, at least on the surface, that the integration of universal and relationship-based corporate finance gives some firms greater access to external finance and may alter their decisions (perhaps even unwillingly) about the various sources of funds to tap as they grow and mature.

At the same time, a significant strand of the historical literature has always emphasized excessive control, abuses of power, and anticompetitive behavior. These sorts of debates raise the possibility that formal banking relationships force firms into decisions they would not otherwise make and that may even be deleterious to their performance.[1] Outside funding also usually brings nonpecuniary costs to a firm – dilution of control or constraints on owners' or managers' decision making. As a result, internal

[1] A more recent strand of the literature raises the issue of related lending, pertaining mainly to modern developing economies (e.g., Mexico), in which bankers lend to companies that they also control via equity stakes. In contrast, Lamoreaux (1994) highlights the benefits of related lending to New England firms in the early nineteenth century.

sources of funds, whether the resources of insider-owners or cash flows from operations, typically comprise the cheapest and therefore most prevalent source of capital for small and emerging firms. Even more advanced firms with easy access to capital markets may prefer internal finance, depending on their assessment of the various costs involved.

Banking relationships, or the potential to create them, might influence firms' decision making about capital structure. Traditional explanations of bank relationships focus on lending by banks and suggest that bank-attached firms should use greater debt than unaffiliated firms. On the contrary, it is also possible that universal banks may gain their board positions as a result of equity underwriting, because they hold temporary equity positions and possibly long-term proxy (indirect) stakes.[2] In that case, bank-attached firms may show relatively high levels of equity finance.

Problems of asymmetric information may also hamper external fund-raising efforts. In extreme cases of credit rationing, firms depend solely on their internal financing – primarily taken from cash flows generated on a year-to-year basis. Theoretical modeling has led some researchers to hypothesize a generally positive relationship between firm investment and cash flow. If bank relationships improve information flows between firms and investors, then firms with bankers on their boards may be rationed less and may therefore invest more on average. Easier and cheaper access to outside funding may also allow firms to invest whenever new projects come along and thereby loosen the hypothetical link between investment and internal cash flows. According to this logic, investment should, therefore, be more sensitive to internal funds for unattached firms' than for attached firms.

Banking relationships, particularly the placement of bank directors on company supervisory boards, may relate to firms' investment programs. Bank relationships may impact firms directly, in that bankers actually cause firms to take actions different from what they otherwise would, or that the bankers' presence permits firms to obtain more or cheaper external financing for investment and thereby allow more rapid growth. Alternatively, bankers may appear on boards because of the changes that firms have already decided to undertake, such as capital expansion. In either case, bank attachment would figure positively in an investment equation.[3] Furthermore, if

[2] Such is a primary finding of Fohlin (2007a) and is noted in Chapter 4 of this book. Whereas it appears that the German banks took to the practice actively, there is little evidence of it at all for Japan, where the banks did not perform much equity underwriting before World War I but also did not often take positions in corporate boards either.

[3] Interacting the attachment variable with each exogenous variable allows a comparison of various coefficients between bank-attached and independent firms within the same regression equation.

the banks advise and provide expertise, their presence theoretically should accelerate firm growth and improve profitability, in comparison with other firms without these advantages. Implicit in the whole idea of banking relationships, however, is some sort of selection into the relationship by banks and firms, making it difficult to determine whether relationships cause or result from differences among firms.

Long-term banking relationships also imply that banks aid firms through difficult periods – by restructuring their financial obligations, providing managerial guidance, or assisting them in networking with other firms. In this view, firms with bankers on their boards may survive longer than their unattached counterparts, particularly if bank connections allow firms to weather severe downturns or crises that they would otherwise not survive. Certainly, the historical literature provides examples of company bailouts in which universal bankers took an active role. Whether or not a firm should be rescued is a more difficult question to answer, because rescue operations may create inefficiencies: The necessary resources may possibly be better directed to other uses. Hence, the mere fact of financial restructuring does not in itself represent a benefit to the economy.

These hypothetical issues surrounding banking relationships and corporate performance sound fairly convincing; however, the historical evidence on the matter offers little support. The previous chapter detailed a number of problems with the standard conception of relationship banking, particularly in the case of Germany. The revised view of how and why bank relationships evolved as they did foretells revision of the presumed consequences of these ties as well. We begin with the classic relationship-banking system of Germany, as the available evidence for that system in the pre–World War I period is now far richer and more comprehensive than for any other financial system of that era.[4] As a result, the chapter is unbalanced, but the alternative would mean essentially throwing out a considerable amount of knowledge that has been gleaned on the German case.

ACCESS TO FINANCE AND CAPITAL STRUCTURE IN GERMANY

Firms finance their activities in several ways, ranging from plowed-back earnings to bank funding to debt and equity securities of various types. For the full range of German nonfinancial corporations, estimated cash flows

---

[4] Most of this section summarizes the results of Fohlin (2007a). The underlying data are available from the author.

averaged between one 1.5 percent and slightly more than 5 percent of total firm assets between 1895 and 1912. German corporations tended to maintain high stocks of financial assets, averaging between 20 and 30 percent of firm assets throughout the period, the great majority of which took the form of liquid assets (cash and bank deposits) and receivables. On average, firms held only 4 to 6 percent of assets in the form of securities of all kinds.

Debt funding, particularly through banks, is often perceived as the most important type of external capital for German firms, both historically and more recently. The universal banks provided short-term capital through bills of exchange and very-short-maturity loans and are widely believed to have offered significant medium- and even long-term credit through rolled-over current account lending. Short maturity financing grew from 9 percent of corporate assets on average in 1895 to 16 percent in 1912. The cost of debt financing varied quite a bit over the industrialization period. Estimated nominal current account rates ranged between 5 and 8 percent and trended up, albeit with great variability, from 1895 to 1913. However, because inflation rates fluctuated widely during this time, real interest rates were highly volatile. Even though the largest swings followed the great foundation boom of the 1870s, firms still faced large year-to-year changes in their real interest rates throughout the period. Real rates fell below 1 percent – notably still positive – in the most inflationary years, but they increased to eight and even ten percent in the deflationary years of the early 1890s, 1903, and 1908.[5] Long-term loans primarily comprised mortgage loans for real estate purchases, frequently funded through mortgage banks (*Hypothekenbanken*) rather than universal banks. These sorts of funds averaged between 15 and 18 percent of total liabilities between 1895 and 1912.

The intensity of debt usage becomes clearer in relationship to the available alternatives, primarily internally generated funds or equity shares. The vast majority of share companies were *Aktiengesellschaften* with mostly common stock. Indeed, nearly all shares issued were ordinary shares, and only 15 percent of firms issued any preference shares. Despite the perception that German firms have typically depended heavily on debt financing, the debt-equity ratios of corporate firms averaged between 44 and 76 percent over the period. Thus, net worth, the majority of which was share capital, comprised two-thirds to three-quarters of total liabilities in the period studied here. The oldest firms were less likely to issue new shares, but overall growth rates of equity capital appear to be independent of age. These results

---

[5] See Fohlin (2006, 2009) and sources cited there on the banking industries of the United States, the United Kingdom, and Germany between 1880 and 1920. Rates were higher in the United States but lower in the United Kingdom.

generally support pecking-order ideas of funding decisions but differ from theories that indicate that bank debt is the first line of funding and is usually de-emphasized as firms create a track record. The German firms follow the expected pattern for debt versus equity in this period, but they appear not to do so in choosing between the two maturity categories of debt.

Counter to debt-monitoring hypotheses, firms with bank attachments did not become highly leveraged in general, but they did decrease their leverage more slowly as they aged. Firms with bankers on their boards actually held less short-term debt as a group, but their short-term debt ratios grew faster than average over time. This pattern does not indicate that bank relationships were unimportant, but rather simply that they do not fit the standard role proposed for them. Companies with bankers on their boards also continued to issue more equity over time, compared to companies without bankers. Still, bank relationships appear not to affect the static level of share capital or decision to increase equity, and stock market listing appears even more important for capital structure than do bank attachments. Firms listed on the Berlin exchange kept significantly lower leverage ratios than unlisted firms and also tended to hold less short-term debt relative to long-term debt. Over time, listed firms also increased their debt ratios less than unlisted firms, at least in part because they were much more likely to raise equity. All of these findings underscore the potential information and liquidity benefits of stock markets.

CREDIT RATIONING AND LIQUIDITY CONSTRAINTS IN GERMANY

Corporate investment is often found to respond to cash flows, controlling for investment potential, and to some extent the same can be said for German firms in the late nineteenth and early twentieth centuries.[6] According to the common interpretation of cash-flow sensitivity, German corporations during this period experienced liquidity constraints. Further investigation, however, demonstrates that firms with greater reserves of internal finance invest more than those with lesser reserves, and controlling for the level of financial assets, firms' investment is actually insensitive to cash flows. Growing revenues are important as well, and together with large stocks of financial assets are the strongest predictors of investment among German corporations in the later stages of industrialization.

Bank board membership is not associated with higher investment rates, and firms with bankers on their boards actually invest much more

[6] See Fohlin (2007a) for details of the analysis.

in the presence of high cash flows than do other firms. Such a finding would, according to many, imply that bank relationships are associated with more severe liquidity constraints. We cannot automatically draw a causal interpretation: Bank representation does not necessarily cause firms to invest, if they otherwise would not have, simply because they have more financial resources at their disposal. Hypothetically, if banks played a debt monitoring-role, attached firms would be predisposed toward liquidity constraints. The analysis in the previous chapter, however, suggests that bank positions appeared as a logical outcome of the organization of German financial markets at the time. This explanation, focusing on the transfer of control rights from shareholders to banks via proxy voting and the engagement of universal banks in the underwriting process, shifts the focus away from bank monitoring and advice and thereby diminishes the hypothetical position of bank board members as an impetus for firm decisions or outcomes.

This line of reasoning still leaves open the possibility of selection bias: If banks disproportionately gain voting rights of large, dispersed firms with listings on the stock exchanges, then these could be firms with particularly active and liquid securities markets and generally good access to credit. But their unattached counterparts may simply represent an alternative form of corporate governance, in which ownership was more concentrated, control more closely held, and both stock market listings and bank board memberships less desirable or frequent. Despite these possible avenues for selection bias, econometric controls for the problem leave the results essentially unchanged. Even accounting for the apparent differences, firms with bank attachments still experience greater liquidity sensitivity than those with no bankers on their boards.[7]

FIRM PERFORMANCE: GROWTH, SURVIVAL, AND PROFITABILITY

On the whole, German firms grew at moderate rates over the later stages of industrialization, with ups and downs, but with only a weak upward trend, over the period studied here.[8] Small, young firms tended to grow

---

[7] See Fohlin (2007a), which uses a two-stage procedure, essentially a "treatment-effects" model, in which the results of a first-stage discrete-choice model of bank attachment feed into the second-stage investment equations.

[8] Firm growth, in this examination, refers to the expansion of revenues or sales. This variable provides the best available proxy for production growth and, in itself, represents a primary goal of industrial enterprises. The typical alternative measure is employment, but few firms report their number of workers in the company reports.

faster than large, old firms. Bank board memberships show no tendency to spur firm growth, and neither do stock market listings.[9] The financial characteristics of firms clearly provide the greatest power in explaining revenue growth. Although firms did not grow at overwhelming rates, they did endure relatively well. Failure rates rose and fell, but even the bad years were not extreme: no more than 2 percent of the sampled firms failed in any one year. Of the joint-stock corporations in existence in 1902, approximately 13 percent entered liquidation in the subsequent decade. Based on this overall failure rate, it is likely that somewhere between 500 and 700 German joint-stock firms failed in the decade before World War I. Births outweighed deaths, though, so that the corporate population grew on net.

Large firms (measured by revenues) were less likely to fail than small ones. This finding highlights the importance of the context of the pre–World War I era: Large, (relatively) young firms are most likely to represent the vanguard of the second industrial revolution – those that are most likely to prosper, and thus least likely to fail. Old-technology firms tended to be smaller. The evidence does not reveal the precise reasons for corporate liquidations, but the patterns evoke the Schumpeterian notion of "creative destruction": small, old firms, in old-technology sectors, with significant debt burden may simply have found it more economical to direct resources to other ventures. Formal bank relationships generally do not alter firm survival, either positively or negatively.

As a group, German corporate firms performed well during the last years of the nineteenth century and the first decade or so of the twentieth century – averaging 3 percent return on assets between 1895 and 1912. Profits varied markedly among firms and over time, with at least 7 percent and up to 22 percent of firms showing negative annual returns (the peak appearing during the stock market crisis of 1901).[10] Stock returns averaged more than 13 percent annually over the period (equally weighted), but the highs and lows made stock investing quite risky. Half of the firms made negative stock returns before dividends in most years, and even adding in dividends, 20 percent of firms made negative annual stock returns. Still, the median firm produced positive dividend-adjusted returns in all but one year (1902).

Bank attachments made little difference for stock returns: Firms with multiple bank attachments yielded the highest returns; those with just provincial banks or just great banks performed the worst (but still more than

---

[9] See Fohlin (2007a) for details. Regressions control for annual fluctuations as well as for unobservable firm characteristics. Selection bias is also mitigated by use of a two-stage model.

[10] See Fohlin (2007a) on the question of cash flow on equity, a useful alternative measure.

10 percent annually) of all. In this case, simply taking the presence of any banker on the board as a quality signal would have produced no relative gain to the uninformed investor, and possibly a relative loss. By modern S&P 500 standards, prewar German firms paid out very high dividends on average, though in any given year at least half of them paid no dividends at all. But dividends still averaged around 3.5 percent over all firms and years in the sample, and 8.4 percent annually for those that paid at least some dividends. Some firms paid out very high dividends: almost a third of the dividend-paying sample distributed at least 10 percent payouts, and sixteen different firms paid dividends of more than 20 percent.

By all available measures, Berlin-listed firms performed better than the rest: They averaged higher ROA, were less prone to showing negative accounting profits, distributed far more generous dividends on average, and yielded much higher dividend-adjusted stock returns (in Berlin compared to the provinces).[11] Such patterns make intuitive sense, to the extent that stock market listing indicates a firm's greater use of outside investors or dispersion of ownership. Highly concentrated ownership, particularly family ownership, suppresses the motive ever to show accounting profits or to distribute dividends, given that there are few or even no shareholders to please and significant income taxes to pay.[12] When ownership is diffuse and largely separated from management, profits and dividends become more important as a measure of success.

If profits measure firm success, then it would not be surprising to find that managerial turnover increases when firms perform poorly. German corporate firms show just such a pattern: high turnover for firms yielding low ROA and even higher turnover for negative ROA. Moreover, when turnover in the supervisory board increased – indicating that shareholders were changing their representation at the firm – executive board turnover increased as well. These phenomena strengthened for firms with Berlin listings: Those firms changed a higher proportion of their boards than unlisted firms, for a given drop in earnings. At the same time, however, bank attachments generally have little discernable impact on turnover and its relationship to firm performance.

As in Germany – perhaps even more than in Germany – formal bank relationships played a prominent role in the story of Italian corporate governance during industrialization. Naturally, one might expect that the active

[11] See Fohlin (2007a) for a multivariate analysis of profitability.
[12] See Fear (2004) on Thyssen, representing perhaps an extreme example of this practice. Thyssen distributed no dividends and took large depreciation expenses to build reserves. He also engaged in other interesting financial accounting practices.

involvement of bankers in these firms had some impact on the way they operated and therefore performed. With the German case already demonstrating a rather neutral influence of bank relationships and with similarly strong connections between the appearance of formal bank relationships and use of stock markets, expectations for the Italian case might be lowered. At the same time, the previous chapter laid out a number of areas of divergence between the German and Italian experiences, so the neutrality of Italian universal banks cannot be presumed. Even though the amount and quality of data does not match that available for Germany, the data are sufficient to reveal many interesting findings.

ACCESS TO FINANCE AND CAPITAL STRUCTURE IN ITALY

In Italy, the interest rate paid on bonds (the only interest rates available), diverged little from 4.5 percent, regardless of bank representation on boards. In the few cases in which rates did deviate from 4.5 percent, it was bank-attached firms paying 4 percent and independent firms paying 5 percent – again, as would be expected. There were regulations constraining the per-firm volume and the interest rates of bonds, but this cannot explain the patterns here. These numbers naturally only capture firms that chose to (or were able to) issue bonds, and as such they may suffer from selection bias.

In contrast to German firms, Italian companies with Comit affiliations used bonds far more than their unattached counterparts: 30 percent of attached firms issued bonds, whereas only 10 percent of unattached firms did so. Because a significant portion of debt consisted of bonds, the larger number of independent firms with no bond financing pulls down the average and median debt-equity ratio for that sample. When conditioned on the existence of outstanding bonds, the debt-equity ratios of the two types of firms are nearly identical.[13]

CREDIT RATIONING AND LIQUIDITY
CONSTRAINTS IN ITALY

Another means of determining the importance of bank affiliation is to investigate the relative liquidity constraints of attached and independent firms.[14] The Italian case suggests conclusions about bank influence similar to those already found for Germany, but there are some important

---

[13] See Fohlin (1998a) for details on the data and analysis reported on in this section.
[14] The results are not completely comparable for the German and Italian cases.

differences. In Italy, firms did experience liquidity sensitivity of investment, but bank affiliation did not offset that effect. Coefficients on liquidity vary depending on the population under consideration. Firms in the early stages of development are likely to need the greatest financial assistance but may also encounter the most difficulty in procuring funds.

The probability of having positive investment is naturally very high when conditioned on status as a start-up firm. Information problems are likely to be more severe in the early stages of a firm's lifespan and are only compounded by the need for a sizeable investment in new plant and equipment. In theory, new firms may have tighter liquidity constraints than established firms, and this effect may be attenuated by bank attachment. Many firms were not investing in fixed assets during the period of the data used in this study. Among those that were investing, liquidity constraints appear to be binding, and were equally tight for bank-attached and unattached firms.

When newly incorporated firms are considered, the findings show a bit more influence of Comit's formal relationships. For the subset of such firms that showed positive investment, liquidity sensitivity is very high – indicating that new firms do experience a great deal more sensitivity of investment to liquidity than older firms. Liquidity sensitivity is far higher for unattached firms than for bank-attached firms in the same category – suggesting that bank connections played an important role for new joint-stock firms.

As with so many other investigations of the effects of bank relationships, selection bias emerges as a concern. Banks might select the most profitable or liquid new firms to underwrite, then gain formalized relationships with the firm and thereby give the false impression that they have attenuated liquidity constraints. Average profits seem to be similar for the two subsamples – though distinctly higher for attached firms in 1908 and higher for unattached firms in 1905. Profits continued to be low for unattached new firms in the late years unpopulated by young, attached firms. Also of note, the rate of new firm creation dropped off significantly immediately following the stock market crash of 1907. Indeed, only two firms in the sample – both unattached firms – were established after 1907.

Unlike the patterns in the entry of new firms and of normalized profits, average normalized stock liquidity is clearly different – much higher – for new, attached firms than for new, unattached firms in every year of the sample. Sample means uncover the same divergence in the full sample, and it is a point worth addressing. There is no way to determine with the current data what proportion of securities was illiquid, and it would be pure speculation to produce an estimate. One might, however, pose the following counterfactual. If bank-attached and independent firms held similar levels of available liquid assets, and if the excess of attached firms' portfolios over that of unattached firms were actually unusable for investment purposes (e.g., a firm might have held shares in a subsidiary for which the new investment was targeted), what would liquidity sensitivity be for attached firms?

Two exercises reveal some useful information for determining the effects of systematic overestimation of attached firms' levels of liquidity. First, reestimating the prior investment equation, but assuming that attached firms' true liquidity was the same as unattached firms on average (in this case, 60 percent of reported levels) yields estimated liquidity sensitivity for attached firms assuming constant levels of investment. This analysis indicates that young, attached firms' liquidity constraints would have been somewhat more binding if the stock of liquid assets were consistently lower. Despite this adjustment, liquidity sensitivity for young, independent firms would remain at least twice as high as that estimated for attached firms. Older, attached firms' liquidity constraints remain unchanged in this exercise.

A second experiment takes the opposite approach and searches for the average level of attached firms' liquidity that produces liquidity sensitivity, for a given level of investment, similar in magnitude to that of independent firms. To equalize liquidity sensitivity for unattached and attached, young firms, 55 percent of attached firms' portfolios must be assumed to be illiquid. Such an assumption stretches credibility, especially compared to unattached firms' portfolios, which are assumed to have been completely liquid. Furthermore, this exercise implies that to equalize liquidity sensitivity across groups, attached firms' average liquidity must fall to 84 percent of independent firms' average liquidity – though this stems partly from the relatively low investment of bank-attached firms.

These two exercises suggest that the high liquidity of bank-attached firms may account for a small part of the difference between the estimated liquidity constraints of attached and independent firms, but that extreme assumptions must be made about systematic overestimation of attached firms' usable liquidity to produce similar liquidity sensitivity for the two samples of young firms. Moreover, manipulations of the liquidity data have little effect for firms that were beyond their first year, and this category comprises the vast majority of the observations.

The fixed-effect methodology used in the liquidity study mitigates the effects of selectivity bias. Therefore, the findings – that liquidity constraints were largely unchanged for the vast majority of bank-attached firms, but that attachment was associated with significantly lower liquidity sensitivity among the youngest firms – are robust to a wide range of assumptions about attached firms' liquid assets. Even advanced econometric techniques that attempt to control for such bias, however, fail to undermine the qualitative results.[15] Furthermore, even if the results stem purely from the biases introduced by membership in a bank network, the findings cast doubt on the notion that bank affiliation provided important oversight functions that improved the efficiency of capital utilization during industrialization. Given the somewhat lower liquidity sensitivity for young Italian firms that were investing, however, the evidence suggests that Comit played a more significant role in this regard than did its German counterparts. The higher liquidity and lower investment ratios of attached firms relative to independent firms suggest that attached firms would require less outside funding relative to size. Thus, going back to the capital structure question, the significantly higher rates of bond issuance by attached firms relative to independents remains puzzling.

FIRM PERFORMANCE: GROWTH, SURVIVAL, AND PROFITABILITY IN ITALY

Median liquidity for Italian firms remained fairly constant over the decade before World War I, but the Italian ratios fell in a similar range as those for German firms during the same period. Given the different stages of the German and Italian economies and the likely age gap between German and Italian industrial firms during this period, however, some divergence might be expected. Reported profits for German and Italian firms relative to fixed capital were significantly lower than liquidity, but the growth rates are similar.

Firms in the Comit network also paid higher dividends (in both levels and percentage terms). As usual, causality and selection are questionable. The higher average dividends – and payments to board members – could simply derive from the higher profits of attached firms. Firm charters typically regulated the percentages of profits to be paid out in dividends and remuneration of board members. However, certain firms may have paid out more than they were allowed or could afford.[16] Higher dividend payments could also relate back to the listing of firms on the stock exchange and the likelihood that those firms were more interested in attracting outside investors.

As in Germany and Italy, Japanese firms of the prewar era financed their activities in several ways, from plowed-back earnings to bank funding to debt and equity securities of various types. Unlike German and Italian

---

[15] Fohlin (1998b) uses a two-stage procedure to account for potential selection biases.
[16] See Cohen (1977).

firms, however, Japanese companies had less formal involvement of bankers in their corporate governance. The *zaibatsu* structure differed from corporate networks in the European continent, though they may have arisen out of similar situations and served related purposes. The data on Japanese firms before World War I is even more sparse and uneven than it is for Italy and is therefore nowhere near the quality and quantity of that available on German firms. A few studies have begun the process of unearthing quantitative evidence, and it is possible to draw some conclusions from them, if only in a provisional manner. The data improve markedly after the start of the twentieth century, so stronger statements can be made about the impact of the corporate governance system in the 1920s and 1930s – a time when Japan was still growing and industrializing rapidly, albeit with some periods of recession and financial crisis.

ACCESS TO FINANCE AND CAPITAL STRUCTURE IN JAPAN

Japanese firms of the pre–World War I era relied little on banks for funding investment. Quite similar to the German and Italian cases, they used substantial financing from equity and retained earnings. Bank borrowing and bonds appeared less prevalently in Japanese corporate capital structure, particularly up through the 1920s. Although the currently available data are far from comprehensive, one small sample shows share capital comprising half to three-quarters of firms' liabilities, and retained earnings amounting to an additional 5 to 18 percent; bond issues and bank loans making up the remainder in roughly equal proportions overall.[17] The railroads fell on the extreme end of the spectrum, with 91 percent of financing from capital stock and 1 percent through bank loans.[18] By other estimates, 30–40 percent of corporate funds came from the capital market, but even in these cases, firms used little financing from financial institutions.[19]

Slightly later data, for 1919 and 1926, show equally low bank debt, with leverage for the most part less than 10 percent of total assets in several different industries; those in the steel machinery industry tending toward slightly

---

[17] See Imuta (1976), as cited in Miwa and Ramseyer 2000, pp. 10. Imuta's highly selective sample included forty-four firms in six sectors, all of which published financial data in the newspaper in the first half of 1898.

[18] See Miwa and Ramseyer (2000). See also the study of Fujino and Teranishi (2000), showing 60–80 percent equity funding.

[19] Okazaki (1993), p. 177.

higher ratios, particularly in the 1920s.[20] Share equity exceeded fixed assets for firms in heavy industry in particular, providing some evidence that bank debt was inconsequential for long-term investment.[21] Japanese figures follow a strikingly similar pattern as the German and Italian ones, suggesting some cross-national consistency in the heavy use of internal funds and equity capital at the time. The fact that these three countries count among those considered the most bank-dominated, makes the reliance on equity financing all the more striking.

The *zaibatsu* tradition (somewhat anachronistically named) sets Japan apart from the others. The *zaibatsu* companies had access to substantial internal funds, largely due to their typical involvement in some of the most profitable industries of the time (mining and overseas trade). The family groups expanded considerably through reinvestment of these internal savings. The various industries outside *zaibatsu* control – cotton spinning and railways, for example – also depended on internal financing, but they did so by borrowing from shareholders and using their stock as collateral.

If Japanese industrial firms met with credit rationing or bumped up against liquidity constraints, there is little evidence of it – quantitative or qualitative – in the sources that have been examined so far. On the contrary, banks found it difficult to dispense of their available funds, and their problems seemingly increased over the first decades of the twentieth century.[22] Firms had access to securities to fund their investment, and the absence of bankers in corporate governance seemingly had no deleterious effects on the financing of Japanese firms. *Zaibatsu* affiliation likely did influence the choice of funds – mostly by keeping the firms under the control of the family-based holding company – but it did not seem to dictate any difference in the availability of finance to enterprises.[23]

---

[20] See Miwa and Ramseyer (2000), p. 14, table 1.B. Their five industries are food and paper, chemicals, steel machinery, mining, and sugar.

[21] Miwa and Ramseyer (2000).

[22] Miwa and Ramseyer (2000), pp. 11–12. Miwa and Ramseyer (2004) uncover (based on a number of in-depth case studies) what looks like credit rationing by banks, however, in the silk industry at the turn of the twentieth century. Because the banks themselves could not assess the collateral (cloth) of the most smaller firms, they lent instead to larger merchants, who could assess cloth quality and thereby had the information necessary to make appropriate advances to the small firms. In other words, the banks used other intermediaries to perform monitoring functions that were too costly for the banks themselves to provide.

[23] See the discussion in Miwa and Ramseyer (2000, 2004). In the first reference, p. 37, they conclude that "... firms with close ties to banks did not enjoy a competitive advantage, and the great zaibatsu groups did not use their banks in order to manipulate capital markets and skew funds to their affiliated manufacturing firms."

FIRM PERFORMANCE IN JAPAN

Firm performance and payout policies varied quite a bit, depending on their governance structures. The Japanese system does not display the typical German and Italian pattern of prevalent bank memberships in corporate boards; questions about the influence of shareholder structure and *zaibatsu* memberships dominate instead. In the Japanese case, the evidence is a bit more cobbled together, so it is more difficult to set out a very coherent story for the late nineteenth and early twentieth centuries.

Large shareholders appear to have played a significant role in firm performance. For example, in the manufacturing and mining sectors, firms with large shareholders outperformed others in the prewar period, based on ROA and growth of total assets. To the extent that these shareholders were outsiders, the findings are consistent with the notion that monitoring by large, outside stakeholders enhanced firm performance.[24] There is some evidence of interlocking directorates between banks and firms, or at least bank-affiliated directors on company boards at the turn of the twentieth century. At least in the spinning industry, board composition had little impact on firms' profits, whether through bank affiliations or via interlocking directorates with other spinning firms.[25] Indeed, controlling for the prominence of board directors, the presence of bank-affiliated directors actually appears to relate to lower profits. There is some similar additional evidence for the interwar years as well. In these years, bank lending – as opposed to bank governance – relates negatively to firm growth and stock returns.[26]

The evidence on the impact of the *zaibatsu* structure of governance is mixed. Having their own group banks, it might be expected that affiliated firms would perform better. But the opposite result could be rationalized as well, given the possibility of "related lending" problems. So far, there is little pre–World War I data on this question, and the evidence on the

---

[24] See Miyajima (2003), who uses a sample of approximately 174 firms. He regresses ROA (defined as the ratio of profit after tax reduction to total assets) on corporate governance variables, some control variables, and ownership structure, using the percentage share held by the largest shareholder unless the largest shareholder was the owner-manager.

[25] Miwa and Ramseyer (1999).

[26] See Miwa and Ramseyer (2000). Using data for six key industries (steel machinery, chemicals, textiles, food and paper, mining, and sugar) for 1919, 1926, 1931, 1936, and 1941, they examine the relation between bank debt and stock prices, and the effect of bank debt on firm growth. For regressions of stock market capitalization on bank-debt/gross-assets, the coefficient on bank debt is negative for all five years and significantly negative for two of them. Regressions using firm growth produce similar results.

interwar years produces partially contradictory results. Whereas one study finds no impact of *zaibatsu* membership on a wide variety of firm performance measures, another finds significant evidence that *zaibatsu* membership did lead to better performance.[27] Yet another study finds that *zaibatsu* firms outperformed their rivals, but the superior performance had no relationship to greater access to bank funding. *Zaibatsu*-affiliated banks do not seem to have routed funds preferentially to group firms. Or at least, the evidence indicates that the *zaibatsu* firms actually borrowed less than other firms.[28]

Like German and Italian firms at the same time, many Japanese firms tended to pay out substantial dividends to shareholders, and these dividends amounted to a large portion of company profits. Many Japanese firms paid out high dividends by tradition, and some did so as explicit policy. Quite similar to the German case, large firms with stock exchanges listings and widely dispersed ownership seem to have paid out higher dividends than others. The pre–World War I evidence comes from the cotton textile industry from 1903 to 1911, an industry that may be unrepresentative because it was particularly successful and used almost no debt financing on average.[29] Still, for later years, and other sectors, dividends remained high. Average dividends reached as high as 70 percent between 1921 and 1936; they correlate closely with profits and use up the majority of those profits, particularly among firms outside of *zaibatsu* groups.[30] Dividends greatly exceeded capital increases for both *zaibatsu* and non-*zaibatsu* firms in the pre–World War II period, so capital increases provided a way of reabsorbing paid-out dividends.[31] Still, *zaibatsu* dividends followed profits less closely; the firms instead smoothed their payout rates over time. The different payout patterns quite likely relate to the more

[27] Frankl (1999) gathered data for 130 firms for 1915, 1921, 1927, 1932, and 1937 and found no significant coefficient of *zaibatsu* membership in regressions of profit-revenue ratios, price-earnings ratios, profit-asset ratios, returns to equity, or sales growth. Okazaki (1999) uses data for 135 large firms from a variety of industries and finds a positive effect in both the 1922–1926 and the 1932–1936 periods. Given the differences in sampling, and possible biases imparted, it is hard to draw strong conclusions from the results.

[28] Miwa and Ramseyer (2000).

[29] See Miwa and Ramseyer (1999), who point out that by 1934, the three largest cotton-spinning firms in the world were all Japanese. Miwa and Ramseyer regressed firm dividends on firm profits, on a dummy equal to 1 if the firm was listed on either the Tokyo or the Osaka Stock Exchange, and on total spindles. The results show that (1) profits held constant, larger firms paid higher dividends than smaller firms; and (2) profits held constant, TSE- and OSE-listed firms paid higher dividends than unlisted firms.

[30] See Okazaki (1993), p. 180.

[31] See Okazaki (1999), table 4.6.

decentralized control typical of non-*zaibatsu* firms, as well as to the long-term, intergenerational perspective of family-dominated *zaibatsu* holding companies.

Family control also played a key role in British corporations throughout the nineteenth and early twentieth centuries. UK Company law was liberalized between 1856 and 1862, yet the number of private companies continued to grow: In 1880, they represented between one-third and one-fifth of all British registered companies and by 1914, their proportion still accounted for 77 percent of all industry.[32] Industrial firms were still largely family concerns by 1914, though the trend toward dilution of family ownership increased during the twentieth century.[33] Even for those firms in which families had sold off their ownership, family members often held onto control via positions on company boards.[34]

ACCESS TO FINANCE, CAPITAL STRUCTURE, AND PERFORMANCE IN THE UNITED KINGDOM

A number of microeconomic studies have been carried out to try and ascertain the state of firms' access to finance in the United Kingdom during the latter half of the nineteenth and early part of the twentieth century. The studies, however, have often yielded conflicting results: Some have found that the capital markets did not impede the development of industry, whereas others argue that market imperfections hindered industry.[35] During the 1870–1914 period, we know that the majority of funds used

---

[32] Watson (1999), pp. 36–37, gives a helpful overview of company law. See Cottrell (1980), p. 163; Gourvish and Wilson (1994), p. 120. Hannah (1976), p. 17, provides similar figures.

[33] See Rose (1999). Cottrell (1980) gives the example of the Truman Hanbury Buxton, a brewery that went public in the late 1880s: "[T]he 12 partners, representing the three families involved, took up all the ordinary capital of £1,215 million and £0,4 million of the debentures, with only the balance of the latter, £0,8 million, being issued to the public." (p. 169). According to Franks, Mayer, and Rossi (2005, p. 11) "dilution of family ownership occurred rapidly throughout the 20th century, primarily due to growth through acquisition [and not to finance internal investments]."

[34] According to Franks, Mayer, and Rossi (2005, p. 3). See Cheffins (2008) on the transformation of UK corporate governance over the twentieth century.

[35] Michie (1990 and 1999) and Watson (1996) take a positive view based on the example of brewing companies – during the "brewing boom," brewers heavily relied on the stock markets. Firms readily accessed new issues markets and raised about three-quarters of their capital needs in that form around 1900 (Watson, 1996, p. 63). However, soon afterward, the brewing companies turned to banks instead. Watson sees, rather convincingly, the functions of banks and stock markets as complimentary. Kennedy (1987) puts forward a very negative view of the role of the stock market.

by firms was generated from the firms' internal sources. Retained earnings financed close to half of fixed investment in manufacturing firms even as late as World War I.[36] The average business resorted little to outside lenders and investors, but the most recent studies indicate that firms could easily use a wide range of external sources of funding but most often did not want to.[37] Even with the widespread adoption of corporate structure and the beginnings of ownership diffusion, firms did not necessarily wish to use significant amounts of external funds.[38]

Surprisingly little is known about general patterns of investment and growth of UK firms in the late nineteenth and early twentieth centuries, particularly for firms without listings on the London stock exchange. In one recent study of listed companies, firms averaged around 26 percent growth (5 percent per year) between 1895 and 1900 and under 10 percent growth (about 2 percent per year) for the next four years; growth rates, however, varied widely among firms.[39] Firms in the electrical supply sector grew fastest, followed with a substantial lag by those in the brewing, extractive, engineering, manufacturing (bicycles, autos, metals), and chemicals sectors. Tobacco, textiles, and railroads experienced the slowest growth, particularly in the earlier period, though textiles grew a bit faster after 1900. What little we know about corporate governance suggests that bankers rarely took positions in the boards of companies, so that there is no sense in looking for differences in firm behavior or performance based on those sorts of bank relationships, as there was for Germany and Italy. There are no Japanese-style *zaibatsu*-like structures to study either. British firms did have informal relationships with banks, and company directors sometimes held positions in other companies' boards.[40] These types of connections did seem to matter: Firms that had well-connected board members or banks in

---

[36] Watson (1999, p. 40) estimates the percentage at 45–50 percent; the figures matches Cairncross's (1953, p. 98) estimates of around half of fixed capital formation coming from reinvested profits.

[37] Watson, Collins, and others.

[38] See Capie and Collins (1992).

[39] See Braggion (2005), who samples 276 listed companies in the first period and 434 in the second. All of the results reported in this paragraph come from that study. Braggion and Moore (2010) develop that analysis further and provide extensive evidence on the position of Members of Parliament on UK corporate boards around the turn of the twentieth century. Cottrell (1980, p. 259, based on C. Feinstein's unpublished dissertation), showed some decline of profitability: The real rate of profit on capital was 18.6% in 1870–1874 and dropped to 11.9 in 1905–1909.

[40] Braggion (2005) counts anywhere from zero to sixty additional board positions for company directors in his sampled firms. The most links appear for company directors in the railroad industry. Again, see also the updated paper, Braggion and Moore (2010).

close proximity do seem to have grown faster than others, particularly in the electrical industry.[41]

Overall, it remains an open question whether British firms suffered considerably from liquidity constraints imposed by lack of funding from external sources. The paucity of data, as well as methodological differences among studies, prevents truly solid comparative analysis between the United Kingdom and the other countries studied here. It does appear, however, that although the financing of British firms in this period differ quite dramatically from patterns that appeared later, the state of affairs does not seem to have differed greatly from that appearing in Germany, Italy, or Japan. Firms in these countries were also mostly family firms, and even those that were not relied heavily on internal financing.

In the United States, as in all of the other countries in this study, the move to the corporate form permitted company growth via a new range of funding sources. Particularly after the 1880s, large manufacturing firms in the leading industries of the day expanded by orders of magnitude to become enormous conglomerates with hundreds of millions of dollars in capital. American corporate giants counted among the largest in the world: The Standard Oil Company was capitalized at $122 million in the 1890s; the American Tobacco Company was capitalized at $500 million by 1904; and most impressive of all, the United States Steel Corporation was capitalized at $1.4 billion in 1901.[42] Still, the American pattern of corporate growth, while perhaps a bit more extreme at the top levels, largely followed a common trend seen in continental Europe and Japan. As in the other rapidly developing industrial countries of the time, a few sectors produced extremely large companies with some separation of ownership and control, whereas the majority remained dominated by small and mostly family-run firms. Among the corporate population around 1900, American industrial firms averaged just short of $5 million

[41] Braggion (2005), based on growth of total assets. Statistically speaking, the author finds that in a regression of asset growth on the interaction of "second industrial revolution" dummy variable and bank proximity, along with other controls, the interacted variable obtains a significant positive coefficient. The "second industrial revolution" variable identifies firms in those sectors that were developing most rapidly at the end of the nineteenth and the start of the twentieth centuries. It does not appear on its own in the reported regression results, but given the growth rates reported in an earlier table, it seems likely that the variable on its own would be positive and significant.

[42] McCraw (1997), p. 320, who notes that the nation's GNP at the time was about $21 billion. See also table 9.1 (Founding dates of Fortune 500 Companies, 1880s–1920s), showing Eastman Kodak, Coca-Cola, and others founded in the 1880s; IBM, Merrill Lynch, and others founded in the 1910s.

in share capital, and the median firm had only around $1.8 million of share capital.[43]

ACCESS TO FINANCE AND CAPITAL STRUCTURE
IN THE UNITED STATES

Observers of corporate finance in the United States during the industrialization period preceding World War I have highlighted the availability of funds via capital markets, the reliance of firms on banks, and the heavy use of retained earnings in financing investment and firm growth. By most accounts, industrialists who wanted to form large enterprises encountered few roadblocks in accessing the necessary capital.[44] The New York market aggregated huge amounts of financial capital to be mobilized by financial institutions and corporations.[45] Capital flowed from both domestic and international sources; the close ties between the London and New York markets, particularly later in the period, contributed to the relatively abundant resources for American firms.

Still, some have argued that American firms of the early twentieth century relied heavily on long-term debt, in part because of the high costs of equity financing.[46] Whether firms easily accessed bank funding remains unclear. At least one study argued that much of the firm financing in the United States (1901–1912) occurred without any intervention from the banks, and that access to bank funds was extremely limited. Small American banks had trouble accommodating large clients, and bank stockholders received preference as borrowers, limiting the amount of capital available to the rest of the firms.[47] At the same time, others point out that American companies relied more on banks for their financing than did British firms. British firms, particularly large ones, relied mostly on retained earnings over the late nineteenth and early twentieth centuries.[48]

---

[43] This figure is calculated by taking a random sample of the 1,551 nonfinancial companies reported in Moody's manual of 1900.
[44] Chandler (1977), pp. 373–74; Navin and Sears (1955); and Sylla (1982). Also see Carosso (1970).
[45] See Sylla (1982), p. 50. Also see the recent work of Mary O'Sullivan (2007) on the expanding role of the New York Stock Exchange over this period.
[46] Calomiris (2000).
[47] Ibid.
[48] McCraw (1997), p. 335. But he also indicates that U.S. firms used less bank finance than either German or Japanese ones. At least in the latter case, and probably in the former as well, this comparison seems flawed, because the Japanese literature suggests low levels of bank financing.

From what scant evidence we have so far, it appears that among the largest firms, debt averaged around 40 percent of total assets, although those proportions varied substantially across firms. Certainly compared to typical German and Japanese corporations at the time, these American firms were highly leveraged. Among these largest of corporate firms, cash flow on equity averaged around 5 to 10 percent of capital stock, exceeding fixed investment rates in many cases.[49] Though large firms may have invested on the basis of retained earnings, it would be hard to argue, based on the little data that has become available, that large U.S. firms suffered severely from financing constraints; the jury is still out on the issue as it pertains to the broader population of American firms.

CORPORATE PERFORMANCE AND BANK INFLUENCE IN THE UNITED STATES

Most of the evidence we have on U.S. corporate finance in the late nineteenth and early twentieth centuries revolves around large firms and prominent bankers, mostly those in New York. Bankers like Morgan played an active role in shaping the destinies of the firms they financed, but it is difficult to say how common these practices were throughout the rest of the firm population or the rest of the country. The New York bankers encouraged consolidations, discouraged "excessive" competition, promoted price stability, and centralized the allocation of capital.[50] The bankers were thought to have extracted excess profits due to their high concentration, interbank coordination, and resulting market power; bankers did not compete against one another for the privilege of lending to the firms.[51] At the same time, what evidence we have suggests that investment bankers that pursued mergers and industrial consolidation benefited the companies and usually did not run contrary to the intentions of corporate managers.[52]

Many contemporary observers viewed Morgan's power as excessive and considered the control of select financiers over industry a fundamental problem of the time.[53] More recent views of Morgan's activities take quite

---

[49] Based on the data reported in Ramirez (1999), table II, p. 669. Firms in this rather small sample are not representative, averaging on the order of fifteen-to-twenty times the share capital of the broader population of corporate firms.

[50] Kotz (1978), chapter 3.

[51] See Carosso (1970, p. 27) and Kotz (1978), p. 26.

[52] Sylla (1982, p. 50), who concludes, "In these respects the American bankers differed from their British counterparts and were much more like the great bankers of Germany" (p. 49).

[53] Brandeis (1914).

the opposite stance, demonstrating that firms with a J. P. Morgan partner on their boards of directors experienced greater stock valuations, superior profitability, and looser liquidity constraints.[54] Morgan-affiliated firms, however, also earned much greater sales (and free cash flow), which would in itself likely weaken the link between investment and cash flows. As always, causal connections prove difficult to pin down. It does seem apparent that the large investment banks worked with industrial firms and railroads to develop profit-enhancing combinations that, through mergers and acquisitions, created the huge "trusts" of the 1890s and early 1900s.[55] As in the German case, the investment banking activities of the U.S. investment banks landed them positions in the new corporate boards. Thus, a clear selection bias emerges between bank board memberships and corporate performance. At the same time, these interlocking directorates were short-lived, as the antitrust and antibanker movements gained steam and culminated in the Clayton Act in 1914.

J. P. Morgan seems to have enjoyed a unique position in American corporate finance. His connections to the London and Paris markets gave him greater access to funds for the companies he helped finance. And his propensity to become closely involved with – one might say micromanage – these associated firms differs notably from the practices of other investment banking houses of the same era.[56] Thus, it remains to be seen how important a role banking relationships more generally played in facilitating firm finance, monitoring firm activities, influencing company policies, or otherwise stimulating superior performance. Most discussions of bank power in the United States pertain primarily to the private New York investment banking houses, or to closely connected large commercial banks, not to the thousands of usually smaller commercial banks throughout the rest of the country. The question of balance of power is tricky, and more recent reassessments that show quite a lot of industrial power in the German

---

[54] De Long (1991) regresses stock prices on a Morgan dummy and other variables; the result is a positive coefficient on the dummy variable for the majority of the specifications attempted. De Long posits that while it is possible to argue that these results are not robust, it is hard to argue that having large financiers on a board of directors actually hurt company's performance. Ramirez (1999) analyzes investment rates and finds less sensitivity to internal funding for Morgan-affiliated firms. Simon (1998) takes a different approach, finding small but significant abnormal returns for J. P. Morgan-controlled firms around Morgan's January 1914 announcement that he would leave the boards of thirty firms on which his firm held positions.

[55] See Simon (1998).

[56] Carosso (1970), p. 27, cited in Ramirez (1999), p. 664. Simon (1998) argues that Morgan did not micromanage his affiliated firms, but rather intervened mainly in financial policy.

context could apply in the U.S. case as well. The evidence so far assembled for Germany, Italy, Japan, and the United Kingdom shows that internal funding prevailed throughout the industrialized, or at least industrializing, world of the pre–World War I period. In comparative perspective, then, U.S. corporate capital structure looks quite ordinary.[57]

Nonetheless, given that Morgan-affiliated firms held approximately $1.7 billion in share capital around 1910, out of the roughly $10 billion held by nonfinancial corporations as a whole, the potential influence of J. P. Morgan alone – whether for good or for ill – should also not be dismissed.[58] This exultation of one individual stands in sharp contrast to the experiences of other countries studied here. In Germany and Japan, the financial elite comprised several competing firms, and even in Italy, where one universal bank took the lion's share of the business, no Morgan-like figure emerged.

CONCLUSIONS

The evidence now available on German firms in the pre–World War I era sheds much light on the possible impact of that country's financial and governance systems, and more specifically of formalized banking relationships, on the way firms behaved and performed. In and of itself, a bank director sitting on the supervisory boards causes no change to most of the patterns investigated here. Banks must have influenced some firms some of the time, perhaps even in extreme ways. In the German case, however, such influence was too uneven to create general patterns of consistently different behavior among affiliated firms. Thus, we cannot infer a significant or definitive role for formal bank relationships in resolving information problems or conflicts of interest, based on this most heavily emphasized case of universal-relationship banking.

The Italian system of corporate finance and governance, and the place of banks within that institutional framework, resembles the German system in a number of ways. Yet the two systems also differed significantly. Italy developed its own version of universal-relationship banking, embedded as

---

[57] Becht and DeLong (2005) underscore the contemporary John Moody's observations that U.S. firms were "normal," meaning like those in other similar countries at the beginning of the twentieth century.

[58] These figures are rough. Total capital of Morgan-affiliated firms comes from multiplying the average capital of Morgan firms reported in Ramirez (1999) by their number (sixteen). Total share capital is estimated for 1900 as the average of $4.88 million for a random sampling of 200 firms multiplied by the total number of nonfinancials reported in the 1900 Moody's. Because total share capital issues increased over the next decade, the 1900 figure of $7.6 billion is surely too low.

it was in a distinct economic, political, legal, and social context. Still, one clear result emerges in common for both Germany and Italy, and that is the very mild influence of formalized banking relationships on the behavior and performance of industrial firms – which is not to say that they held no sway over some firms. It does appear that the Italian universal banks – at least the largest of them – may have had a slightly greater role than the German universal banks. More remarkable, however, is the similarity in the links that appear among stock markets, ownership dispersion, and bank relationships. These connections suggest fundamental revisions to common views of bank relationships and their role in the promotion of industrial development. The Japanese case compounds the need for revision. Its pre–World War I (and up to World War II) history demonstrates little formal role for banks in overseeing firms and thereby influencing their activities or performance.

In all three universal banking cases, capital markets played a significant, even critical, role in financing corporate firms in the later stages of industrialization. It would be tempting, based on the German and Italian cases, to ascribe this fact to the intermediating role of the universal banks. It may well be that the German and Italian universal banks facilitated firms' access to equity financing. Whether that role hinged on their combination of services is less clear. Japanese firms and British firms also accessed capital markets, and they did so very often through direct subscriptions (especially in Japan) or through investment banks. What these countries lacked was the extreme level of concentration in the investment banking industry – the apparent domination of one individual over access to equity capital – that emerged in the United States. If such concentration of power stemmed from inefficient and poorly integrated capital markets, as some have suggested, then the American experience – particularly in contrast to the German and British ones – surely suggests that the factors that shape corporate finance and governance systems are myriad and complex, making it difficult to boil the history down to a very tidy story about a small number of types or categories of financial systems.[59]

---

[59] On the late integration of capital markets, see Davis (1966). Also see the more recent work – which, however, can be seen as partly contradictory for the antebellum period – by Bodenhorn (2000).

PART II

THE BIGGER PICTURE

6

Classifying Financial Systems

Financial systems have evolved along different paths in different places around the world and over time, raising the question of whether some systems have performed consistently better than others. Before we can consider the relationship between financial system design and economic performance, we must understand how actual financial systems are structured, or were in the past. In particular, it would be helpful to be able to divide up the world's systems into a small number of categories, so we could use those categories as a quantifiable measure in explaining desirable outcomes such as economic growth.

Classification of financial systems typically follows a binary approach, and most often focuses on the relative dependence of corporate finance on capital markets or banks: A system is either bank-based or market-based. This system dichotomy has tended to subsume other institutional features that characterize banks and financial systems, such as scope of banking services (universality), engagement in relationship banking, corporate governance mechanisms, markets for corporate control, or capital structure of corporate firms.

In the idealized view, each institutional feature possesses two types, say "A" and "B," and every financial system falls into one of two distinct theoretical categories. So, a system that is type A for one feature is type A for all other characteristics as well. For example, if a system is bank-based, then its banks are universal, not specialized, and those banks engage in relationship banking, not arms-length lending. In reality, however, not only are these distinctions not clear-cut – that is, we see a continuum – but also a country's financial system may combine institutional characteristics from more than one canonical system type, muddying the classification scheme. For example, banks may simultaneously organize themselves as universal banks and behave in an arms-length fashion. In practice, therefore, we must classify financial systems separately along several different typology spectra, so we end up with far more than two types of financial systems – perhaps even an infinite number, depending on how finely we want to differentiate types. To add to the challenge, most systems support multiple types of financial institutions, and these characteristics may also change over time.

Despite all this complexity, we may still try to recover some sense of order and identify certain repeated patterns in how systems are organized. Alexander Gerschenkron (1962, 1968) offers the best-known general hypothesis about the genesis of financial institutions. He argued that banks played a more important role in industrialization for "moderately backward" economies than they played for the earliest country to industrialize, Great Britain. According to Gerschenkron, financial institutions led the industrialization of much of northwestern continental Europe. In situations of extreme underdevelopment, however, such as Russia, financial institutions were insufficient to support the transition to modern industrialized economies. In those cases, he argued, centralized institutional intervention, typically by government, was required.

Gerschenkron's work remains influential in modern thinking about financial system design, but recent work has also questioned his heavy emphasis on economic factors in determining the shape and role of financial institutions. Although economic backwardness may be a cause of rapid financial development during industrialization, likely other institutional factors constrained real as well as financial development up to the point of industrialization. Instead, much of the variation in financial system structure may be generated by peculiarities of financial system regulation. In particular, government intervention may hinder development or promote certain institutions at the cost of others. For example, some have argued that government regulation in Germany in the 1890s simultaneously promoted the large, universal banks and hampered operation of securities markets. Conversely, limitations on banking activities in the United States, particularly after the passage of the Glass-Steagall Act, may have hamstrung banks while spurring financial market development.

To determine the factors that systematically influence financial system design, we first need a classification of financial systems by type. This chapter therefore starts with a discussion of the characteristics of financial systems, to break down overarching terms into their component parts. Next, I categorize the types of financial systems exhibited by 26 different countries through a period of 100 to 150 years.[1] As it turns out, however, few banking

---

[1] I include these twenty-six countries because they are the full set of countries for which the relevant data are available over a long time horizon. They provide a wide sample of

systems fit the extreme paradigms of the universal-relationship or special-ized arms-length banking: Most are hybrids. Because institutions and sys-tems are very difficult to categorize definitively – as the first part of this book highlighted in depth – the chapter uses several different categories, and the results are variable.

The classification exercise demonstrates that modern financial systems, particularly those in highly developed western economies, are highly path-dependent. With some notable exceptions, most countries that industrial-ized in the pre–World War I period have similar overall financial system structure now as the one they had at the turn of the twentieth century. Therefore, to understand the current structure of financial institutions, we must consider the legal, political, and economic forces at play in *both* the distant as well as in the more recent past – that is, in the nineteenth century as well as the twentieth. To be sure, saying that today's financial systems find their roots in the past does not mean that institutions and systems do not change over time. Quite to the contrary, myriad influences continue to mold financial institutions over time, and many financial systems under-went significant institutional change during the upheaval of the middle third of the twentieth century.[2]

CHARACTERISTICS OF FINANCIAL SYSTEMS

Financial systems can be characterized by various metrics. Traditionally, the literature focuses on the distinction between bank-based and market-based financial systems or on universal-relational and specialized arms-length financial systems. This distinction, however, does not fit empirical observation: Most systems are better characterized by specific components of one or the other system rather than these broad terms.

Universal and Specialized Banking

Commercial banking systems are commonly divided into two main types: universal or specialized, depending on the scope of services offered. The fundamental characteristic of universal banking is the provision of a wide range of financial services by the same institution. A true univer-sal bank is allowed to provide almost any product and typically combines

---

both industrialized and industrializing countries with various types of legal, political and economic frameworks.

[2] Rajan and Zingales emphasize the 1930s as a key turning point.

standard commercial banking functions (short-term credit, deposit taking, payments clearing, bill discounting) with underwriting and trading in securities. Modern universal banks also sell insurance, mortgages, and investment funds, although they usually do so through affiliates. The necessity for investment banking services naturally grew with the onset of free incorporation and the development of secondary markets on which to trade securities. Thus, universal banking emerged in many countries only in the mid- to late nineteenth century. Germany has come to exemplify this institutional form, though it has existed in nearly all continental European countries to some extent.

Universality spread over many parts of the world in the nineteenth century, but it did not completely supplant other types of institutions. For example, the case of Belgium displays a pattern common in many moderately industrialized countries of the mid- to late nineteenth century: a small number of large-scale, typically limited-liability universal banks augmented by generally smaller specialized banks focusing on a narrower range of services. To varying degrees, this mixture of institutions emerged elsewhere in continental Europe (at least in Denmark, France, Greece, Italy, the Netherlands, Spain, Sweden, and Switzerland), parts of Latin America (Argentina, Brazil, and Mexico, for example) and, in a limited way, even in Australia, New Zealand, and the United States before various financial crises and regulatory actions damped it out. Germany, with its dozen or more large-scale universal banks, remained at the extreme until the major concentration movement of World War I. Even in Germany, however, many joint-stock banks that could legally provide any service in fact participated infrequently and to a limited extent in investment banking.[3]

Specialized banking, on the other hand, refers to banks that restrict their activities to one or a small portfolio of services such as the exclusive provision of loans or investment services. American banks (between the onset of Glass-Steagall and its repeal in 1999) and British banks (until the end of the twentieth century) provide counterexamples to the universal system and might be classified as specialized. In the United States, the Glass-Steagall Act passed in 1933 prevented commercial banks from undertaking investment banking services. The Bank Holding Company Act, passed in 1956, extended the restrictions on what type of nonbanking activity a bank could engage in and instituted restrictions on buying banks in other states. The restrictions on banking activity implied by the Glass-Steagall Act and the Bank Holding Company Act altered profoundly the development of

[3] Fohlin (2007a).

the American financial system. These restrictions also effectively ensured that the banking system in the United States would remain specialized until the late 1980s, when bankers began lobbying for change. The landmark Travelers Insurance Company-Citicorp Bank merger in 1998, which created the world's largest financial services company, served as a catalyst for the eventual repeal of Glass Steagall.

In contrast to the United States, UK financial institutions specialized by function from the beginning, without explicit regulatory impetus. The investment banks and merchant banking houses evolved separately from the commercial banks in part as a natural consequence of the extent of the markets for those services, and the fact that the early investment banking services revolved heavily around government finance with little possibility to gain from economies of scope between investment and commercial banking.

Relationship versus Arms-Length Banking

Relationship banking is believed to at least partly explain the industrial success of Germany and several other continental European countries in the early twentieth century, as well as Japan and Germany in the post–World War II reconstruction, but what it exactly is remains quite vague in the literature on financial system design.[4] The three main characteristics of relationship banking systems are proxy voting, equity shares, and board positions. The proxy-voting system (Germany is the typical example) allows shareholders to deposit their shares with a bank and grant the bank power of attorney over their shares, resulting in additional voting power for the banks. Even in 1990, German banks held on average approximately 24.3 percent of effective voting rights due to direct equity holdings and 29.5 percent, on average, owing to proxy voting rights at general meetings of their current clients.[5] From this example, it is clear that potentially, the proxy-voting system provides banks with significant power over firm management.

In addition to holding power of attorney over voting shares, banks in a relationship banking system may take direct equity stakes in firms for which they also provide financing. In some cases, bank representatives may

---

[4] See Chapter 3 in this book, along with the extensive reviews in Fohlin (2005, 2007a). On Germany, relationship banking characteristics were brought to light most notably in Jeidels (1905) and Riesser (1910) and many that followed, including the better-known work of Gerschenkron (1962).

[5] Elsas and Krahnen (2003) report these figures on the basis of a sample of large German firms' general meetings minutes in 1990.

be members of supervisory boards of firms as well. Such board positions are more common in some banking systems than others, and here again, modern-day Germany is a key example: 70 percent of sampled firms had a bank representative on their board in 1990.[6] Even in the United States, usually seen as the archetype arms-length banking system, one-third of large firms have a banker on the board.[7] This latter pattern suggests that the presence of bankers on corporate boards does not necessarily signal a full-fledged relationship-banking system of the traditional conception (or that the U.S. system is more relationship-oriented than commonly assumed).

There is no standard way of determining whether a particular set of banking institutions constitutes a relationship-banking system, but categorization typically leads to a common understanding based on at least a perception that banks in that system engage in some mixture of the three primary attributes: bank representatives on firm boards, direct equity shares held by banks, and proxy voting. Among firms that are organized without publicly traded equity, such as the German GmbH, relationship banking takes the form of a "house-bank" relationship. These relationships cannot be formalized in the same manner but may actually prove stronger, owing to the firms' possibly limited access to capital market alternatives. The crucial point is that banks' activities gain them significant formal control over the management decisions of nonfinancial firms; ownership, or rights to the companies' cash flows, takes a lesser priority. Presumably, relationship banking ought to also imply that banks provide helpful advice to young firms, but that sort of criterion is both difficult to formalize and troublesome to measure.

Relationship banking can also be defined by what it is not: It is the absence of arms-length banking. The latter describes bank-firm relationships that are based solely on the bank in its role as financier. In an arms-length system, banks take no enduring corporate governance role in nonfinancial firms. Throughout its financial history, the United States has typically been characterized as an arms-length system, J. P. Morgan notwithstanding. For most of the twentieth century, legal restrictions such as those on equity stakeholding or board memberships have often prevented banks from developing close and formal relationships to their clients. The situation in the United States likely results from the government's drive to support competitive markets and its active prevention of any type of collusive behavior. Trust-busting began in the United States almost as soon as trusts emerged.

[6]   1990 data taken from a survey of 144 firms. Quoted in Elsas and Krahnen 2003.
[7]   Kroszner and Strahan (1999).

In the United States and other "market-based" systems, typically the market provides an incentive for information gathering that supersedes the need for closer monitoring by bankers. It is worth noting, however, that the United States pioneered the development of intensive relationship banking in the form of venture capital firms. This institution is easily explained within the market framework by the realization that venture capitalists fund predominantly untested projects for which the market has yet to enter the picture and therefore market participants cannot reveal information.

Relationship banking (sometimes called relational banking) is often erroneously considered either part of universal banking or a necessary component of universal banking. The prominence of the German case as an example of universal banking has likely led to this error: Germany not only had one of the largest and most complete universal banking systems but also developed relationship-banking practices of various sorts. Relationship banking (versus arms-length banking) implies rather vaguely that bankers maintain close relationships to their finance clients. Banks typically formalize and maintain these relationships through some combination of practices: long-term equity stakes in companies they finance, proxy voting of their customers' shares (often in firms to which the bank lends or for which the bank underwrites issues), or sitting on the board of the client firm.

Prior to World War I, however, formalized relationship-banking characteristics developed gradually and unevenly. As Chapter 4 pointed out, the relationship building often associated with the German banks was actually far less common than might be expected. Until the 1860s and 1870s, when incorporation became freer in many parts of the world, and corporate governance institutions like supervisory boards gained prominence, few opportunities arose for formal bank connections. There are actually very few studies that quantify the extent of these practices, but the qualitative descriptions available suggest that most banks played a small role in nonfinancial corporate governance for most of the nineteenth century.

Thus, even in countries with universal banks, practices that are now seen as enforcement mechanisms for long-term bank-firm relationships, such as equity stakes and board seats, varied quite a bit in their origins and importance. At least in Germany, and apparently also in Belgium, France, and likely elsewhere, the first universal banks in the 1850s often took over the capital of a few firms for which the banks were managing a new issue. The downturn in the markets of the mid- to late 1850s left the banks holding major stakes in a few firms, and the ensuing losses taught these banks to avoid such costly mistakes in the future (prominent examples include the French Credit Mobilier and the German Discontogesellschaft and

Darmstädter Bank). These participations were largely accidental, in this case a result of the market declines, and were not pursued as a means of corporate control. In fact, historical studies highlight the dismay of bank shareholders when bank funds became tied up in long-term equity holdings.

Many countries took to relationship-banking practices much more actively around the turn of the twentieth century, long after the advent of universality; but even then, it appears that long-term, direct equity stakes and board positions were limited to a small proportion of firms. Certainly German, Austrian, and Italian universal banks took positions on firms' boards, but the vast majority of at least German joint-stock companies received no representation from banks.[8] Bankers also took up board positions in primarily specialized systems, such as Canada, Finland, Greece, Japan, the United States, and probably also Belgium, France, and Italy during the middle of the twentieth century, when many of these countries underwent regulatory restraints on universality.

The fact that universal banking existed without widespread and comprehensive relationship banking (at least nine of the twenty-six cases of universal banking) suggests that the latter is not necessary to ensure the viability of the former. Moreover, in many cases, it is clear that firms developed relationships with multiple banks. Because of the size of their securities issues, the largest public firms in particular used financing from, and often received board representation from, several different banks. Thus, the historical experience also suggests that relationship banking is not even clearly based on exclusive, long-term interaction with firms. This institutional independence is important because some have hypothesized that formal institutions help enforce repeated interaction between individual firms and a single bank – the *Hausbank* idea – that in turn yields informational economies of scope and lower costs of finance for industrial firms.[9] Likewise, the engagement of specialized banks in board positions further indicates that relationship banking was motivated by factors other than ensuring informational economies of scope.

Where Does Branching Fit?

Branching over extensive geographic areas (or nationwide) is sometimes identified as a characteristic feature of universal banking as well, but geographic scope actually arises distinct from functional scope. Size may improve the viability of universal banking by making it more feasible to

---

[8] See Fohlin (1997b, 1999b, 2007a).
[9] See Calomiris (1995) for a review of these and related arguments.

perform several functions in one institution, but branching is neither a necessary feature of universal banks nor a predictor of their success. The first universal banks were in fact unit banks: For example, in Germany, unit banks offered a wide range of services within single offices for several decades before branching. Branching appeared first and most prevalently in the United Kingdom, the quintessential specialized system, but emerged in most of Europe and Japan in the 1870s or later. Branching generally remained limited and poorly integrated at a national level until the start of the twentieth century. At that point, branching spread through almost all highly developed financial systems, whether they had universal or specialized banks, or both.

The primary benefits of branching come from geographic diversification and increased growth potential – assuming that banks grow on the basis of increasing deposits and that customers want to deposit their money nearby. Both size and geographic span increase a bank's asset diversification potential, and therefore branching may benefit both universal and specialized banks. Although geographical diversification may not necessarily reduce risk in all cases – it may increase risk as banks branch outside the territory with which they are familiar – it is typically identified with diversifying risks and creating economies of scale.[10]

Given the near ubiquity of branching among the countries surveyed, it is clear that these hypothetical ideas hold up under empirical scrutiny. Branching practices are related neither to the institutional structure of commercial or industrial banks nor to the political-legal system in each country. National branch networks evolved in most cases at the very end of the nineteenth century, most likely in response to the increased pressure for size. Technological advances during the last quarter of the century – both in products and processes, such as electricity – encouraged increasing scale of industry. The growing scale of firms, new and old, led in turn to greater magnitudes of financial capital demanded from financial institutions. Anecdotally, at least, banks also felt the need to improve their bargaining position against large industrial firms, and doing so meant becoming larger themselves and to some extent circumscribing competition from other banks. Fairly quickly, enlarging an individual bank's resources began to depend on its gathering resources from a widening base, much of which was little concerned with equity ownership. Hence, branching arrived hand in hand with the pursuit of the deposit business by commercial banks.[11]

---

[10] Kroszner (1998) points to this sort of risk from loss of expertise.
[11] On changes in banks' funding sources in Germany, Italy, and England, see Fohlin (2001b) and (1999a).

Taking over another bank offered the quickest means of branching, and doing so typically meant branching into new geographical regions.

Banks may also have actively sought regional diversification of both assets and liabilities to smooth out local cycles specific to their home regions and better match – or, rather, offset – the demands of their depositors and borrowers. For example, in a highly agricultural district, a bank may face simultaneous withdrawals of deposits and demands for loans surrounding idiosyncratic events in the local harvest calendar. In more extreme cases, where a bank's assets are dedicated to a homogeneous group of borrowers, a severe drought or other catastrophe may jeopardize the bank's solvency. By opening branches in areas with different industrial bases, a bank may use surpluses in one area to finance deficits in another and shield it from the problem of insolvency.

Certainly, these sorts of motivations for growth and diversification appeared as soon as banks did, but the process of identifying the problem and its solution took time. Limited liability and incorporation facilitated the process of expansion, and most governments liberalized the relevant regulations only in the second half of the nineteenth century. Diversification goals may have also accelerated in response to the widespread financial crises of the early 1890s. These economic influences pervaded most of the industrialized or industrializing world and in nearly all cases superseded the special interests generated by fragmented political power and the centrifugal forces of common-law traditions.

Where national branching did not occur with great frequency, most notably in the United States, we can often point to a heavily regulated financial system. In the U.S. case, interstate and intrastate bank branching was well established primarily in the South prior to the Civil War.[12] Both types of branching disappeared thereafter.[13] Regulation also prevented banks from opening branches outside of the city or state where they were incorporated. The pent-up demand for branching is abundantly clear in the United States over the later twentieth century. As states and then the federal government loosened regulation on branching, banks became large regional players and some have quickly become national in their reach. This rush to network building suggests that branching is an advantage that banks will pursue when they are permitted to do so, regardless of the type of banking system in place.[14]

---

[12] Calomiris (2000).
[13] Chapter 3 gives a detailed account of branching in the United States.
[14] The branching and consolidation movement preceded the deregulation on banking scope (Gramm-Leach-Bliley) and has involved many banks that have not gone "universal" in the wake of the deregulation of scope.

Market-Based versus Bank-Based Financial Systems

In addition to being characterized along the parameters already discussed, financial systems are commonly distinguished on the basis of their emphasis on capital market versus bank financing. Systems supporting large, active securities markets, and in which corporate firms use market-based financing, are often referred to as "market oriented." Systems in which banks provide the majority of corporate finance are known as "bank based." Typically bank-based financial systems correspond to countries in which corporate banks are universal, whereas market-based systems correspond to those with specialized banks. Thus bank domination has become nearly synonymous with universality, whereas market orientation has become linked to specialization.

This oversimplified characterization (bank- or market-based) and the presumed association between universality and bank dominance provide a partial picture, accurate only during particular periods of financial system development, when there were often regulatory restrictions on bank practices. While it is exceedingly difficult to gather accurate and comprehensive historical measures of securities market activity, the qualitative evidence and the data available for a few countries both undermine this neat classification. Before World War I, most industrializing economies supported thriving secondary markets for securities. Even some of the poorest economies, such as India, Russia, and Brazil, had one or more relatively active financial markets. Only a few countries – Finland, New Zealand, and Norway, for example – had virtually no capital markets.

Clearly, financial markets emerged regardless of banking design. At the same time, emerging equity markets likely face a path-dependency issue. The countries that developed the strongest equity markets first could draw foreign firms to list securities with them, reducing the role of national securities markets in other European or North American countries. Countries that led the prewar monetary system, such as Great Britain, France, the United States, and Germany, also took the leading role in international financial markets of the late nineteenth and early twentieth centuries. So, London, Paris, New York, and Berlin topped the list of financial markets around the turn of the twentieth century. In 1905, moreover, approximately 30 percent of the 5,500 German joint-stock companies (*Aktiengesellschaften*) held listings on one or more German exchange – with the majority of these listings in Berlin. Thus, the archetypal universal banking system, Germany, was quite heavily market-based.[15]

---

[15] Fohlin (2007a and 2007b).

It should actually come as no surprise that universal banking systems support active securities markets, if one considers the primary characteristics
of universality: a combination of investment and commercial banking. The
existence of full-scale universal banks requires the use of securitized financial
instruments. A universal bank will have little investment banking business
if it has no underwriting and brokerage services to perform. The existence
of markets in which to trade securities facilitates the use of these claims and
therefore promotes the investment side of the universal banking business.

There are also obvious ways in which banks and markets compete, in
both the initial placement and the ongoing trading of securities, and there
are probably cases in which the activities of universal banks impinged on
the operation of the market. For example, universal banks that provided
brokerage services may have traded securities among their customers and
taken only the net transaction to the market. In the German example, a tax
loophole that failed to impose trading taxes on all orders, even those executed through banks, allowed Berlin-based universal banks to offer savings
to their customers who traded through them instead of through smaller
intermediaries or brokers. The more trades the banks could gather and net
out within their own client networks, the further the eventual net trading
fees were spread. This loophole was closed by 1900, but even before that, it
did not prevent the expansion of the Berlin exchange. This example, however, may say more about the idiosyncratic influences of government than
the innate substitutability of financial markets and universal banks.[16]

The list of true bank-based systems might dwindle down to nothing.
Even Japan is not viewed as an entirely bank-based system, but a hybrid of
bank- and market-based systems plus the addition of the *zaibatsu* (before
World War II) or *keiretsu* (post–World War II) as an extra complexity.[17]

Relationship with Securities Markets

The literature on financial system design touts bank-based systems as more
conducive to contests for corporate control and to long-run economic
growth.[18] This assumption stems from the view that banks play a positive

---

[16] Germany provides a wealth of examples of government intervention in financial markets
and institutions, including requirements on stock market listing, levying of taxes on issues
and trades, and imposition and removal of a ban on futures trading on nearly all industrial
shares. See Fohlin (2000).
[17] Dietl (1998) and Hoshi and Kashyap (2001). See Morck and Nakamura (2005) for an
exhaustive treatment; they explain the (substantial) differences between the modern *keiretsu* and the prewar *zaibatsu*.
[18] See Levine (2002) for a summary.

role as intermediaries in collecting and disseminating information, in managing risks of various dimensions, and in mobilizing large amounts of capital quickly. By playing this regulatory and information-sorting role, banks arguably enhance investment efficiency and thereby economic growth (Allen and Gale 1999), improve capital allocation and corporate governance (Diamond 1984; Gerschenkron 1962), and mitigate the effects of moral hazard (Boot and Thakor 1997). In this view, the long-run relationships that banks form with their clients enable them to smooth the flow of investments and reduce transaction costs and asymmetric information distortions. If banks in these systems internalize market functions, however, they may not support very liquid equities markets, implying a lower level of market development.[19] In contrast, market-based systems by definition support large, liquid equities markets. Markets may enhance growth because they increase incentives to acquire and profit from information about firm performance; under market-based systems, managerial compensation may be more easily tied to firm performance and markets may reduce inefficiencies associated with bank control.[20]

As the previous discussion underscores, however, setting up banks and markets as opposites misses the fundamental complementarities between them and ignores their complexity and heterogeneity. The banks-versus-markets dichotomy therefore provides a false sense of clarity in comparing national financial systems, as the next section makes very clear.

BROAD PATTERNS OF DEVELOPMENT

With a rather negative prospect for classifying financial systems having been set out in the first half of this chapter, it is now necessary to attempt just such an exercise. The classification scheme for financial systems discussed here relies on a set of indicators for financial system types. Another way of characterizing countries is to consider the laws and regulations regarding universality, relationships, branching and equity markets. Because regulations constraining banking operations vary in their intensity and enforcement, and as well, systems have historically differed even in the absence of regulatory restraints, the de facto approach may better capture actual rather than theoretical differences among systems.

Rather than commonly accepted notions of national system types, however, the bases for the categories described in Table 6.1 come from a careful

---

[19] See Bhide (1993) and more recently Levine (2002).
[20] See Levine (2002).

Table 6.1. *Banking system characteristics, nineteenth and twentieth centuries*

Country	Time period	Universality	Bank seats on company boards	Equity share holdings by banks	Proxy voting by banks[a]	Extensive branch networks[b]
Argentina	esp. after 1890	mixed	some	few	?	1
	1990s	restricted	restricted	restricted	restricted	1
Australia	before 1890s	1	?	some	?	1
	1895–1950s	0	?	few	?	1
	1990s	unrestricted	some	some	some	1
Austria-Hungary	pre–WWII	1	1	1	1	1
	1990s (Austria)	1	1	1	1	1
Belgium	1830s–1934	mixed	?	1	?	1
	1934–1970s[c]	0	?	0	?	1
	1990s	mixed	restricted	restricted	restricted	1
Brazil	1850–1900	mixed	0	some	?	1
	post-1900	1	some	0	0	1
	1990s	mixed	restricted	restricted	restricted	1
Canada	1900–1913	mixed	some	some	?	1
	esp. after WWI	0	some	few	?	1
	1990s	mixed	restricted	restricted	restricted	1
Denmark	1870–1913	mixed	some	some	?	0
	1990s	unrestricted	unrestricted	unrestricted	unrestricted	1
England	esp. after 1850s	0	few	few	?	1
	1990s (UK)	unrestricted	unrestricted	unrestricted	unrestricted	1

Finland	pre–WWI	0	some	few	1	1
	1920s–1980s	1	1	some	1	1
	1990s	1	some	some	some	1
France	1800–1880	1	few	few	?	0
	1880–1913	mixed[d]	1	some	1	1
	1941–1984	0	?		?	1
	1990s	mixed	1		1	1
Germany	pre-1880	1	few	few	?	0
	esp. after 1890s	1	1	some	1	1
	1990s	1	1	1	1	1
Greece	pre–WWI	mixed	some	some	?	1
	1928–1962	0	1	1	?	1
	1990s	mixed	unrestricted	unrestricted	unrestricted	1
India	esp. after 1850s	0	?	few	?	1
	1990s	mixed	restricted	restricted	restricted	1
Ireland	esp. after 1850s	0	?	few	?	1
	1990s	unrestricted	unrestricted	unrestricted	unrestricted	1
Italy	1890s–1920s	1	Top banks	1	?	1
	1930s–1980s	0	?	0	?	1
	1990s	1	1	1	1	1
Japan	pre–WWII	1[h]	few	few	?	1
	post–WWII	0	1	1	?	1
	1990s	restricted	restricted	restricted	restricted	1

(continued)

Table 6.1 (*continued*)

Country	Time period	Universality	Bank seats on company boards	Equity share holdings by banks	Proxy voting by banks[a]	Extensive branch networks[b]
Mexico	1897–1913	few	some	some	?	1
	1990s	mixed	0	0	0	1
Netherlands	1860–1920s[g]	mixed	1	1	?	1
	1990s	1	1	1	1	1
New Zealand	1870–1895	mixed	?	some	?	1
	1895–	0	?	few	?	1
	1990s	mixed	unrestricted	unrestricted	unrestricted	1
Norway	pre–WWII	0	0	0	?	0
	1990s	mixed	some	some	some	1
Portugal	1890s–WWII	1	1	some	?	few
	post–WWII	1	1	1	?	1
	1990s	1	some	some	some	1
Russia	1890s–WWII	1	1	1	?	1
	1990s	mixed				
Spain	esp. after 1890s	mixed	1	1	?	1
	1990s	1	1	1	1	1
Sweden	esp. after 1850s	mixed	1	some[f]	some	1
	1990s	1	restricted	restricted	restricted	1
Switzerland	esp. post-1890s	mixed	1	some	?	1
	1990s	1	1	1	1	1

United States						
before 1914	1^i	1	1	?	0
1914–1933	1	some	few	?	some
after 1933	0	some	0	?	some
1990s	restricted	restricted	restricted	restricted	some

Notes:

a In many cases the extent of proxy voting by banks is difficult to measure accurately.

b In most cases, branching proceeded slowly until after the second half of the nineteenth century or even later.

c Or since World War I.

d Some universal banks, some specialized. French universal banks moved more toward straight deposit banking after 1880.

e After 1934, mixed banks were required to split into deposit banks and holding companies, and the banks could not hold shares.

f Intentional acquisition of shares was illegal until 1909. Shareholdings could result from collateral held on bad loans.

g Some universal, some primarily commercial. (Jonker argues that Dutch banks were universal only between 1910 and 1920. After about 1924 and through World War II, the Dutch banks reverted to primarily commercial banking, with some low-risk company flotations.)

h Japanese banks combined commercial and investment banking but underwrote little corporate equity; they were prohibited from acting as dealers in secondary markets.

i Bank structure varied considerably. Services were combined through commercial bank subsidiaries of investment banks. Compliance to (or interpretation of) the new laws also varied.

Source: For most of the countries listed, the determination of banking characteristics stems from the author's evaluation based on searches of secondary literature as well as discussions with several scholars who have studied these systems. For Germany and Italy, and to a lesser extent the United States and the United Kingdom, the determination is based also on the author's own original research. Gaps remain where information is too sparse to support a certain categorization.

examination of financial systems of 26 countries spanning the last 150 years.[21] The set of countries reflects data limitations; ideally we would like to have as broad a range of countries as possible and as long a time series as possible. But for many countries, there are few records on the evolution of their financial systems. The resulting set of twenty-six countries includes South American (Argentina and Brazil), European (France, Germany, United Kingdom, Denmark, among others), North American (United States, Canada, and Mexico), and East Asian (India, Japan) countries. The data begin in the mid-nineteenth century for some countries (beginning about 1850), and at various later points for the rest.

The classification scheme follows the characteristics and practices described in the previous section (Tables 6.1 and 6.2):

- Universality (whether commercial banks also perform investment services)
- Bank seats on company boards
- Bank shareholding in nonfinancial firms
- Proxy voting of nonfinancial shares
- Extensive branching networks

These facets of financial institutions most clearly distinguish among types of financial services along dimensions that hypothetically matter to the performance of the system and the broader economy.

Universality

Germany, Austria-Hungary, and Portugal were the only countries to develop a universal banking system in the late nineteenth century and maintain it continuously into the late twentieth century. Germany is associated most closely with the universal bank, whose beginnings were observable from about the mid-nineteenth century to maturity after German unification (1871) and the creation of a common currency (1876). The German universal bank provided investment and credit functions for its clientele, primarily composed of corporations and large private enterprises. In Italy, the financial system remained compartmentalized until the early 1890s, when it suffered a severe crisis and the failure of many banks (see Chapter 2). The crisis prompted the establishment of a central banking system and the importation of German-style universal banking.

---

[21] For most of the countries listed, the determination of banking characteristics stems from exhaustive searches of secondary literature as well as discussions with several scholars who

Table 6.2. *Persistence of banking system characteristics during the twentieth century*

Country	Universal in 1913? 0–2 (subjective)	Universal in 1990s? 0–2 (subjective)	Universal in 1913? 0–1 (subjective)	Universal in 1990s? 0–1 (subjective)	Bank-based in 1990s? 1 = yes	Structure index for 1990s	Development of equity markets in 1913? 0–2 (subjective)
Argentina	1	0	0	0	1	−0.18	1
Australia	0	2	0	1	0	0.80	1
Austria-Hungary	2	2	1	1	1	−1.27	1
Belgium	1	1	1	1	1	−0.17	1
Brazil	2	1	1	1	0	1.01	1
Canada	1	1	0	0	0	0.82	1
Denmark	1	2	1	1	0	0.17	1
England	0	1	0	0	0	1.24	2
Finland	1	1	1	1	1	−0.76	0
France	1	1	1	1	1	−0.17	2
Germany	2	2	1	1	0	0.17	2
Greece	1	1	1	1	1	−0.66	n/a
India	1	1	0	0	1	0.14	1
Ireland	0	2	0	1	0	0.33	n/a
Italy	2	2	1	1	1	−0.55	1
Japan	1	0	1	0	0	0.86	1
Mexico	1	1	0	0	0	0.90	1
Netherlands	1	1	1	1	0	0.33	1
New Zealand	0	1	0	1	0	0.49	0
Norway	1	0	0	0	1	−0.23	0
Portugal	2	1	1	1	1	−1.43	1
Russia	2	n/a	1	n/a	n/a	n/a	1
Spain	2	2	1	1	1	−0.31	1
Sweden	1	2	1	1	0	0.80	1
Switzerland	1	2	1	1	0	1.58	1
United States	1	0	0	0	0	1.34	2

Sources: Same as in Table 6.1 plus structure index from Levine and Zervos (1998).

In the 1890s, several countries developed universal banking: Finland, Spain, Sweden, Ireland, and Switzerland. Some consistently mixed or partially restricted their systems (Argentina, Belgium, Brazil, Canada, Greece, India, Mexico, New Zealand, Norway, and Russia). Other countries, such as Australia, France, Netherlands, Belgium, Italy, Russia and the United States, developed universal banking practices in the nineteenth century but then restricted or abandoned them at various points later on. Notably, the United States began the twentieth century with universal banking but sharply restricted it with the passage of the Glass-Steagall Act in 1933 and the Bank Holding Company Act in 1956, both as responses to the Great Depression–era bank failures. Even into the 1990s, the United States did not develop unrestricted universal banking or in fact national branch networks. The Glass-Steagall Act persisted until its repeal in 1998, after much debate and as financial and political reality overtook the antiquated law.[22]

Relationship Banking

A deeper examination of historical cases demonstrates that not all universal banks perform the complete range of relationship-banking functions, and not all financial institutions that provide some of these functions are universal banks. As discussed earlier, relationship banking is defined by the closeness of a bank's relationship with its clients and measured by the following: seats on company boards, equity share holdings, and proxy voting.

Again, the strength and prevalence of relationship-banking practices varies across countries and across time periods. In the late nineteenth century, Austria-Hungary was the only country (for which there is data) that engaged in widespread relational banking under the complete definition (seats on company boards, equity share holdings, and proxy voting; note that the latter criterion is difficult to collect data on). In Italy, the Netherlands, Russia, Spain, and the United States, banks in the late nineteenth century also took seats on company boards and held equity share holdings. In all of these cases, there is no data on proxy voting. German banks held board positions and proxy votes but few equity stakes. Thus, we can surmise that these six countries in addition to Austria-Hungary had some large degree of relational banking.

have studied these systems. For Germany and Italy, and to a lesser extent the United States and the United Kingdom, the determination is based also on my own original research. Gaps remain where information is too sparse to support a certain categorization.

[22] The merger between Travelers Insurance Group and Citibank in early 1998 was a direct challenge to the early-twentieth-century banking acts.

After World War II, Austria, Germany, Greece (to some extent – there is no data for proxy voting), Japan (also no data on proxy voting), Netherlands, Portugal, Spain, and Switzerland all had some degree of relational banking practices. In the late twentieth century, Italy, France and Finland also developed relational banking. At the same time, these practices became restricted in Japan. Most countries whose banks held seats on company boards allowed them to have equity share holdings in nonfinancial firms. On the whole, these two characteristics of relationship banking did appear to go together, but the extent of long-term stakeholding did vary a great deal. When equity stakes coincided with board representation, the motivation was simple to understand: Through board seats and equity stakes, banks could provide corporate oversight and simultaneously manage their investments.

The data on proxy voting is sufficiently patchy to make observations of broad patterns meaningless. In Germany, however, the data and qualitative evidence on proxy voting (testimony from contemporary observers) suggests that throughout most of the twentieth century, banks held significant control over corporate governance via proxy voting. It is worth noting that U.S. regulation prevented banks from holding equity in companies to which they provided financing – an arms-length relationship, as discussed earlier.

Branching

The clearest pattern in the countries examined here is the prevalence of extensive, national branch networks around the world by the early twentieth century. Only Portugal, Denmark, Norway, and the United States failed to develop such branching before World War I. Explaining the absence of branching is easy for the United States but less simple for the other three countries. While the United States imposed a variety of restrictions on branching, the first three countries did not. Their lack of branching might be attributed to lack of economic development, except that many far poorer countries, such as India, Brazil, Mexico, and Japan, did maintain branch networks.[23] Moreover, although these three nonbranching countries were on the European periphery, so were several branching countries: Spain, Russia, Finland, and Sweden, for example. Finally, even though these three countries were small and had small industrial sectors, so were New Zealand, Finland, Ireland, and Greece. In any case, by the early post–World War II

---

[23] Apparently, Brazil imposed restrictions on interstate branching by domestic banks but permitted branching within states. Foreign banks could branch as they pleased.

years, only the United States perpetuated the unit banking system in many
parts of the country – but even then branching within states was taking
hold in several states, to the degree it was permitted.[24]

The findings here also support my earlier contention that branching is neither necessary nor sufficient for universal banking to arise. Indeed, universality arose in most
places in the middle of the nineteenth century, long before the impulse to branch
struck. Despite some modern arguments to the contrary, universality of banking
services required a very modest minimum scale of operations, as evidenced by the
success of many private bankers operating in a range of commercial and investment
banking services. Even joint-stock universal banking succeeded in (nearly) unitary
organizations into the twentieth century. Two cases illustrate this point: Germany
developed joint-stock universal banking at least by 1848 but, like most other countries, created widespread branch networks only in the 1890s; England, on the other
hand, maintained specialized deposit and investment banking even throughout
most of the twentieth century, but developed an extensive nationwide branching
system even earlier than the universal-banking countries.

Financial System Evolution over the Twentieth Century

The identification of universality with bank domination and specialization
with market domination likely stems from two forms of myopia: focus on
the post–World War II era and narrowness in the range of cases examined.
The typology is usually based on comparisons of the United States, Great
Britain, Germany, and sometimes Japan in the 1950s through 1980s. The
first two countries, having hosted the most important international financial markets for much of the twentieth century and having eschewed both
universal banking and formalized bank relationships for most of that time
(particularly in the postwar United States), head up the market-based, specialized, arms-length group. Germany and Japan, with their enormous
banks (in the 1950s through the 1980s, at least) and widely cited networks
of clients and house-bank relationships, lead the bank-dominated, universal, relational group. Even these cases, however, defy rigid classification, because closer scrutiny has revealed a number of contrary facts: for
example, a lack of widespread, exclusive house-bank relations in Germany;
the unraveling of interlocking directorates and unwinding of equity stakes
in Germany recently; the frequent appearance of bankers on American
boards of directors (approximately one-third of large U.S. firms have at
least one bank representative on their boards); the lack of universality in

---

[24] See Calomiris (2000) for a collection of his previous articles dealing largely with branching
and relevant political and regulatory debates.

post–World War II Japan; and the large size and high level of activity of the securities market in Japan.

Moreover, many systems underwent significant upheaval in the aftermath of the two world wars, so that some systems changed significantly during the interwar and early postwar years. Banking institutions in a number of countries suffered both political and economic consequences of war and depression. Many countries enacted legislation in response to political pressure in the 1920s and 1930s, and countries such as Belgium, Greece, Italy, Japan, and the United States went so far as to legally prohibit full-scale universal banking. At the same time, economic and political crises hit financial markets, particularly in the early 1930s and during and after World War II. Rajan and Zingales (1999) suggest that governments, because they could exert less control over markets than over firms, and because of the growing discontent of their constituents, found ways to effectively hinder or even shut down markets of all sorts. These authors argue further that the extent of the antimarket backlash varied most significantly with the legal-political system, civil-law countries being more susceptible to centralizing command and control than common-law countries.[25]

Germany presents, again, one of the most striking examples. The fall-out after World War II included the cession of vast portions of eastern German industry and resources, along with the very site of the primary stock exchange (and important provincial exchanges), and the near obliteration of the vibrant Berlin market of the pre– and early post–World War I era. The weight of foreign occupying powers, the urgent bailouts of industrial firms by financial institutions, the strengthening of the social-welfare state, the imposition of hefty capital gains taxes on sales of shares, and other exigencies of postwar reconstruction conspired to produce a financial system in which banks were extremely large, industry partly subordinated its ownership and governance to financial institutions and the government, and markets failed to flourish. Yet, given the country's unique position in the events of the 1930s and 1940s, Germany's path is unlikely to reflect the experiences in most other countries – even those with universal banks. Thus, concentrating on Germany as the paradigm case of a universal banking system, even if it was the originator, likely skews the perception of the organization and operation of such systems in general. Particularly salient is the observation of a reunified Germany in the last ten-to-twenty years that has moved away from the universal house-banking format to some extent, demonstrating that its existence may be more related to the economic and

---

[25] Sylla (2006) offers a critical appraisal of the Rajan and Zingales "great reversals" thesis.

political realities of postwar Germany than to some innate distinction in the feasibility of a particular system.

Elsewhere, the move away from universality varied in its implementation and lasted only a few decades even where it was enforced. By the 1990s, most systems had deregulated and reverted to something resembling their pre–World War I state (see Table 6.2). Using the traditional meaning of universal banking – the combination of investment and commercial banking by one institution – banking structure in 1990 is extremely highly correlated with structure in 1913. For those countries that had begun to industrialize by the mid-nineteenth century, the correlation persists back to at least 1850. Of the 26 cases surveyed, no system clearly and permanently switched from one category to the other over this period of 100 to 150 years. This evidence of path-dependency is all the more impressive in light of government interventions specifically intending to alter institutional design.

Despite much continuity, of course, bank structures, activities, and instruments have evolved over time. Most banking systems, whether universal or not in the prewar era, underwent a conglomeration movement starting in the 1970s. This development created quasi-universal banking in nearly all industrialized countries, in the sense that financial institutions of several types began operating under the umbrella of bank holding companies. Thus, even the steadfastly specialized system of England is home to financial services conglomerates. Likewise, the traditionally universal systems of Germany, Belgium, and many other continental European countries have outgrown the centralized universal banking form, so that the commercial and underwriting arms of banks are less closely integrated.

CONCLUSION

The goal of this chapter is to broaden the existing perspective on the factors involved in the design and development of national financial systems. The classification of the twenty-six sampled countries by type of financial system yields several interesting patterns.

From this analysis, it is clear that attempting to fit particular countries into a few narrowly defined, overarching categories of financial system – for example, Germany as a universal banking system – can be misleading. Most financial systems have a mixture of characteristics and do not fit neatly into narrow classifications. Many economies undergoing industrialization in the mid- to late nineteenth century supported a small number of large-scale universal banks but simultaneously maintained many more specialized banks. Nationwide branching appeared in most countries between the 1890s and World War I; only the United States persisted with widespread unit banking after World War II, and this persistence is related to regulatory factors. Relationship banking was more common in universal systems, but the two institutional features also existed separately from each other. In addition, there has been no link between branching and the design of financial institutions.

The distant history of banking systems reveals that the relationship between universal banking and limited securities markets, to the extent that it exists, is a post–World War II phenomenon. Indeed universal banking came about because financial markets existed in which to trade securities. Most industrialized economies maintained significant securities markets in the prewar era, and some of the most important markets of the time were embedded in at least partially universal systems (e.g., the Berlin, New York, Paris, and Vienna stock exchanges).

The loss of active markets is much more persistent than changes in banking design. Among the countries surveyed, no system permanently switched from universal to specialized; banking structure exhibits path-dependency, or path reversion, over the past 100 to 150 years. At the same time, financial conglomerates with fairly distinct functional units have emerged in most industrialized countries. This relatively recent phenomenon appears to be driving the convergence of financial system design: Formerly specialized systems are becoming more universal, whereas traditional universal banks are less truly universal. Over the past 150 years, banking systems in industrialized countries have become remarkably similar, regardless of their initial development, and many systems have evolved back to their pre-regulation configuration. Almost all countries today have extensive branch networks. And in most countries, there are at least some universal banks and some of the attributes typically associated with relationship or *Haus*-banking, even in systems that would not typically be associated with either institutional form.

Bank-Based or Market-Based: Does It Matter?

One of the more important characteristics of financial systems in terms of their hypothesized impact on economic growth is whether a system is bank- or market-based. The strict dichotomy between market-based and bank-dominated systems that appears in the literature on comparative financial systems, although useful for organizing debate, is far more stylized than the reality. Financial systems can be considered neoclassical (market-based) or relational (bank-based), with examples of hybrid systems comprising characteristics from both polar cases occupying the middle ground.[26] According to this typology, financial systems can be characterized as more market-based (neoclassical) or more bank-based (relational). But the market-based or bank-based distinction does not necessarily translate into a specific set of characteristics such as universal or relationship banking, even if in some cases they may. History offers interesting insights into the multiplicity of financial system designs and the lack of tight links among various banking characteristics. Many systems combine universal banking with active securities markets, particularly before World War II, whereas others support both large-scale universal banks and more specialized banks. It may be more useful, therefore, to consider financial systems as an amalgamation of a set of indicators rather than as monoliths with overarching types such as market- or bank-based.

Tracing these indicators of banking system types across countries for various time periods highlights a number of clear patterns. For example, by the early twentieth century, national branch networks were prevalent in almost all moderately industrialized countries. The results highlight long-run consistency in institutions but also turn up quite a lot of change over time: Many industrialized countries evolved from universal and often relationship banking to specialized and sometimes arms-length systems, and back again. Even if these systems returned to the original forms, the transitions took time. Therefore it would be incorrect to identify particular countries and their financial systems at a single point in time and assume permanent adherence to that form. It is necessary to consider development over time as well.

These results highlight the two themes discussed in the introduction: the weight of history in determining the growth and design of financial institutions and markets, and the importance of idiosyncratic forces that change institutions over time. This observation brings us to the next problem: examining what sorts of institutional factors – economic, political, and legal – determine, or at least influence, what type of financial systems emerge. The next chapter turns to the question of identifying the factors that led some countries to take on certain sets of institutions while others turned to a different type of system.

---

[26] Dietl (1998).

Appendix 6.1. *International comparisons of financial system structure, circa 1990*

Country	Securities	Insurance	Real estate	Nonfinancial firms	Stock market cap	Structure index	Market
Argentina	3	2	2	3	0.05	−0.15	0
Australia	1	2	3	2	0.43	0.09	1
Austria	1	2	1	1	0.07	−0.23	0
Belgium	2	2	3	3	0.26	−0.13	0
Brazil	2	2	3	3	0.12	0.03	1
Canada	2	2	2	3	0.46	0.12	1
Switzerland	1	2	1	1	0.71	0.12	1
Germany	1	3	2	1	0.19	−0.14	0
Denmark	1	2	2	2	0.22	−0.08	0
Spain	1	2	3	1	0.18	−0.17	0
Finland	1	3	2	1	0.18	−0.16	0
France	1	2	2	1	0.20	−0.17	0
United Kingdom	1	2	1	1	0.76	0.21	1
Greece	2	3	3	1	0.08	−0.18	0
India	2	4	3	3	0.13	−0.07	0
Ireland	1	4	1	1	0.27	0.15	1
Italy	1	2	3	3	0.12	−0.19	0
Japan	3	4	3	3	0.73	0.06	1
Mexico	2	2	3	4	0.15	0.13	1
Netherlands	1	2	2	1	0.41	−0.04	0
Norway	2	2	2	2	0.15	−0.15	0
New Zealand	2	2	2	1	0.40	0.07	1
Portugal	1	2	3	2	0.08	−0.23	0
Sweden	1	2	3	3	0.38	0.07	1
United States	3	3	3	3	0.58	0.17	1

Note: The variables securities, insurance, real estate, and nonfinancial firms may take values 1–4 as follows:
1 Unrestricted; banks can engage in the full range of the activity directly in the bank.
2 Permitted: The full range of those activities can be conducted, but all or some of the activity must be conducted in subsidiaries.
3 Restricted: Banks can engage in less than full range of those activities, either in the bank or subsidiaries.
4 Prohibited: The activity may not be conducted by the bank or subsidiaries.
Stock market capitalization is given as a share of GDP. Market equals one if the structure index is positive and zero otherwise. All variables come from Levine and Zervos (1998).
Source: Levine and Zervos (1998).

7

What Shapes Financial Structure?

A number of countries that underwent heavy industrialization at approximately the same time developed very different financial systems. Although the countries of northwest continental Europe and North America all began large-scale industrialization in the early to mid-nineteenth century, for example, they developed financial systems quite distinct from one another. It remains unclear, as both a historical and an economic question, why the genesis and development of financial systems differed across countries that were, at first glance, relatively similar in their economic development.

Gerschenkron (1962) was among the first to attempt an explanation for the observed differences among financial systems that emerged over the latter half of the nineteenth century. His arguments hinged on economic factors as the crucial determinants of the particular form that financial systems took at that early phase of development. Gerschenkron hypothesized that a country's stage of economic development and the particular national economic conditions dictated the sort of financial and banking systems that could take root. These sorts of theories held sway for several decades. More recently, however, a broader set of considerations has emerged in the literature on financial system design. Some argue that a country's legal tradition factors critically into the type of financial organization that can arise and flourish.[1] Others argue further that not only legal environment, but more proximally political environment, is significant or even crucial for determining the characteristics of financial systems.[2] Each of these

---

[1] La Porta et al. (1997, 1998) and Dietl (1998).

[2] Rajan and Zinagales (2003), although they focus on the changes taking place over the twentieth century. Verdier (1997, 2002) builds an argument about the political origins of financial systems in the nineteenth century. Both of these hypotheses are discussed further in the next section of this chapter. Besley and Persson (2009) present a theoretical

competing explanations has some intuitive merit for understanding the types of financial systems observed in today's industrialized countries and their origins in the distant past. What is missing in the discussion, however, is a thorough examination of all three categories of theories for the birth and growth of particular financial systems across various industrialized countries. Moreover, the literature so far has turned up little or no quantitative evidence or tests of the theories in explaining or predicting outcomes. This chapter takes up these problems and sets the stage for a careful analysis of the consequences of financial system design in the following chapter.

The analysis in this chapter shows that, even though political and regulatory intervention must influence system design, political system type does not have any systematic or predictable effect; it is idiosyncratic across countries. Economic and legal factors show greater relationships to financial system design and development, but causality is difficult to establish. Hence, although social and political contexts play important roles in shaping institutions, it is difficult to pinpoint reliable, consistent relationships among economic, political, legal and financial variables. Still, the path-dependent nature of financial systems suggests that the initial conditions and historical evolution of the financial system are important for determining the modern result in a unique way.

ECONOMIC, LEGAL, AND POLITICAL THEORIES
OF FINANCIAL SYSTEM ORIGINS

Economic Factors

Although most of the literature addresses the impact of financial system organization on economic growth, a smaller line of research investigates the underlying impetus for financial development and structure. Gerschenkron (1962) offered probably the best-known general hypothesis about the genesis of financial institutions.[3] In essence, he argued that banks played a more important role in industrialization for "moderately backward" economies than they had played for the earliest industrializer, Great Britain. According to his schema, financial institutions played a critical role in the

---

model of state capacity that develops a connection between fiscal and legal development and their further connection to financial development. Their analysis underscores distant historical roots of financial development and growth.

[3] Gerschenkron (1962, 1968). Sylla (1991) reviews Gerschenkron's theories and related work. Knick Harley (1991) addresses Gerschenkron's idea of "substitution for prerequisites" of industrialization.

industrialization of much of northwestern continental Europe. In situations of extreme underdevelopment, as in Russia, however, financial institutions were insufficient to support the transition to modernized industrial activity; such cases demanded centralized institutional intervention, mostly from government.

The role of financial institutions comprises only part of Gerschenkron's overall thesis. He saw banking as one factor in many that varied with general economic conditions in direct relation to a country's degree of backwardness, namely:

1. the speed of industrial growth;
2. the stress on bigness of plant and enterprise;
3. the composition of the nascent output, that is, the degree to which "heavy" industries were favored;
4. the reliance on technological borrowing and perhaps financial assistance from abroad;
5. the pressure on levels of consumption;
6. the passive role of agriculture;
7. the role of banks and state budgets;
8. the virulence of ideologies under the auspices of which the industrialization proceeded.[4]

Gerschenkron argued that because of their ability to adopt technologies from industrialized areas, relatively "backward" economies modernized faster than their role models. This situation appeared to be the case in Germany, where even though industrialization came somewhat later, relative to Britain, the speed of industrialization was much greater – particularly over the late nineteenth century. The scale of factories and firms required to compete, however, was so large as to prohibit self-financing. Follower economies therefore needed institutions capable of mobilizing a high volume of capital from disparate sources and also that were able to compensate for a shortage of entrepreneurship. In Gerschenkron's view, the German universal banks were just such an institution, as his widely cited commentary suggests: "The German investment banks – a powerful invention, comparable in economic effect to that of the steam engine – were in their capital-supplying functions a substitute for the insufficiency of the previously created wealth willingly placed at the disposal of entrepreneurs."[5]

Inherent in this view is the idea that lack of economic development necessitated special characteristics and growth-promoting practices of banks: mobilizing capital through large networks of branches, screening potential

---

[4]　Gerschenkron (1968), pp. 98–99, cited in Sylla (1991).
[5]　Gerschenkron (1968), p. 137. Less clear is the causal connection.

entrepreneurs, providing long-term lending, deciding on investment and production strategies, monitoring the progress of clients' investments, promoting and reorganizing industries, arranging and enforcing industrial combinations, and diversifying away the inherent risk. We now know that the German banks did not do all of these things, at least not on the grand scale that these older accounts described. Other universal banking systems operated in a variety of ways, often not at all in line with the traditional view. But these idealized conceptions, however weak their evidentiary basis, have continued to influence more modern thinking about the emergence of financial systems. The appeal is strong, particularly because modern theoretical models of financial systems based on resolving problems of asymmetric information seem to mesh well with the classic view of what universal-relationship banking systems do.

In the Gerschenkron-inspired vein, Allen (1992) and Allen and Gale (2000) argue, in part, that the historical experiences of Britain and the United States support the idea that markets are preferable in situations of complex decision processes and rapidly advancing technology, whereas banks should dominate where optimal investments are agreed on and primarily just need monitoring.[6] Applying these notions to the cases of Germany, Italy, and Japan, for example, where industrialization occurred not only late, but more rapidly than in the United Kingdom, does seem to fit on the surface. Large-scale, heavy industry was largely concentrated in the hands of a small and powerful group of industrial leaders. In Germany, the argument goes, this "state-capitalism" that took hold during industrialization left little place for small and medium-sized firms and the rise of the bourgeois entrepreneurial class that had occurred in other European nations.[7]

Gerschenkron's work does remain influential in some quarters, but recent work has also questioned his heavy emphasis on economic factors in determining the shape and role of financial institutions. Economic backwardness may be a proximal cause of – or more accurately, may precede – rapid financial development during industrialization; but other factors are likely to have constrained real and financial development up to the point of industrialization. Some have argued that the Gerschenkron-inspired view underemphasizes the role of political and legal factors in the development of financial systems. Legal provisions arguably kept the British

---

[6]   Boot and Thakor (1997) and Thakor (1996) address the question of financial system structure and innovation.

[7]   See, for example, Dahrendorf (1967). For a more recent view, taking issue with the traditional conception, see Herrigel (1996).

banks excessively small and conservative early on, and at least some of the deleterious effects endured after the removal of the initial impediments.[8] Even though British banks went on to become the largest in the world in the later nineteenth and early twentieth centuries, they are often criticized for excessive conservatism in their investment and lending strategies. Moreover, the lack of dependable lender-of-last-resort facilities reinforced the reluctance of bankers to engage in risky transformation of short-term liabilities into potentially illiquid assets.[9] The standard view holds that the German Reichsbank, in contrast, both squeezed other banks out of much of the short-term commercial business and facilitated those banks' provision of riskier investment services. A more recent study of central banking, however, argues that the lender-of-last-resort function became dependable in continental Europe only after the turn of the twentieth century.[10] Thus, there is still some debate over the timing, and therefore potential influence on industrialization, of central banking activities.

Legal and Regulatory Factors

In the past several years, financial system research has turned its attention to legal and regulatory factors. Much more than the research of the 1950s through the 1980s, the newer line of inquiry postulates that the observed variation in financial system structure may result from peculiarities of financial system regulation. Government intervention may hamper all development or might promote certain institutions at the cost of others. Some have argued, for example, that government regulation in Germany simultaneously promoted the large, universal banks and hampered operation of securities markets.[11] Similarly, limitations on bank operations may have spurred financial market development in the United States, especially during the twentieth century. Regulation of nonbank institutions – such as securities markets, corporate chartering, limited liability, and bankruptcy – may have further altered the shape of financial systems. For example, laws that protect investors, contracts, and property rights might be argued to encourage the development of all kinds of financial institutions, and particularly atomistic market arrangements.[12]

---

[8] The Bubble Act of 1720 and the monopoly of the Bank of England over limited-liability banking until 1825, for example.

[9] Ziegler (1993), Kennedy (1992), and Tilly (1994b).

[10] Forrest Capie (1999).

[11] Tilly (1995). In earlier work, I even hinted at this possibility (Fohlin, 1997b).

[12] On Germany, see the edited volume by Horn and Kocka (1979), especially those by Horn, Friedrich, and Reich.

The legal framework influences, and in some cases determines, the type of banking practices that are more likely to dominate. For example, where shareholder rights are not well protected by a legal framework, either due to lack of potency in the law or lack of effective enforcement, relationship-banking practices – formal arrangements in which banks are able to monitor firm activities, exert influence, and thereby protect their investors' interests – are more likely to emerge. Conversely, where there are tough laws on creditor and investor rights that are also enforced in a rational manner, arms-length banking practices are theoretically more likely, and stock markets are more likely to develop as vibrant institutions.

The enactment of laws is not exogenous. The regulatory process depends on both legal and political conditions, and certain legal systems produce more enabling legislation than do others. Some have argued for the importance of legal traditions in determining the development of financial markets.[13] The modern evidence suggests that countries adhering to a French civil law system have both the weakest investor protection, through both legal rules and law enforcement, and the least-developed capital markets. Common-law countries fall at the other end of the spectrum, so that American and British economies or societies have led to market-oriented financial systems. Similarly, Dietl (1998) lays out the poles, admittedly highly stylized, of neoclassical versus relational regulation. These extremes map directly to common-law and civil-law legal systems, respectively. In Dietl's schema, neoclassical systems focus on allocative efficiency with the objective of eliminating capital market imperfections. This legal environment leads to strictly enforced accounting regulations and effective prohibitions on insider trading, market manipulations, and anticompetitive behavior, along with regulatory roadblocks to true universal-relationship banking. Relationship-based systems focus on coordinative efficiency with the goal of enhancing corporate governance and reducing the costs of financial distress. The results, in the extreme, contrast starkly with the neoclassical system: weak or vague laws on accounting, insider trading, market manipulations, anticompetitive behavior, and banking scope. Connecting the arguments of LaPorta and colleagues and Dietl results in the hypothesis that neoclassical, or

---

[13] See the series of papers, LaPorta et al. (1997, 1998, 1999). In Besley and Persson's (2009) model, if the cost of protecting property rights is lower under common law than under civil law, then common law would allow for more credit as a share of GDP. Pagano and Volpin (2005) make related arguments, discussed subsequently in the "Political Factors" subsection of this chapter. Of course, by now, many others have used a similar legal tradition indicator to help explain a number of financial and economic phenomena.

common-law, legal-regulatory systems encourage market-based financing with specialized banking and a short-term investment perspective; relational, or civil-law, systems yield the opposite.

In between these polar extremes lie the tradition of German civil law and Scandinavian civil law that provide an intermediate level of rights for shareholders and creditors. It is interesting to note that enforcement of these laws – in recent decades – is highest in Scandinavian and German civil-law countries and weakest in French civil-law countries.[14] Overall, in the late twentieth century, common-law countries have provided the best legal protection to shareholders whereas French civil-law countries have provided the worst. Additionally, common-law countries have provided creditors with the strongest legal protections against managers – suggesting that corporate oversight by bankers may not be as critical in these countries.[15] The German civil-law countries produce mixed results. La Porta et al. (1998) conclude that countries that provide weak laws for creditor or shareholder protection or weak enforcement of those laws develop substitute mechanisms, such as concentration of ownership, to safeguard owners' rights. Acemoglu and Johnson (2005) argue similarly that individuals adapt their financial intermediation approaches to fit the constraints placed by contracting institutions.

If legal institutional framework is critical for legal protection and enforcement of shareholder and creditor rights, then it could be expected that legal tradition plays a role in the development of types of financial systems. Clearly, if shareholders either do not have clear rights over their investments or their rights are not protected through legal enforcement, this situation provides an impediment to the development of well-functioning stock markets.[16]

As convincing and intuitive as many of these findings may seem, it is well to bear in mind the limited amount of information that can be mustered to support them, even in the most recent periods. Furthermore, there is no comprehensive evidence of their validity before the end of the twentieth century. Thus, in using these ideas as general theories that stretch back to the origins of financial systems, they should clearly be seen as hypotheses waiting to be tested.

[14] See La Porta et al. (1998). Besley and Persson (2009) find that German and Scandinavian legal origin relates positively with financial development (private credit and credit access) and with investor protections.

[15] Enron and WorldCom notwithstanding.

[16] Djankov, McLiesh, and Shleifer (2007) conclude that the recent evidence demonstrates that legal creditor rights as well as information-sharing institutions substantially promote the development of private credit.

Political Factors

Rajan and Zingales (2003) propose a related theory for the determinants of overall financial system development and specifically contrast legal and political influences. Directed primarily at the LaPorta et al. series (1997, 1998), Rajan and Zingales point out that, except for the outlier – Britain – the most-developed countries in 1913 maintained similar levels of financial development, regardless of legal system.[17] These authors argue that not legal systems, but political contexts – the support of financial institution growth by government and interest groups – determine the course of development. Landed gentry, for example, typically oppose financial development, whereas industrial bourgeoisie champion the cause. The government itself may also harbor incentives for or against financial development. Examples such as the 1848 bourgeoisie revolutions in continental Europe (promoting financial development) and the dictates of the Japanese government in the 1930s (impeding financial development) bolster this impressionistic account of financial and political history.[18] As the discussion reveals, characteristics of political systems, such as centralization of power or strength of interest groups, may at least partly depend on legal tradition: Common law aids the devolution of power to the periphery, whereas civil law more likely thwarts it. Yet the authors note that civil law can, if motivated, replicate the common-law outcome, thus implicitly raising the question of underlying motivations for legal systems.

The authors' discussion can be read as equating financial development with the expansion of financial markets, primarily securities markets. From this idea, one could perhaps infer, in the spirit of Gerschenkron, that hierarchical forms of financial institutions, such as banks, evidence lack of financial development. Thus, whereas Dietl's dichotomy places neoclassical (common-law, market-based, specialized arms-length banking) systems on an equal footing with relational (civil-law, hierarchy-based, universal-relationship banking) systems, Rajan and Zingales' hypothesis (ala Gerschenkron) suggest an unequal ordering.

Verdier (1997, 2002) hits on similar themes, but lays out a political-economic view of the development of financial systems. In doing so, he takes

---

[17] On the advanced level of financial development in Britain, Schultz and Weingast (2003) argue that the emergence of liberal democratic political institutions in the seventeenth century prompted a financial revolution that expanded credit availability (government debt at that stage).

[18] The German Stock Exchange Law of 1896 could go in the antifinancial development category as well, because it was the agrarians who imposed the strict limitations on futures trading (Fohlin, 2007b).

direct aim at Gerschenkron's hypothesis about the relationship between the extent of economic backwardness and the role of financial institutions. In this view, political structure, not relative backwardness, determines the shape of financial systems. In particular, universal banking arose in the coincident presence of two conditions: (1) a segmented deposit market, dominated by nonprofit and provincial banks; and (2) a reliable lender-of-last-resort facility ensuring liquidity in the banking system. Furthermore, Verdier argues, these two preconditions for universality emerged simultaneously only when state centralization was sufficient to provide a strong central bank (with credible lender-of-last-resort status) but limited enough to permit coexistence of provincial and, in his parlance, "center" banks. The issue of legal system does not appear in Verdier's analysis, but the other work reviewed here suggests a possible connection. As Verdier concedes, however, political centralization was neither solitary nor decisive in determining financial structure in most cases. Thus, whether or not Verdier correctly characterizes the relationship between political and financial development, he does not clearly subvert Gerschenkron's hypothesis.

Neither political nor legal structure is clearly independent of economic development, and the three factors may be mutually enhancing rather than mutually exclusive. For example, Pagano and Volpin (2005) find that proportional voting systems yield less shareholder protection (and greater worker protection) than majoritarian systems, and vice versa. These arguments resonate with those in Besley and Persson (2009), who relate similar financial development with legal origins.

Thus, the existing literature leaves room for all three types of factors – economic, political, and legal – in determining the shape of financial development. So far, neither formal theoretical research nor cogent empirical research has rationalized the endogenous development of distinct financial system designs and their persistence in the absence of regulation. Answers to such puzzles may hinge both on making advances in theoretical modeling and on assembling a wider range of evidence.

TESTING THEORIES OF FINANCIAL SYSTEM ORIGINS

The preceding section raised a number of theoretical and empirical questions on which further analysis may shed some light. In particular, it remains to be determined whether systematic relationships emerge among legal, political, economic, and financial characteristics of countries. Creating testable hypotheses and assembling data with which to implement the resulting models poses a challenge in the historical context, particularly in light of the difficulties of categorizing financial systems that emerged in Chapter 6. Nonetheless, the exercise is worthwhile, and the subsequent analysis reveals a number of interesting insights into the origins of national financial systems.

Empirical Models

Economic Factors Model

As appealing and intuitive as Gerschenkron's work is, it yields few concrete implications that can be implemented as statistical tests. One hypothesis, however, can be construed from his work: The more backward the economy at the outset of industrialization, the greater is the role for financial institutions to play. David Good (1973) offered early testing of this and related hypotheses. Specifically, Good interpreted Gerschenkron as implying either that the level of banking development at the end of the so-called great spurt of industrialization or the growth rate of the banking sector during the great spurt relates positively to the extent of backwardness at the time of initiation of industrialization. Gerschenkron insisted that his theory applied only to continental Europe in the nineteenth and early twentieth centuries, therefore tightly constraining the number of cases available for empirical tests. It is worth noting, in addition, that the narrowness in the applicability of his hypothesis naturally limits its usefulness in drawing lessons from history. It is helpful therefore to seek more general hypotheses linking economic conditions to the development and design of financial systems – for example, by investigating other areas and time periods.

Before taking steps toward an empirical model, it also important to clarify the issue of the onset of modern industrial growth. One problem with this whole line of research is the notion of a "great spurt" of industrialization. More and more, researchers are determining that industry developed more gradually and with less discontinuity than was thought in the 1950s and 1960s. Still, it is clear that certain economies had reached a much more developed state by the last quarter of the nineteenth century than had others. By examining the level of financial development around 1880 and its growth in the succeeding twenty years, we can capture the parabolic relationship between economic and financial development. For Europe around 1880, the most- and least-developed economies should have the lowest rates of financial system growth, whereas the moderately advanced economies should have the highest rates. Based on the theoretical framework, the level of financial development may be high in the most-industrialized economies, but it should certainly be high in the moderately advanced economies and low in the least advanced.

Rates of economic growth, in contrast to levels, should yield an essentially linear relationship between economic and financial development: The fastest-growing economies should have the most rapid financial development. In the traditional view, slow growers include both those that have passed their earliest phases of industrialization and those that have so far failed to industrialize. If the hypothesis is true more generally, then the U-shaped relationship between financial system growth and economic development should hold in different time periods and for all countries. The results of these tests (discussed subsequently) can neither prove nor disprove Gerschenkron's hypothesis about economic backwardness and financial institutions, but they will at least provide some tentative evidence for or against.

Political Factors Model
Verdier's argument relates political structure to universality of banking, and again specifies a nonlinear relationship. Universality is hypothesized to be more likely the stronger the lender-of-last-resort facility of the central bank, but less likely the more centralized the market for deposits is. These proximal causes for universality therefore imply an inverted-U correspondence between state centralization and universality. Verdier's argument is couched in a historical perspective, and it is not clear that it applies generally. More specifically, the argument relates to the role of state centralization at the inception of the financial system; it does not specify a permanent relationship between the two variables. The argument should hold well in the 1880–1913 period, when financial system development was fresh, but might hold more loosely thereafter. For example, changes in state centralization may not alter the shape of the financial system if institutions exhibit strong path-dependency. Alternatively, exogenous shocks may alter financial system design, even though state centralization remains stable. Also along the lines of political structure, Pagano and Volpin (2005) relate financial development to proportional versus representative types of government.

Legal and Regulatory Model
Implicit in La Porta et al. (1997, 1998) and Dietl (1998) is the idea that, for reasons related primarily to investor protection and tendencies for centralization of power, the growth (and, implicitly, the design) of financial systems are correlated with legal tradition. In general, financial development proceeds faster and markets supersede banks in common-law

countries. Rajan and Zingales (1999) argue that the causal link is weak and may relate more to the role of state centralization (as in Verdier). Nonetheless, civil-law traditions may favor greater centralization of power, making it difficult to disentangle the links among legal, political, and financial variables.[19]

Variables and Data

Financial System Variables
The foregoing sets of hypotheses specify three different types of financial system variables: financial development, market orientation, and universality of banking.

Financial system development. Financial system development is measured as both the level and growth rate of aggregate financial assets (normalized by GDP) in a country at a given point in time or over a specific period of years. Because of the lack of sufficient data on stock market capitalization for the current sample of countries, the figures here include Goldsmith's (1969) compilation of assets held by financial institutions.

Market orientation. Market orientation is more difficult to measure. The composite measure in Beck, Demirgüç-Kunt, and Levine (2000), is aimed at distinguishing bank-based from market-based systems in the 1990s, but the variable provides a few puzzling results. For example, using the binary indicator variable formed by breaking the continuous measure at the median, Brazil, Denmark, Germany, the Netherlands, Sweden, and Switzerland are all classified as "market-based," despite the traditional presence of large-scale universal banks in these countries. This mismatch may be interpreted two ways: Either the banks-versus-markets dichotomy corresponds poorly to the universal-versus-specialized split (as I argued in Chapter 6), or this particular measure fails to capture either phenomenon. Given the extremely high correlation between the binary system variables for 1913 and 1990 demonstrated in Chapter 6, I assume for the sake of argument that the continuous variable in Beck, Demirgüç-Kunt, and Levine (2000) applies similarly in 1913. I emphasize that I am not assuming that the variable accurately represents the *absolute* level of "market orientation" in 1913, but rather that the variable roughly approximates the *relative* extent of "market orientation" of the systems at that time. In the absence of the necessary data

---

[19] Acemoglu and Johnson (2005) distinguish further between property rights institutions and contracting institutions. Empirically, they find that the former affects financial development generally, whereas the latter primarily affects the form of financial intermediation.

to create such a composite – quantitative variable for 1913 – this measure provides the next best proxy.

The figures presented in Rajan and Zingales (1999) demonstrate similar problems. Their calculations of stock market capitalization relative to GDP in 1913 place the United Kingdom, Japan, and Germany as the top three markets, followed closely by Switzerland, Italy, and Norway. The United States and France, considered two of the most important markets of the time, appear in the same league as Belgium and Spain and lie closer to Finland and Hungary than to their qualitative peers. Given the number of countries not covered by the underlying sources, I do not use these data in the econometric analysis.

Universality. Chapter 6 noted the difficulty of classifying countries using a binary financial system variable, yet other recent research indicates the trouble inherent in quantitative measures. Verdier (1997), for example, uses the ratio of commercial bank equity to deposits as a proxy for universality, but again, that measure corresponds inconsistently to a qualitative assessment of the prevalence of universal banks in the economy. The analysis here uses the two- and three-choice indicator variables given in Table 6.2, as well as Verdier's equity-deposit ratio.

Endogenous Variables

Economic factors. Economic factors are the most straightforward to quantify, although of course data availability, particularly for the early to mid-nineteenth century, varies from country to country. Gross domestic product per capita, measured in 1990 Geary-Khamis dollars, comes from Maddison (1995). From these figures, I measure growth rates of GDP per capita for several subperiods as the coefficient estimate on a time trend when the log of GDP per capita is regressed on a constant and that trend variable. Employment in various sectors of the economy – agriculture, industry, and finance or commercial – comes from Mitchell (1983). After constructing the ratio of industrial-to-agricultural employment, I calculate the percentage growth of the ratio from 1880 to 1913. These measures permit quantification of the distribution of resources to different sectors and the development of industry relative to agriculture. Finally, industrial development is measured as the product of GDP per capita and the industrial/agricultural employment ratio. The purpose of this variable is to measure not just the wealth, but the combination of wealth and industrial development in the sample of countries.

Legal factors. Legal factors boil down to common-law versus civil-law traditions, measured by a simple binary indicator taking the value 1 for common law countries and zero for all versions of civil law. Given the small sample of countries, further division into types of civil law would divide the sample too finely for statistical inference to yield robust results.

Political factors. Political characteristics mean the nature of the political system, not the frequency or nature of individual political events. Centralization of power is the main feature of importance in the theories presented. Verdier (1997) measures centralization by the share of total government revenues collected by the central government. It is difficult to quantify centralization, of course, yet this variable seems a reasonable proxy. Unfortunately, lack of data on government revenues in the prewar period limits the number of cases that can be included.

Testable Hypotheses and Results

Given that we are dealing with national data in a period before large-scale government accounting, the sample is naturally limited. The problem is severe enough in the period before 1880 as to essentially rule out statistical analysis of the data. Nonetheless, several clear relationships emerge in the data, and they offer important insights into the three sets of hypotheses laid out previously.

Economic Factors

In the theoretical framework, "economic factors" refers to the level of economic development at the time of industrialization. If economic development does influence financial structure as hypothesized, then we should expect to find an inverted-U-shaped relationship between GDP per capita in 1880 and the level of financial system assets in both 1880 and 1900. Such a relationship does emerge among the fourteen-to-nineteen countries for which there is sufficient data (Table 7.1). The coefficient estimates, based on robust regression (using a Huber/biweight limited-influence estimator), are much more statistically significant for 1900 than for 1880. The industrial development measure performs relatively poorly.

Along this same line of reasoning, the growth rate of financial assets should be negatively associated with the level of GDP per capita in 1880. This hypothesis is borne out for the growth of financial assets both from 1880 to 1900 and from 1900 to 1913. The level of GDP per capita in 1900 is also negatively related to financial system asset growth over the succeeding thirteen years. Particularly interesting is the rate of growth of GDP per capita from 1880 to 1900, which relates very strongly and positively to the growth of financial system assets over the following period (1900 to 1913).

Table 7.1a. *Economic factors in financial development*

	FI/GNP (1880)	FI/GNP growth (1880–1900)	FI/GNP (1900)	FI/GNP growth (1900–1913)	Market orientation, 1990s
Real GDP per capita, 1880	0.06 *0.16*	-0.001 *0.05*	0.10 *0.05*	-0.0001 *0.02*	-0.001 *0.13*
Real GDP per capita – squared, 1880	-0.01 *0.30*		-0.02 *0.09*		0.0003 *0.09*
Industrial development, 1880	0.05 *0.25*	0.00 *0.44*	0.07 *0.12*		
Industrial development – squared, 1880	0.00 *0.35*		0.00 *0.21*		
Real GDP per capita, 1900				-0.001 *0.03*	-0.001 *0.11*
Real GDP per capita – squared, 1900					2.41e-07 *0.06*
Real GDP per-capita annual average growth rate, 1880–1900		-5.31 *0.79*		12.23 *0.04*	

	(1)	(2)	(3)	(4)	(5)	(6)	(7)	(8)	(9)	(10)	(11)	(12)	(13)
Industrial/ agricultural employment, 1913													0.44 *0.04*
Constant	−23.49 *0.60*	34.18 *0.14*	2.46 *0.01*	0.64 *0.00*	0.57 *0.05*	−25.87 *0.57*	52.52 *0.01*	0.51 *0.00*	0.60 *0.00*	0.06 *0.49*	1.15 *0.16*	1.08 *0.16*	−0.37 *0.15*
Number of observations	14	14	14	14	14	18	19	19	20	20	22	24	17
P(F)	0.08	0.46	0.05	0.44	0.79	0.06	0.22	0.02	0.02	0.04	0.16	0.07	0.04

Note: All columns, except column three, use Huber/biweight limited-influence estimation, for which no R^2 statistics are reported. The adjusted R^2 for column three is 0.23. P-values of t-statistics are reported in italics below coefficient estimates. FI/GNP is the ratio of total assets of financial institutions to GNP, and the growth of that ratio is calculated as the difference in the ratio between the end and base years, divided by the ratio in the base year. GDP per-capita annual average growth rate is calculated as the estimated coefficient of a time trend when the log of the ratio is regressed on that trend variable and a constant. The industrial development variable is the product of real GDP per capita and the ratio of industrial to agricultural employment. The final column includes European countries only.

Source: Original results from author's regression analysis. GDP data from Maddison (1995). Employment and financial institution assets data derive from Mitchell (1983 and 1992) and Goldsmith (1969), respectively.

Table 7.1b. *Economic roots of modern financial system structure*

	Market orientation (1990s)		Bank type (binary)				Bank type (three-choice)	
							specialized	*universal*
Bank type (binary), 1913						0.002 *0.05*		
Real GDP per capita, 1880	−0.10 *0.13*		0.10 *0.35*					
Real GDP per capita – squared, 1880	0.03 *0.09*		−0.02 *0.38*					
Real GDP per capita, 1900		−0.10 *0.11*		0.21 *0.05*			0.20 *0.29*	0.71 *0.02*
Real GDP per capita – squared, 1900		2.41e−05 *0.06*		−3.9e−05 *0.05*			−3.57e−05 *0.29*	−1.26e−04 *0.02*
Real GDP per capita, 1913					0.19 *0.08*			
Real GDP per capita – squared, 1913					−2.41e−05 *0.15*			
Industrial/ agricultural employment, 1913		0.44 *0.04*						
Constant	1.15 *0.16*	1.08 *0.16*	−0.37 *0.15*	−0.77 *0.50*	−1.89 *0.14*	−3.80 *0.02*	−3.02 *0.19*	−8.91 *0.01*
Number of observations	22	24	17	25	26	26	26	
P(F)	0.16	0.07	0.04	0.64	0.12	0.01	0.20	

Note: The first set of columns uses robust regression (Huber/biweight), the two-choice model uses probit regression, and the three-choice model uses multinomial logit regression, with quasi-universal banking as the comparison group. P-values of the t and z statistics are reported in italics below coefficient estimates.

Source: Original results from author's regression analysis. GDP data from Maddison (1995). Employment and financial institution assets data derive from Mitchell (1983) and Goldsmith (1969), respectively.

The reverse relationship – from financial system asset growth to GDP per-capita growth – does not appear.

A corollary to this hypothesis is the idea that market orientation is related to the level of development. Indeed, in the current sample, a U-shaped relationship emerges between the structure index reported in Beck, Demirgüç-Kunt, and Levine (2000) and GDP per capita in both 1880 and 1900. For most of the range of GDP per capita, the structure index is increasing, suggesting that for the most part, market orientation is increasing in the level of development. Economic growth in the nineteenth century is closely associated with rapid industrialization and the movement of labor from agriculture to industry. The ratio of industrial to agricultural employment therefore offers an added measure of economic development on the eve of World War I and should also relate positively to market orientation. Despite the small sample, just such a relationship arises in the data.

Political Factors
Given the results and discussion in Verdier (1997), it is not surprising that a U-shaped relationship does not emerge between the equity-deposit ratio and state centralization for the fourteen countries for which the data are available (Table 7.2). This statistical weakness may stem from a lack of an underlying relationship or simply from the dearth of data. It is interesting that the economic variables included as controls attain markedly higher statistical significance than does state centralization. Columns three and four indicate that universal banking was more likely in countries with lower levels of GDP per capita in 1880 and with higher rates of growth of GDP per capita between 1880 and 1900. While this finding tends to support a Gerschenkron-inspired view of the importance of large-scale industrial banking for late-nineteenth-century industrializers, the statistical significance varies depending on the measure of universality used. Somewhat contrarily, growth of industrial employment relative to agriculture (from 1880 to 1913) relates negatively to the probability of universality. One would expect, in the traditional line of thinking, that the opposite relationship would hold. Again, however, the statistical power is low.

In line with expectations, state centralization (in 1880) relates very significantly and negatively to market orientation (in the 1990s). Given the long time lag between the dependent and independent variables, the findings further bolster the idea of path-dependency in financial system structure.

Legal Tradition
Adherence to common-law principles is argued to promote market development and support financial markets in particular. The results here suggest that market orientation (as measured by the 1990s structure index) is far higher in common-law countries, and that financial institution growth in the pre–World War I period was higher (albeit statistically not very significantly) in civil-law countries. Common law is also seen as possibly hampering the centralization of state power, but the findings here support this idea very weakly: The ratio of central to total government revenues is only

Table 7.2a. *Political factors in banking structure and market orientation*

	Two-choice indicator		Three-choice indicator			Equity-deposit ratio			Market orientation	
State centralization, 1880	2.54	-1.15	-11.06	-11.99	18.86	-23.95	-2.03	-9.05	-2.13	-4.06
	0.88	*0.93*	*0.68*	*0.67*	*0.42*	*0.19*	*0.89*	*0.45*	*0.02*	*0.49*
State centralization – squared	-0.15	2.19	7.59	8.08	-17.72	21.41	3.93	8.99		1.65
	0.99	*0.85*	*0.74*	*0.71*	*0.39*	*0.16*	*0.75*	*0.38*		*0.74*
GDP per capita, 1880	-0.001		-0.002			-0.001				
	0.25		*0.04*			*0.17*				
GDP per-capita growth, 1880–1900	84.22		236.26			-17.48				
	0.17		*0.11*			*0.77*				
Industry/agriculture employment growth, 1880–1913		-0.68			-1.96			-0.70		
		0.22			*0.11*			*0.27*		
Constant	-0.16	-0.87	10.87	3.05	-1.03	8.86	0.69	3.23	1.64	2.14
	0.98	*0.81*	*0.24*	*0.70*	*0.86*	*0.17*	*0.85*	*0.37*	*0.01*	*0.20*
Number of observations	17	18	17	18	18	14	15	15	18	18
P (chi-squared or F)	0.21	0.37	0.07	0.18	0.25	0.27	0.54	0.34	0.02	0.07
Pseudo/adj. R²	0.19	0.13	0.39	0.25	0.21	0.11	-0.06	0.05	0.24	0.20

Note: P-values are entered below coefficient estimates. Two-choice models use probit regression, three-choice models use logit regression, and the equity-deposit models use OLS. State centralization is measured as the ratio of central to total government revenues. GDP per-capita annual average growth rate is calculated as the estimated coefficient of a time trend when the log of the ratio is regressed on that trend variable and a constant. The industrial-to-agricultural employment growth is calculated similarly. Market orientation is the structure index given in Levine and Zervos (1998) and Beck, Demirgüç-Kunt, and Levine (2000).

Source: Original results from author's regression analysis. GDP data from Maddison (1995). Employment and financial institution assets data derive from Mitchell (1983 and 1992) and Goldsmith (1969), respectively. Market orientation is the structure index given in Beck, Demirgüç-Kunt, and Levine (2000). Verdier (1997) provides equity-deposit ratio.

Table 7.2b. *Political factors in modern financial system structure*

	Securities activity (0–2)			Market orientation (1990s)		
State centralization, 1880	11.93			−2.13		
	0.03			*0.02*		
Government expenditures/	0.22	0.45		−0.002	−0.01	
GDP, 1980–1992	*0.19*	*0.07*		*0.61*	*0.19*	
OECD membership,	1.34			−0.08		
1980–1992	*0.55*			*0.29*		
Real GDP per capita,		−0.14				5.46e–03
1900		*0.05*				*0.04*
Real GDP per capita, 1980	−0.04			−1.63e–03		
(Summers-Heston)	*0.03*			*0.05*		
Constant	−2.82	1.88	−0.65	1.64	−0.10	−0.03
	0.35	*0.38*	*0.80*	*0.01*	*0.13*	*0.74*
Number of observations	18	44	32	18	64	33
P (chi-squared or F)	0.03	0.05	0.13	0.02	0.23	0.11
Pseudo/adj. R^2	0.40	0.20	0.20	0.24		

Note: P-values are entered below coefficient estimates. Three-choice models use logit regression, and the market orientation models use robust regression. State centralization is measured as the ratio of central to total government revenues. Securities activity is 0 if there are no laws regarding bank involvement in securities business, 1 if there are laws requiring at least part of the securities business to take place under subsidiaries, and 2 if at least some portion of the securities business is prohibited for banks (see Levine and Zervos, 1998). Market orientation is the structure index given in Levine and Zervos (1998) and Beck, Demirgüç-Kunt, and Levine (2000).

Source: Original results from author's regression analysis. GDP data from Maddison (1995). Employment and financial institution assets data derive from Mitchell (1983) and Goldsmith (1969), respectively. Market orientation is the structure index given in Beck, Demirgüç-Kunt, and Levine (2000). Verdier (1997) provides equity-deposit ratio.

slightly higher in civil-law countries than in common-law countries (0.69 vs. 0.58), and the p-value of a one-sided t-test is only 0.15 (Table 7.3). The cross tabulation results indicate clearly that full-scale universal banking is absent in common-law countries, while completely specialized intermediaries did not arise in civil-law countries. It is tempting to argue that market promotion tends to foster the development of institutional substitutes, so that we should expect to find that civil-law countries are more prone to universal banking than are common-law countries. On the other hand, it may be more realistic to point out that the common-law countries are virtually all related to England in various ways and adopted and adapted many institutions and norms from the mother country. In this sample, the four strictly specialized systems are England, Australia, New Zealand, and Ireland. When the 1913 world is divided into just two camps,

Table 7.3. *Legal tradition, banking structure, financial development, and GDP growth*

	Common law	Civil law	Total/P(t-test)
Cross tabulations:			
Specialized banking	7	3	10
Universal banking	0	16	16
Specialized banking	4	0	4
Partial universal banking	3	12	15
Universal banking	0	7	7
Total	7	19	26
T-tests:			
State centralization, 1880	0.58 (6)	0.69 (12)	0.15
Equity-deposit ratio, 1913	0.22 (4)	1.17 (11)	0.10
Market orientation, 1990s	0.74 (7)	0.01 (18)	0.02
FI/GNP growth (1880–1900)	0.57 (5)	0.96 (10)	0.30
FI/GNP growth (1900–1913)	0.17 (6)	0.37 (14)	0.12
GDP per-capita growth, 1820–1850	0.011 (5)	0.005 (12)	0.03
GDP per-capita growth, 1890–1900	0.008 (8)	0.016 (19)	0.03
GDP per-capita growth, 1900–1913	0.014 (9)	0.016 (27)	0.26
GDP per-capita growth, 1950–1980	0.024 (12)	0.035 (29)	0.01
GDP per-capita growth, 1980–1992	0.019 (12)	0.017 (29)	0.42

Note: The third column reports total number of observations for the cross-tabulations and significance (p-values of t-statistics) for the t-tests. The t-tests are one-sided (testing that the larger mean is significantly larger), based on a 95 percent confidence interval. The number of observations used to calculate each mean is reported in parentheses.

Source: Original results from author's regression analysis. GDP data from Maddison (1995). Employment and financial institution assets data derive from Mitchell (1983 and 1992) and Goldsmith (1969), respectively. Market orientation is the structure index given in Levine and Zervos (1998) and Beck, Demirgüç-Kunt, and Levine (2000). Verdier (1997) provides equity-deposit ratio.

the specialized category includes also Canada, the United States, and India. Argentina, Mexico, and Norway – all with arguable ties to England, but with civil-law traditions – round out the specialized group of countries.

Long-Term Impact

The results are particularly remarkable for their support of the idea of path-dependency in financial system design: The explanatory variables predate the market orientation variable by 90 to 120 years. The analysis also points toward path-dependency of banking institutions: One of the strongest predictors of modern banking type is actually past banking type (Table 7.1). Banking type is also connected to past economic performance, at least among those countries industrializing before World War I. Again, the relationship is U-shaped, with the poorest and wealthiest countries circa 1900 tending to have specialized banking (or not purely universal banking) at the end of the twentieth century. State centralization circa 1880 relates very significantly to both contemporary market orientation and promulgation of legislation regarding bank involvement in the securities business. Countries that were strongly centralized in 1880 tend to be less market-oriented in the late twentieth century and are more likely to have free involvement of banks in the securities business (universal banking). Modern measures of government expenditures provide no prediction of market orientation but are positively related to full universality of banking (Table 7.2).

The split between universal and specialized banking is most relevant and pronounced in the historical period before the conglomeration movement of recent years. Regardless of the underlying impetuses for universality or specialization, the findings here (the three-choice indicator) once again emphasize the fact that the majority of financial systems fall somewhere in between the two extremes, and that systems in highly developed economies have been moving toward the middle ground over the past few decades. Among the countries without pre-1913 data, only Uruguay severely restricts universality. Even the United States, the only common-law country maintaining mostly specialized banks after 1990, moved significantly toward integration in financial services with the deregulation of the 1990s.[20]

CONCLUSIONS

This chapter presents and contrasts three types of theories for the development of financial systems: economic, political, and legal. The analysis uncovers several patterns in the development of financial systems and helps disentangle the various forces involved. All three categories of theories display some power in explaining the genesis and development of financial systems. Clearly, the analysis returns economic factors to the fore: the stage of economic development does partly predict the type of banking system that subsequently developed among the pre–World War I industrial nations and also factors into the strength of financial system development. The fact that the converse relationship does not hold is a particularly interesting result in light of the still-heated debates over the causal relationship between financial and real growth – the subject of the next chapter. The inverted-U-shaped relationship between financial institution assets and GDP per capita

---

[20] The financial crisis of 2008–2009 raised concerns over that liberalization and reactionary calls for reregulation, even the reenactment of Glass-Steagall provisions.

lends support to the idea that the moderately industrialized countries of the time depended more on financial institutions to mobilize capital than did the most and least advanced economies.

The experiences of late-nineteenth-century industrializers such as Germany, Italy, and Japan on the one hand, and the earliest industrial nation, Great Britain, on the other, highlight the pattern. Whereas Britain developed a specialized arms-length banking system, continental Europe and Japan propelled industrialization via universal banks.[21] The statistical relationships hold all the more robustly when non-European countries are included. Given the small sample sizes, it is difficult to determine whether this added statistical strength stems solely from the increase in the number of countries included. Whether these tests address the so-called Gerschenkron hypothesis is open to debate, but the results do seem supportive of his general ideas.[22] Economic forces alone, however, cannot provide the basis for understanding the different types and depths of systems outside of some special cases. Moreover, the "economic backwardness" line of reasoning cannot explain the emergence of very broad and active securities markets in Germany and the United States in the last quarter of the nineteenth and the start of the twentieth century.

Quantifiable political factors, such as government centralization, provide very little power in explaining banking system design, but do strongly relate to market orientation. Nonetheless, many individual countries' histories make it clear that political forces played important roles in shaping regulations that in turn altered the course of financial institutions and markets. Some potentially important political factors – the ability of incumbents to oppose financial development or openness to trade – are difficult to capture in quantitative terms. To the extent that interest-group politics and their interaction with national institutions coincide with state centralization, the analysis can shed light on these theories. Interest-group politics may help explain why, by some measures, financial system development followed a generalized decline during much of the twentieth century. But these theories cannot explain the emergence of particular financial system characteristics and the fact that in many countries, these characteristics have stayed relatively constant, even as incumbent interests have changed over time. The results in this chapter suggest that political factors vary a

---

[21] But as Chapters 2 through 5 laid out in detail, these systems differed substantially from one another, and the Japanese universal banks in particular were not providing extensive equity underwriting services as the German and Italian banks were.

[22] The consistency of the relationship over different time periods offers a useful avenue for future research.

great deal and do not consistently impede or encourage financial development. In other words, political forces appeared inconsistently and had no traceable, uniform relationship to the overall political system in place in the nineteenth century.

Legal traditions, in contrast, correlate highly with both market orientation and banking institution design (but not with government centralization). It seems very likely, however, that the legal system variable may coincidentally proxy for the true source of influence on the financial system – whether adoption from colonizing powers, adaptation from neighbors or trading partners, or innate cultural and social beliefs. Most problematic, the hypothesized causal links between legal tradition and financial development – that is, specific investor and creditor protections and their enforcement – came into being around the same time or even after financial systems were taking shape. In this sense, it is less surprising that legal orientation exerted little impact on financial institution growth at the turn of the century. Although the diversity of legal structures across countries could explain why some countries would be likely to develop stronger equity markets and arms-length banking systems whereas others developed relational systems that depended more heavily on banking institutions, they cannot explain why the level of financial development has been unstable over time. If structural explanations are correct and complete, once a country has achieved a certain level of financial development, it should maintain that level coincident with the demand for financing. However, after the Great Depression and World War II, most countries faced a decline in financial system development. Moreover, there have been reversals in the rankings of countries in terms of financial development, which should not occur if legal structure is what explains the level of development completely, as legal structure should remain relatively stable over time.[23] The historical record suggests that structural factors, such as the endowment of the legal system (and enforcement), cannot provide a complete theory for financial system development. Other theories are needed to explain both the cross-sectional and the time-series variation.

Economic, political, and legal factors most likely work together, and some combination of the rather distinct theories is required to explain the shape of financial systems at their origins and their development over the past century and a half. Undoubtedly, as the case study chapters very clearly

---

[23] See Fohlin (2000, 2002b) and Rajan and Zingales (2003). As Rajan and Zingales (2003) put it: "If some countries have a system that is pre-disposed toward finance, that predisposition should continue to be relatively strong since structural factors are relatively time-invariant."

illustrate, idiosyncratic factors – particular regulations, specific events, mixes of natural resources and human capital, perhaps even national culture – also matter for explaining the emergence and persistence of financial system characteristics. Whether we can pin down and classify systematic influences, history clearly matters for financial system structure.

8

Does Financial Structure Drive
Industrial Growth?

Economic historians have always underscored the influence of institutions – economic, political, legal, social, and even cultural – in the processes of industrial development and economic growth. In the last decade, economists more broadly have turned their attention to similar factors underlying the differential economic growth witnessed across countries.[1] Much of the recent literature on the determinants of long-run economic growth focuses on financial institutions as critical factors.[2] In particular, the current literature focuses on the role of political and legal systems in providing the environment that allows financial institutions to allocate capital and services efficiently.[3] This literature takes as a given that functioning financial institutions are important preconditions for economic growth, which is sometimes called the finance-leads-growth perspective. In contrast, in the mid-twentieth century, the dominant view held that financial development responded to demand or real economic activity.[4] The finance-leads-growth perspective has begun to hold sway, although some have recognized the dual directions of causality: In the long run, increases in industrial activity will feed back into the financial system, thereby increasing the demand for financial services. In this case, in the long run, the causality from economic growth to financial development goes both ways.

Financial development can imply a variety of processes and can envelop numerous different institutions. Fully functioning financial systems must

[1] See, for example, Acemoglu, Johnson, and Robinson (2004).
[2] See, for example, Beck, Levine, and Loayza (2000), Berkowitz, Pistor, and Richard (2003), and Carlin and Mayer (2003).
[3] The most important papers in this regard are Rajan and Zingales (1998) for political institutions and La Porta et al. (1998) for the relevance of legal structure. Persson and Tabellini (2009) identify democracy as a positive factor in economic growth.
[4] Most prominently, see Joan Robinson (1952).

do at least three basic things: provide credit for entrepreneurial projects, independent of personal connections; instill confidence in investors that they will earn a fair expected return; and spread risk across investment projects.[5] A mature financial system should provide all of these services at a low cost. In economic terms, these conditions imply complete markets for insurance and financing based on market factors; low "outside risk" – that is risk associated with factors such as political or institutional instability (like political revolutions or bank failures); and low transactions costs for obtaining financial services, such as borrowing, securities issues, or insurance. Low transaction costs are typically also associated with the existence of arms-length financing opportunities as these can be competed for on merit, disclosure laws (i.e., transparency in financial deals), and contract enforcement that ensures creditor repayment or punishment. Several studies have offered evidence that this sort of financial development provides an impetus for economic growth. These studies have focused primarily on the past thirty years, however, and they therefore neglect the structures that have evolved over longer periods that may be more important for understanding why some countries grow faster than others.[6]

The rest of this chapter begins by laying out the facts of economic growth over the past 100 years for a panel of countries that industrialized before World War I. A review of the prevailing theories of the role of financial system design for long-run economic growth then sets the stage for an assessment of how well these available theories explain the empirical link between finance and growth. The analysis shows, in fact, that although institutional factors may be important in determining economic growth, they are not pivotal. Many of the financial development indicators viewed as important for economic growth were put into place long before countries diverged in their growth performance.

THE DATA ON LONG-RUN GROWTH

During the mid- to late industrialization period – approximately 1880–1900 for most European countries and their colonial offshoots – real GDP per-capita growth rates averaged approximately 1 percent (Table 8.1). Over the subsequent decade and a half, growth rates increased to approximately 2 percent on average, and even higher without the slow growers such as India (0.5 percent growth). This set of relatively advanced economies maintained

[5] These three factors are suggested by Rajan and Zingales (1998).
[6] Two of these are Levine (1998), and Rajan and Zingales (1998).

Table 8.1. *Growth rates of real per-capita GDP*

Country	1820–1850	1850–1880	1850–1913	1880–1900	1880–1913	1900–1913	1870–1994	1900–1994
Argentina						.029		.011
Australia	.095	.050	.073	-.01	.003	.025	.011	.015
Austria	.035	.031	.100	.02	.016	.016	.017	.022
Belgium	.047	.068	.110	.01	.010	.010	.014	.018
Brazil	.009	.007	.025			.013		.024
Canada	.053	.041	.167	.02	.026	.030	.021	.022
Chile						.023		.013
China		.013	.044					
Denmark	.046	.028	.107	.02	.018	.029	.019	.021
Finland	.016	.042	.131	.02	.018	.019	.024	.028
France	.044	.031	.098	.01	.014	.016	.019	.022
Germany	.040	.047	.131	.02	.018	.017	.019	.022
Greece								
India	.005	.010	.031			.005		.006
Indonesia	.011	.001	.051			.018		.009
Ireland	.052	.043	.096					
Italy	.012	.038	.011	.004	.015	.030	.021	.024
Japan	.002	.016	.095			.015		.032
Mexico		.017	.121					
Netherlands	.026	.067	.098			.009		.019
New Zealand						.017		.014
Norway	.011	.042	.107		.012	.019	.022	.027
Portugal		.006	.030					
Russia	.030	.009	.071	.012				
Spain	.011	.046	.096			.006		.021
Sweden	.010	.050	.122	.016	.017	.016	.021	.024
Switzerland						.013		.022
United Kingdom	.040	.053	.097	.012	.010	.006	.013	.015
United States	.048	.075	.143	.01	.017	.016	.018	.019
Average	.029	.035	.094	.013	.015	.017	.018	.020

Source: Author's original regression estimates based on GDP data from Maddison (1995).

an average annual growth rate of 2 percent for nearly a century and a quarter – 1870 to 1994.[7] The quickening pace of growth and the fact that substantial growth occurred even over the long run meant that standards of living in industrialized countries improved dramatically in this time.

[7] Similarly, if we just consider the average long-run growth rate over most of the twentieth century – 1900 to 1994 – the growth rate is also 2 percent. These growth rates are calculated by estimating the coefficient of GDP on a time trend.

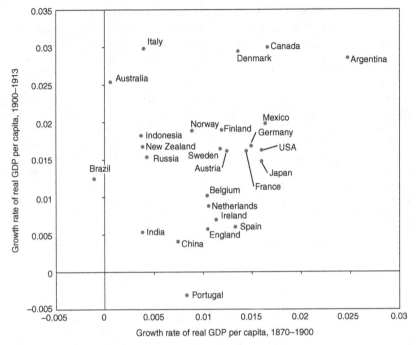

Figure 8.1. GDP per capita growth, 1870–1900 and 1900–1913.
Note: Real GDP per capita is calculated in 1990 Geary-Khamis dollars.
Source: Maddison (1995).

Moreover, whereas some countries, such as India and Mexico, did not catch up to the growth leaders, most European and colonial countries did grow at very similar rates, particularly when viewed over the long run. In fact, countries with very different institutional structures, in terms of legal systems or banking characteristics, such as Germany and the United States, still grew at very similar rates over the past 100 years.

Given the sparseness of the pre-1870 data, the growth rates and averages for that period should be interpreted with caution. Even so, we can say that the standard of living in 1880 vastly improved the status of 1820, particularly for the early industrializers – the United Kingdom and France.

A simple scatterplot of growth rates of GDP per capita from 1870 to 1900 versus those from 1900 to 1913 demonstrates the positive relationship between GDP growth rates in these two adjoining periods (Figure 8.1). Countries that grew slowly from 1870 to 1900, such as India, China, and Portugal, continued to grow slowly in the second period. Countries that were growing faster in the earlier period, such as Canada, the United States, the United Kingdom, Denmark, Japan, and France, continued to grow

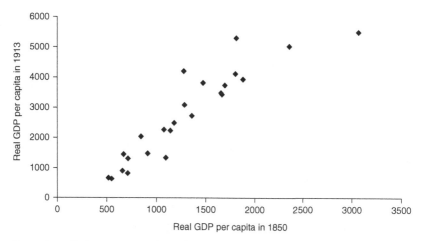

Figure 8.2. GDP per capita, 1850 and 1913.
Note: Real GDP per capita is calculated in 1990 Geary-Khamis dollars.
Source: Maddison (1995).

relatively fast in the second period. There are several countries, however, that do not fit this positive linear relationship – Italy, Austria, and Brazil, for example, grew slowly in the earlier period but much faster in the later period. Because of the small numbers of countries involved, we can only say for sure that there is a weak positive relationship between growth rates when comparing across countries during the middle and later stages of the industrialization period. In a more absolute sense, however, most countries did improve their performance over time. Those whose growth rate increased in the later period outnumber those whose growth rate declined by about two to one. And only two countries – Spain and Portugal – slowed down by more than half a percentage point.

Levels of wealth appear to have been set a bit more firmly and very early on. All of the sampled countries – a select group, to be sure – expanded over this period, and most became substantially better off. But GDP per capita in 1880 relates very closely to that in 1820. Even in 1913, the level of GDP per capita relates very positively to GDP per capita in 1850 (Figure 8.2) and even as far back as 1820.[8] Even though they cannot provide causal evidence, these correlations do indicate that for the developing economies of the pre–World War I era, the level of national wealth toward the end of the

---

[8] A Spearman test shows a correlation of GDP per capita of 0.95 between 1820 and 1880 and 0.94 between 1850 and 1913. The tests clearly reject the hypothesis that the two series are independent at the 1 percent confidence level. The correlation between the level of GDP per capita in 1820 versus 1913 is still 0.87.

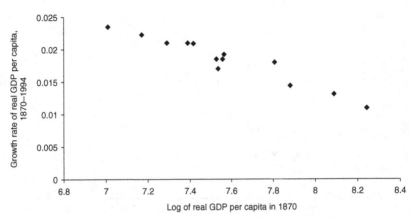

Figure 8.3. Log GDP per capita in 1870 versus growth rate for 1870–1994.
Note: Real GDP per capita is calculated in 1990 Geary-Khamis dollars.
Source: Maddison (1995).

industrialization period relates closely to a country's wealth many decades, and even a century, before. For these particular countries, those that were initially wealthy continued to stay wealthy, whereas poor countries remained poor. And contrary to convergence hypotheses, income disparity actually grew between 1850 and 1913 (Figure 8.2). Divergence appears to be the very-long-run trend in aggregate growth as well, given that inequality between countries rose from 1820 to 1950 and also during the 1960s.[9] The idea is also borne out by the fact that the slow-growing, poor countries of the nineteenth century continued to remain poor and slow-growing throughout much of the twentieth century. Without an acceleration in growth, there would be no means for these late developers to catch up to the early industrializers. There is new evidence that convergence in aggregate growth between countries began in the late twentieth century.[10] In contrast, but consistent with modern theories of economic growth, growth rates over the long run relate negatively to the level of GDP per capita at the beginning of the period – whether 1870 or 1900 – suggesting that highly developed countries grew slower than poorer countries (Figures 8.3 and 8.4). This analysis is suggestive, but the focus on long-run growth neglects important variations in growth rates that occurred at various times. For example, for various subperiods, poor countries grew slower than wealthy ones.

The Great Depression and World War II altered the course of many economies and financial systems. By some measures – the ratio of deposits at

---

[9] See Pritchett (1997) and O'Rourke (2001).
[10] See, for example, Lindert and Williamson (2003).

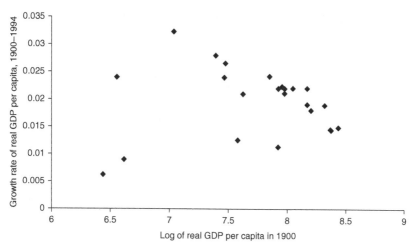

Figure 8.4. Log GDP per capita in 1900 versus growth rate for 1900–1994.
Note: GDP per capita is given in 1990 Geary-Khamis dollars.
Source: Maddison (1995).

banking institutions to GDP, for example – financial development reached an apex prior to the stock market crash in 1929, declined through much of the twentieth century, and only returned to 1929 levels in the late 1990s.[11] Stock market capitalization as a ratio to GDP reached its apex a bit later, in 1938, and then also declined for the most part throughout the twentieth century, and also returned to its old level only in the late 1990s.[12] Changes in financial institution assets as a ratio of GNP offer a broader way to look at financial system development (Table 8.2). In 1860, for example, the average ratio of financial assets to GNP was 40 percent. In 1913, the average was 109 percent, indicating almost a tripling of financial assets as a percentage of GNP over fifty years.

Financial development, in other words, proceeded with marked ups and downs over the past century and a half and with significant variation across countries. Any cogent theory of the relationship of financial development to economic growth must account for these very clear, long-run patterns. Moreover, the theory should account for the fact that economic growth continued throughout the twentieth century, even as financial activity waxed and waned.

[11] Measuring financial development by deposits is an imprecise measure that may in fact be meaningless in some cases, except as a rough indicator of development, due to the fact that some countries naturally had a higher level of deposits than other countries due to regulatory reasons.
[12] At which point, it then expanded rapidly and then contracted again precipitously twice in the first decade of the twenty-first century.

Table 8.2. *Financial institution assets as a percentage of GNP*

	1860	1880	1900	1913
Argentina			44	66
Australia			108	98
Austria				
Belgium		71	94	109
Brazil				36
Canada		43	87	96
Chili				
Denmark		95	147	184
Finland				
France	19	50	96	104
Germany	40	73	114	158
India		2	4	7
Indonesia				
Ireland				
Italy		36	61	97
Japan		13	82	97
Netherlands		46	62	83
New Zealand		100	109	121
Norway		107	136	166
Spain			37	35
Sweden		89	123	136
Switzerland	56	153	184	287
United Kingdom	57	95	93	103
United States	28	49	86	91
Average	40	68.1	92.6	109.2

Sources: Author's original analysis based on GDP data from Maddison (1995) and financial institution assets data from Goldsmith (1969).

WHAT EXPLAINS ECONOMIC GROWTH?

The patterns of real economic growth and financial development are relatively clear, but the links between them are as yet less well understood.

Theoretical Debate

In most theoretical general equilibrium models of economic growth, financial intermediaries improve the efficiency with which investment capital is allocated in the economy. Financial intermediaries are, in principle at least, better able to acquire and process information about the innovative activities of entrepreneurs or about the aggregate state of technology. These information advantages allow them to fund more promising projects on the whole. Because of their size and scope, financial intermediaries are also able to pool risk across investment projects, thus promoting growth through the provision of higher and safer returns to investors.[13] Moreover, to the extent that pooling projects from multiple sectors mitigates risk from industry-specific shocks, then portfolio diversification may in fact encourage specialization and further productivity growth.[14] These primary functions of financial intermediation may thereby promote or enhance real economic growth.

Empirical studies on the relationship between long-run growth and financial intermediation show that increased intermediation, or financial development more broadly, significantly increases growth. Intermediaries presumably lower costs of investment by diversifying idiosyncratic risk and by exploiting economies of scale in information processing and monitoring; they also provide insurance for entrepreneurs who cannot diversify their risk on their own.[15] Large fixed initial investment costs – research and development (R&D), for example – can force entrepreneurs to seek external financing; without financial intermediaries, agency problems could make the cost of finance too high, discouraging innovation (and therefore growth). Joseph Schumpeter argued in 1912 that financial intermediaries promote innovative activities, decrease transaction costs, and improve allocative efficiency; in this manner, the financial sector becomes the "engine of growth." Without intermediaries, the cost of R&D projects would be prohibitively high. Financial intermediation also lowers the required rate of return on innovation by lowering fixed costs, thereby spurring growth through investment in R&D.

Bank Based versus Market Based – or Something Else?

Chapter 7 explored the differences between bank- and market-based financial systems and set out the many potential costs and benefits of systems

[13] This view may be faulty if higher returns on investment reduce saving and therefore investment.

[14] Banks and insurance companies may also reduce the need to hold liquid savings (which are unproductive), providing additional funds for investment into productive capital. Alternatively, if investments provide higher returns due to the efficiency of financial intermediaries, saving may decline.

[15] These propositions surely seem almost preposterous in light of the crisis of 1907–1909 (and the financial crisis of 2007–2009). The severe drop in economic growth following the loss of liquidity and the general malfunctioning in the financial sector actually underscores the key part that a properly functioning financial system plays in permitting economic growth. Gaytan and Ranciere (2006) develop an overlapping generations model that incorporates liquidity crises and demonstrates a variable relationship between financial development and growth.

dominated by one or the other sort of institution.[16] Particularly important for the problem of growth, powerful banks may be more able to force firms to repay debt, particularly in countries with weak contract-enforcement capabilities.[17] Moreover, strong bank involvement in their investments, as well as enforcement of their contracts, may encourage foreign direct investment in countries with otherwise underdeveloped institutions and where investors typically would be hesitant to enter due to enforcement concerns.[18] Still, many tout the advantages of market-based systems and point to pitfalls of systems dominated by powerful banks with few regulatory restraints.[19] Competitive capital markets may play a particularly

[16] At least hypothetically, bank-based systems may offer a number of advantages in promoting economic growth: acquiring private information about firms and managers, thus improving capital allocation and corporate governance; managing and diversifying cross-sectional, intertemporal, and liquidity risk, therefore enhancing economic efficiency and hence growth; mobilizing capital to exploit economies of scale; monitoring firms and reducing postlending moral hazard; and exerting control over bank managers because they (possibly) hold equity shares for the long term (unlike most market investors). For a general discussion, see Levine (2002). See also Ramakrishnan and Thakor (1984), Allen and Gale (1999), Sirri and Tufano (1995), and Boot and Thakor (1997) for a discussion of specific points.

[17] A good example of this phenomenon, in the past decade, is examined by Tornell, Westermann, and Martinez (2004). They determine that much of Mexico's stagnation in GDP and exports can be blamed on the lack of judicial and structural reform after 1995. In particular, they point to a decline in contract enforceability and an increase in nonperforming loans as one of the key factors in Mexico's poor growth performance. See also Gerschenkron (1962).

[18] See Levine (2002) for empirical results. Chakraborty and Ray (2006) develop an endogenous growth model in which systems that use predominantly bank lending outperform systems using markets. This result seems somewhat at odds with Baliga and Polak (2004), whose theoretical model shows that a market-based finance system (bonds) can only persist if it is efficient, but an economy can get stuck in an inefficient bank-based financing system. In a related dynamic general equilibrium model where firms may raise money through external finance via monitored bank loans and arms-length borrowing, Chakraborty and Ray (2007) identify initial inequality, investment size, and institutional factors as determinants of financial development; findings that they argue support empirical findings in LaPorta et al. (1997, 1998) and Levine (2002), namely that institutional and legal factors are important determinants of financial structure.

[19] For example, market-oriented systems provide greater incentives for individual investors to research firms in which they intend to invest (because of the profit opportunity provided); enhance corporate governance through the facilitation of takeovers and the ease of tying managerial compensation to firm performance (when the company's shares trade on the market); and facilitate risk management. For a discussion of the advantages of market-based systems, see Levine (1991) and Obstfeld (1994). Banks may reduce innovation by extracting informational rents and protecting established firms with close bank-firm ties from competition (Hellwig 1991; Rajan 1992); collude with firm managers against other creditors, thus impeding efficient corporate governance (Hellwig 1998); and may fail to aggregate information signals and transmit them efficiently to investors as markets do (Allen and Gale 1999).

positive role in aggregating information signals and transmitting them efficiently to investors, thereby facilitating firm financing and encouraging economic growth.[20]

Between these two perspectives is the financial services view that emphasizes how financial arrangements (contracts, markets, intermediaries) *all* reduce market imperfections in the provision of financial services.[21] All of these financial arrangements develop to provide essentially the same "goods": assessment of potential investment opportunities, exertion of corporate control, facilitation of risk management, liquidity enhancement, and allocation of savings/investment funds. The role of all financial systems, whether market- or bank-based, is to provide such services effectively. In this perspective, the focus is on creating an environment where intermediaries and markets provide effective financial services, not on whether the system is bank- or market-based. A special case of the financial services perspective focuses on the legal environment as the "glue" that produces and sustains the financial system, whatever it may be.[22] Finance can be considered as a set of contracts, defined and made effective through legal rights and enforcement mechanisms that facilitate the operation of markets and banks, improving efficient allocation of resources and ultimately therefore of economic growth.[23] According to the financial services perspective, the distinction between bank-based and market-based systems is immaterial for long-run growth outcomes – a proposition that is also borne out by the data, in that the two archetypical bank-based systems, Germany and Japan, had largely the same long-run growth experience as the two archetypical market-based systems, the United States and the United Kingdom. There is also no cross-country empirical support for either the bank-based or the market-based view: Neither the bank- nor market-based financial system is uniquely effective in generating growth.[24] Even when comparing extremes, countries with very well-developed banks but poorly developed capital markets do not perform significantly differently from countries with the reverse financial system or even those with more evenly balanced systems in terms of bank and market activity. Even an allowance for the possibility that financial structure changes as countries develop, and that legal systems

---

[20] For example, see Hellwig (1991), Rajan (1992), Hellwig (1998), and Allen and Gale (1999) for the problems associated with bank-based systems.
[21] Merton and Bodie (1995, 2005) and Levine (1997) discuss the financial services view.
[22] La Porta, Lopez-de-Silanes, Shleifer, and Vishny (1998) were the first to demonstrate the importance of legal systems in establishing functioning efficient financial systems.
[23] Such is the view proposed by La Porta et al. (1998).
[24] See Levine (2002).

evolve over time, does not materially change the results, suggesting that the distinction between bank-based and market-based financial systems is not an analytically useful tool for understanding cross-country differential rates of economic growth.[25]

At least in the more recent past, better-developed financial systems (whether bank- or market-based) do seem to promote economic growth. Moreover, the part of financial development defined by legal rights of investors and efficiency of contract enforcement is strongly associated with growth, therefore supporting the idea that the legal system is critical in determining financial development whereas financial structure is not.[26] In other words, strengthening the rights of investors and improving contract enforcement is more relevant to economic growth than developing a particular financial system. In particular, common-law countries seem to provide shareholders and creditors with the strongest legal protection, whereas French civil-law countries provide the weakest legal protection.[27] French civil-law countries appear to be weakest in law enforcement, whereas Scandinavian and German civil-law countries provide the highest-quality legal enforcement. These institutional differences may bear importantly on finance and growth. French civil-law countries have highly concentrated ownership, whereas common-law countries have highly dispersed ownership, indicating that the legal system affects the financing system: Arguably, the more legal protection offered to investors, the more likely is the development of stock markets and the ability to spread investment risk. Legal origin also seems to affect law enforcement and accounting standards.[28]

The recent literature on law and finance brings to the fore questions about the economic consequences of legal system design over the long run. This strand of literature advances the idea that particular legal systems promote

[25] Rajan and Zingales (1998) argue that bank-based systems are better at promoting growth in countries with poor legal systems, whereas market-based systems become the better growth promoter as legal systems develop. Tadesse (2002) finds that bank-based systems promote higher growth rates in less developed financial systems, whereas market-based systems spur more growth in more developed ones. The analysis, however, is based on thirty-six countries over the 1980s to mid-1990s. Deidda and Fattouh (2005) provide theory and evidence arguing that the growth effect of financial development is ambiguous at low levels of development, and eventually becomes positive in later stages of development.

[26] Levine (2002).

[27] La Porta et al. (1998) consider a sample of forty-nine countries that they divide into four groups depending on legal origin of modern commercial laws: common law (English), French civil law, German civil law, and Scandinavian civil law.

[28] These factors were discussed in Chapter 7, where we looked at financial system design and its relationship to historical institutional factors such as the legal and regulatory structure. See also Fear and Kobrak (2006) on the development of accounting standards in Germany and the United States.

greater efficiency and economic well-being than others, at least in part via better-functioning financial contracting. Yet the typical measure of prosperity of an economy – the growth of GDP per capita – does not vary systematically with the adherence to a particular legal system. Simple correlations display a negative relationship between legal system type and the growth of GDP per capita, and available evidence cannot reject the hypothesis that legal system type and GDP per-capita growth are independent. Levels of GDP per capita do correlate significantly to legal tradition. Although such simple correlations do not constitute proof of any relationship, they do suggest strongly that GDP growth rates relate only weakly to legal system type. If common-law tradition constituted a causal factor in growth, then it should appear consistently as a predictor of GDP per-capita growth rates. The long-run data show, however, that whereas common-law countries grew faster in some subperiods, civil-law countries grew faster in others. These periodic advantages and disadvantages trace back to obvious origins, such as periods of rapid industrialization or postwar reconstruction. Once the tumult of the first three quarters of the twentieth century passed – that is, during the 1980s and early 1990s – growth rates became statistically identical across legal types. A historical perspective, therefore, leaves the strong impression that legal tradition matters little for economic growth over the long run. What appears to matter more in promoting investment and economic growth is that whatever laws there are, they are understood by participants in the financial system and are enforced by a legal authority. Further supporting this viewpoint is the fact that for the first countries to industrialize, legal system structure was often not set into place until some time after industrialization began. This would imply that legal system design in itself cannot constitute a fundamental cause of differential long-run growth rates.

Legal system design is not monolithic. On the contrary, it encompasses much more than just the type of laws enacted and their enforcement and often proxies well for cultural factors that may in fact matter more. Colonies offer an interesting testing ground for the role of culture versus formal institutions like legal systems, as the legal system is often imported from the imperial power. In these cases, institutional framework may depend less on the legal origin of the country and potentially more on whether the legal framework imposed by the colonial ruler was embraced by the colony: Was the ruled country receptive to the institutions of the colonial ruler? At least for the post–World War II period, colonial acceptance of imported (or imposed) institutions proves to be crucial to the effectiveness of legal institutions; legal effectiveness in turn helps explain financial development.[29] Religion and language may proxy for culture, and may therefore help explain such legal institutions as shareholder rights or creditor rights.[30] In Weberian fashion, it seems that Protestant countries in general offer better creditor protection than Catholic countries, and because strong creditor rights facilitate development of banks and debt markets, religion may relate to financial and therefore economic development.[31]

Disentangling the Causality: Empirical Evidence

Schumpeter's (1912) view – that well-developed financial systems promote growth by channeling credit to its most productive uses – is now viewed as conventional wisdom. Financial development may affect real sectors in varying ways depending on institutional design. The growth and finance literature primarily tries to determine whether financial intermediaries impact, or in some sense, cause economic growth.[32] If financial systems do have an impact on growth, then the next questions are what type of system has the most beneficial impact and what determines financial system development in a given country. Answering these questions involves a number of statistical and econometric questions, and past researchers have attempted a number of different methodologies and models.[33]

Cross-Country Growth Models

In the cross-country regression approach, subsequent growth rates of percapita GDP are regressed on initial income, other variables controlling for the steady state and measures of financial development of the economy.[34] Studies of post–World War II data have shown a prominent role for measures of financial development in predicting growth rates.[35] Cross-country studies present two critical concerns that need to be addressed in any

---

[29] See Berkowitz et al. (2003), for example, who consider the origin of institutions. Adoption or acceptance of imperial rule adds explanatory power to regressions that seek to explain the effectiveness of legal institutions.

[30] See, for example, Stulz and Williamson (2003). Culture helps predict shareholder rights, but the significance drops by adding legal origin. Religion is more robust in predicting creditor rights.

[31] De Long (1988) noted the significance of religion in predicting productivity growth and convergence.

[32] A group of studies beginning with King and Levine (1993) have found evidence in favor of such a view.

[33] Beck (2008) provides an extensive survey of the empirical literature with a focus on econometric techniques. See also Ang (2008), Trew (2006), and Levine (2002).

[34] See Barro (1991).

[35] King and Levine (1993) and Levine and Zervos (1998), for example.

empirical work. First, it may be inappropriate to pool countries with different levels of industrialization, if the estimated effect of finance on growth is unstable across countries at different stages of development. Second, the effect of financial development on growth may prove difficult to isolate; the causal (directional) link between finance and growth may therefore be impossible to establish definitively.

Establishing a definition of financial development is the first step in such an analysis. Financial development can be assessed using a variety of metrics: the ease with which an entrepreneur or company can obtain finance, the confidence creditors or investors have in adequate returns, the ability to gauge and spread risk, and the ability to find credit at low cost.[36] As natural as these factors seem, however, they turn out to be largely unobservable, and in practice, their intangible or qualitative nature raises the problem of finding good proxies. Often, researchers resort to measuring the size of the banking sector or the liquidity of stock markets. The research that has resulted over the past decade establishes a positive association between initial size of national banking sectors and subsequent economic growth in the past thirty years or so.[37] In particular, some have found that bank development and stock market liquidity are independently and robustly linked with contemporaneous and future economic growth, while the volatility of stock returns and international migration are found to be insignificant.[38] Historical studies, although a bit sparse, show a strong positive effect of financial intermediation in the pre–Great Depression period in particular.[39] In one such study, however, finance loses much of its explanatory power for growth when legal origin appears in the regression.[40] Yet none of the legal-origin factors is statistically significant, suggesting that if legal origin matters for growth, it does so through financial development. Moreover, political variables (proportional-representation election systems, frequent elections, infrequent revolutions) correlate with larger financial sectors and higher conditional rates of economic growth.

[36] See, for a recent example, Rajan and Zingales (2000).
[37] King and Levine (1993) sparked a decade of empirical testing with their cross-country growth regression methodology (based on Barro 1991).
[38] Levine and Zervos (1998), test two specific hypotheses: first, that banks and equity have an independent first-order effect on economic activity; and second, that the risk-reduction function of the financial sector is the particular channel through which financial development affects growth. Stock market liquidity is measured by the ratio of the value of shares traded to market capitalization (as well as to GDP). Economic growth is measured by real GDP growth per capita, rate of capital accumulation, and rate of productivity growth.
[39] Rousseau and Sylla (2003) do a similar exercise as King and Levine for seventeen countries from 1850 to 1997.
[40] Bordo and Rousseau (2006).

The cross-country method is not without critics, and some have argued that the approach suffers from statistical bias due to the endogeneity of the explanatory variables. Typical techniques require often unrealistic assumptions about the properties of underlying variables, and, in any case, the models can only uncover an "average" effect of financial development.[41] As a result, the estimated parameters prove difficult to interpret and most likely prevent any kind of generalization about how financial and economic developments have coevolved in the past or how they could interact in the future. Various methodologies have been employed in the literature to control for the potential endogeneity of financial variables and also for reverse causality – whether financial development "causes" economic growth or vice versa. In one typical approach to the causality problem, researchers have used legal origin dummies as instruments for financial development.[42] The legal origin variable stems from the idea that differences in legal protection for investors and creditors have an implication for corporate governance, the financing patterns of firms, the concentration of share ownership, and ultimately for economic growth. An alternative approach involves isolating the effect of finance on growth by looking at the effect of banking sector deregulation on economic growth in various U.S. states during the 1970s and 1980s.[43] In this case, financial development seems to show a positive effect on growth.

Still, the instrumental variables approach cannot establish causality, particularly if there are variables omitted that correlate with both financial development and growth. Even though the evidence available so far suggests a correlation between financial development and various aspects of the legal system, it may be that financial development is highly correlated with other institutional factors. These factors that are omitted from the statistical models bias the coefficients estimated for financial development.[44] A closer examination demonstrates some weakness in the empirical foundation of the idea that finance causes growth.[45] In particular, financial intermediation influences growth more in non-OECD countries, where bank financing is important, although it also appears that finance correlates more closely with growth after a country reaches a certain level of economic

---

[41] See Quah (1993), Caselli, Esquivel, and Lefort (1996), and Manning (2003).

[42] Levine (1998), Rajan and Zingales (1998), and Carlin and Mayer (2003), for example.

[43] See Jayaratne and Strahan (1996).

[44] The evidence appears in La Porta et al. (1997).

[45] Manning (2003) identifies this problem in two influential recent studies: Rajan and Zingales (1998) and Levine and Zeros (1998).

development.[46] Still, it is difficult to disentangle the effect of financial development from the effects of other correlated factors – legal, cultural, and political. Moreover, the apparent impact of financial development on growth depends heavily on the strong performance of the Asian Tiger economies during 1980s, underscoring once again the importance of a longer-run perspective.[47]

Finance seems to influence growth at the firm level as well, particularly in a broader view of financial development that envelops the size of the stock market and accounting standards, as well as the size of the banking sector. Broader measures of financial development have the advantage of reflecting the potential for obtaining financing rather than just the actual amount of financing raised. What evidence we have supports the idea that the extent of industry's dependence on external financing – and the accounting standards of the country in which it operates – exerts a positive effect on industry value added.[48] Similarly, firm growth appears to relate to specific features of a country's legal and financial system, such as active stock markets (high level of turnover) and well-developed legal systems.[49] In other words, differences in the effectiveness of legal and financial systems seem to lead to systematic differences in firms' access to external finance and therefore differences in firm-level growth. The relative strength of banks versus capital markets, however, seems not to affect the overall availability of external finance, although it does relate to the composition of financing between short and long maturities.

The fact that the empirically determined causal structure underlying the aggregate relationship between the financial and manufacturing sectors varies widely across countries suggests the importance of historical and institutional factors, as well as international capital flows, in the interaction between industrial and financial sector. Small countries, for example, may import capital, so that for them, financial intermediation may not serve the same purpose as it does in large, diverse countries. Moreover, the link between finance and growth seems to differ depending on a country's level of development, appearing most significant in modern periods for countries at earlier stages in economic development. In these cases, it appears that bank finance is particularly important.

---

[46] See Rioja and Valev (2004).
[47] The Asian Tiger economies include Hong Kong, Singapore, South Korea, and Taiwan.
[48] See Rajan and Zingales (1998) and Beck and Levine (2002). On a related note, Beck, Demirguc-Kunt, Laeven, and Levine (2004) find that finance promotes growth more in sectors where firm size is naturally smaller.
[49] See Demirguc-Kunt and Maksimovic (1998 and 2002).

Time-Series Evidence

Time-series evidence for individual countries offers an alternative approach to the problem of modeling the long-run relationship between financial intermediation and growth and can permit more conclusive inferences on the causal relationship between financial development and growth than is possible with cross-sectional studies. It seems clear that financial systems vary substantially, and that patterns of causation differ among countries or perhaps even within a single country at different stages of its development. Using time-series approaches for individual countries might reveal long-run relationships between real per-capita GDP and measures of financial development, and help address the statistical question of causality. The results of such investigations turn out to be mixed. Banking system development and output levels in Germany show bidirectional relationships, whereas stock market development shows some sign of pushing output in the long run.[50] In the United States, by contrast, real GDP seems to influence finance.[51] In less-developed economies, financial development appears to push real economic growth without bidirectional causality.[52]

Several other recent studies have found innovative methods for circumventing criticisms of omitted variables and endogeneity bias.[53] Some include a variety of additional controls and measure financial depth using all types of intermediaries in an attempt to measure the financial sector as a whole. Characterizing financial intermediation as completely as possible means including assets held in commercial banks, savings and loan associations, investment banks, pension funds, and life and casualty insurance companies.[54] Moreover, using GDP of these sectors allows the measures to encompass both off-balance-sheet and capital market activities. Considering the entire financial sector in this fashion solves the problem of biasing results toward countries with universal or unit banking systems. A final refinement tightens the focus on the manufacturing sector, under the assumption that productivity-enhancing investment projects in manufacturing technology depend heavily on outside finance and are likely to

---

[50] Statistically speaking, stock market development is weakly exogenous to output.
[51] See Arestis, Demetriades and Luintel (2001), for example.
[52] Christopoulos and Tsionas (2004), based on panel cointegration tests using ten countries over the period 1970–2000.
[53] For example, Kugler and Nuesser (1998), Levine, Loayza and Beck (2000), Levine and Zervos (1998).
[54] The variables in Kugler and Neusser include deposit and credit business by commercial banks, service charges, commissions related to stocks and bonds, and off-balance-sheet activities, but excluding real estate activities.

face the more extreme sort of principal-agent problems that intermediaries might help mitigate.

The results of this approach so far suggest that the role of the financial sector varies considerably across countries. For example, the financial sector grew faster than the manufacturing sector in most countries, but not in three of them – France, Denmark, and Sweden.[55] In Germany and the United Kingdom, however, financial sector growth was high even when manufacturing growth remained below average. Financial sector expansion spurs growth of the manufacturing sectors most significantly in the United States, Japan, Germany, and Sweden, and to a somewhat lesser extent for most other countries.[56] Whereas models linking financial development and growth typically predict that along the balanced growth path, manufacturing total factor productivity and the financial sector should grow at the same rate, newer evidence runs contrary to that result for some countries.[57] From a statistical standpoint, financial sector activity is shown to cause manufacturing total factor productivity in the United States, Germany, and Australia, but not in other countries. Moreover, the story is a bit more complex than these unidirectional links let on: Manufacturing total productivity also feeds back into financial sector GDP, so it appears that causality may also run from manufacturing total factor productivity to financial sector activity for many countries, including the United States, Germany, France, and Japan. The feedback loop shows up most significantly for Canada, France, Australia, and Finland. In other words, despite sophisticated statistical techniques, it is extremely difficult to determine which event comes first: financial system development or manufacturing growth.[58] Particularly

---

[55] Consistent with the world development report of the World Bank (1989).

[56] More accurately, the financial sector "Granger causes" manufacturing growth. The statistical relationship is strongest for the United States – at least for the post–World War II period.

[57] In other words, a cointegrating relationship usually exists. In Kugler and Nuesser, the null hypothesis of no cointegration between the log of manufacturing GDP and the log of financial sector GDP cannot be rejected.

[58] Levine, Loayza, and Beck (2000) and Beck, Levine, and Loayza (2000), use a dynamic panel methodology proposed in Arellano and Bond (1991) that uses lagged values of the explanatory variables in the regression as instruments. They have a panel of seventy-four countries where they average the data over seven five-year periods between 1961 and 1995. Their studies focus on size measures of financial intermediation. Both studies find that exogenous components of measures of financial intermediation are positively and robustly associated with economic growth and the sources of growth. These estimates depend critically on having adopted the correct model specification, and they may also still suffer from omitted variables problems. In fact, Favarra (2006) recalculates the relationships using the same data as LLB and finds no clear evidence that finance spurs economic growth. Furthermore, the relationship is highly heterogeneous across countries.

due to the feedback process, it is quite likely impossible to make a general statement about whether financial development is an engine of growth or just a sign or symptom of the evolution of the whole economy due to independent factors. In Germany, for example, it appears that the financial sector reacts to the manufacturing sector, where it is then manufacturing productivity that drives economic growth; among the G7, however, U.S. and Japanese financial institutions play an especially proactive role in promoting manufacturing growth.

Far less analysis is available on historical patterns, but the evidence available so far continues to point to highly variable relationships between financial development and economic growth. In the United States, the United Kingdom, Canada, Norway, and Sweden – five countries undergoing industrialization between 1870 and 1929 – financial intermediation leads output, but output does not immediately feed back into finance. Causality seems to run from financial intermediation to output growth and not vice versa, although the relationship is stronger for some countries than for others.[59] More recent studies demonstrate similar relationships for the Dutch Republic (1600–1794), England (1700–1850), the United States (1790–1850), and Japan (1880–1913).[60] Over the very long run – 1850–1997 – robust correlations appear between financial factors and real sector development.[61] Even though considerable uncertainty persists, overall, the evidence leads to the conclusion that real economic growth is at least in part "finance-led."

MORE EVIDENCE FROM HISTORY

Most studies examining the relationship between financial system development and growth limit themselves to the past few decades. For most industrialized countries, and for some undergoing industrialization, political, legal, and financial systems were already in place, whether in fully developed or nascent form, since at least the turn of the twentieth century. For many industrialized countries, particularly the early industrializes – England, Germany, France – legal and financial systems were fully functioning by

---

[59] See Rousseau and Wachtel (1998). In statistical terms, financial intermediation Granger causes real per-capita output in their VAR systems. They find a single cointegrating relationship between per-capita levels of output, money, and intermediary assets as a measure of financial development. They find that output does not Granger cause intermediation. However, the finding of a single cointegration relationship is significant only at the 15% level for Norway and 15% or less for Canada and Sweden, casting some doubts on the robustness of the results.

[60] Rousseau (2003).

[61] Rousseau and Sylla (2003).

the late nineteenth century (in England, this date is even earlier). Therefore to understand how financial system design impacts industrial development and long-run economic growth, we need to consider a much longer horizon where possible to do so. For a considerable number of countries, it is feasible to investigate the history of economic growth in the last 100–150 years, in particular to examine how historical growth rates are able to predict modern growth rates. In this way, we can then isolate events that occurred in the financial and legal systems of these countries more than 100 years ago as predictors of subsequent economic growth.

Cross-Country Evidence

Financial and economic development levels clearly relate to each other in countries that had begun industrialization in the formative pre–World War I era. For the twenty-one countries with the necessary data, simple Spearman tests show a positive correlation (0.47) between the level of GDP per capita in 1880 and the ratio of financial assets to GNP in the same year, and that independence of the series can be rejected at the 10 percent level. Similarly, the level of GDP in 1913 correlates positively (0.49) with the ratio of financial assets to GNP in that year as well; independence is even more confidently rejected (1 percent level), possibly due to the increased number of countries for which data are available. Given the relatively small sample size – from a statistical standpoint – the correlations and lack of independence are notable.

Simple linear regressions of GDP growth per capita from 1880 to 1900 add a bit more complexity to these correlations (Table 8.3) and show some importance of prior accumulation of financial assets in this early period.[62] Even for this rather small set of countries, it appears that levels of financial assets in 1880 relate positively to subsequent growth. The ratio of industry to agriculture in 1880 – a measure of industrial development, as opposed to wealth that could be accumulated from expanding agriculture – also relates significantly to economic growth.[63] In other words, economies that,

---

[62] Due to the small number of countries and time periods for which reliable data are available, it is impossible to use dynamic panel methods to more thoroughly analyze causality. See Musacchio (2008) on long-run effects of legal origins.

[63] Interestingly, the ratio of finance and industry to agriculture relates negatively to growth in this population, after controlling for the level of industrial development. The small sample size (fourteen countries) may weaken the results, but they at least reflect the patterns of all countries that can be considered for such an early period. If the square of real GDP per capita is included in the regression for 1880 with the industry/agriculture, the coefficients lose their significance.

Table 8.3. *Cross-country growth regressions: 1880–1900 and 1900–1913*

	1880–1900			1900–1913	
Log initial real per-capita GDP	0.317** *0.097*	0.551 *0.433*	−0.003 *0.006*	0.235* *0.115*	0.174* *0.100*
Square of log real per-capita GDP 1900	−0.021** *0.006*	−0.036 *0.028*		−0.016* *0.008*	−0.011* *0.007*
Financial Assets/ GNP 1880		0.0001 *0.0001*		−0.0001 *0.0001*	
Financial Assets/ GNP 1900				0.0000 *0.0001*	0.0000 *0.0001*
Ratio of industry/ agriculture employment in base year (1880 or 1900)			0.100* *0.049*		
Ratio of (finance+industry)/ agriculture employment in base year (1880 or 1900)			−0.091* *0.047*		
Number of Observations	13	9	13	15	18
R-squared	0.57	0.48	0.52	0.50	0.23

Note: the dependent variable is percentage growth of per capita real GDP 1880–1900 and 1900–1913. Robust standard errors are in italics. * indicates significance at the 10 percent level and ** indicates significance at the 5 percent level.

Source: Author's original analysis based on GDP data from Maddison (1995) and employment and financial institution assets data from Mitchell (1983 and 1992) and Goldsmith (1969), respectively.

by 1880, had undergone more of the transition from agriculture to industry grew faster overall in the subsequent two decades. The same cannot be said for the first thirteen years of the twentieth century. This period brings in a wider range of countries with a greater variation in levels of financial development and rates of growth. In this period, and for this wider set of countries, the link between financial development and real economic growth weakens and even disappears. Baseline levels of economic advancement become the most important correlate in this era. The relationship is nonlinear, however, because the effect tapers off for the fastest growers.[64]

---

[64] The level of GDP per capita obtains a positive and significant coefficient, whereas the square of the level obtains a negative and significant coefficient. The square of the ratio of financial assets to GNP does not produce significant results.

Countries that had already attained moderately high levels of GDP per capita in 1900 – but not necessarily the richest ones – grew fastest in the years leading up to World War I. This result also holds constant the level of financial development at the start of the period.

One partial solution to the shortage of data is to pool the cross-sections covering the period from 1850 to 1913 (Table 8.4).[65] GDP growth rates remain as the dependent variable, but now it is possible to include a few more explanatory variables. Including the base year level of GDP per capita for each time period reduces the potential for reverse causality from growth to additional finance. This technique cannot completely eliminate the simultaneity problem, but it ensures that all regressors are predetermined and therefore constitute plausible determinants of subsequent growth.[66] In this new specification, logged real GDP still relates positively (and significantly) to growth, and its squared value relates negatively.[67] In this broader context, levels of financial development show little influence on subsequent economic growth rates, and neither do ratios of industrial to agricultural employment.

Naturally, these results do not eliminate the possibility that economic factors also influence financial development. Indeed, financial depth in 1900 does relate very positively to the level of economic development and to the level of industrialization twenty years earlier (Table 8.5). Financial development also grew faster between 1900 and 1913 for countries with relatively high real GDP per capita in 1900.[68] It is interesting to note, however, that financial assets actually grew more slowly relative to GNP between 1900 and 1913 for countries that had comparatively high levels of GDP per capita in 1880. These results highlight the tapering-off effect, for the wealthiest countries in 1880 were generally the earliest industrializers. They produced

---

[65] Hausman tests indicate that fixed effects is the more efficient model (compared to random effects) at the 1 percent confidence level. Given the small number of countries, and the missing observations for certain variables in some years, it is not possible to implement dynamic panel estimators. Extending the time period would add more statistical power but would obviously prevent us from drawing inferences solely about the industrialization period.

[66] As Rousseau and Sylla (2003) note.

[67] Using a simple regression of growth rates on the log level of real GDP per capita and real GDP per capita squared, coefficients are significant at the 10 percent level. Adding the square of the ratio of financial assets to GNP still does not make its level significant on its own. Universality in 1913 is statistically insignificant when included along with legal structure.

[68] In the first model, financial assets as a ratio of GDP in 1900 are regressed on real GDP in 1880. The growth rate of the financial asset ratio from 1900 to 1913 is then regressed on various GDP levels and growth rates. The regressions use Huber/biweight limited influence estimation.

Table 8.4. *Pooled cross-country growth regressions, 1850–1913*

	Dependent Variable: % Growth of Per-Capita GDP				
	(1)	(2)	(3)	(4)	(5)
Log of initial real GDP	0.335**	0.178*	0.380**	0.296**	0.258*
per capita	0.055	0.088	0.100	0.095	0.110
Log of initial real GDP	−0.022**	−0.025**	−0.025**	−0.020**	−0.017*
per capita squared	0.004	0.007	0.007	0.006	0.007
Financial assets to GNP		0.000	0.0001	0.0001	0.000
		0.000	0.0001	0.0001	0.0001
Legal structure (civil or			0.013**		
common law)			0.004		
Universality in 1913				−0.01*	
				0.004	
Structure index for 1990s					0.005
					0.003
R-squared	0.86	0.89	0.93	0.92	0.91
(Number of Observations)	60	31	31	31	31

Note: The table reports coefficients from pooled regressions with standard errors in italics. The dependent variable is the growth rate of real per-capita GDP. * and ** denote statistical significance at the 10 and 5 percent levels, respectively.

Source: Author's original analysis based on GDP data from Maddison (1995) and employment and financial institution assets data from Mitchell (1983) and Goldsmith (1969), respectively. Structure index for 1990s comes from Beck, Demirguc-Kunt, and Levine (2000).

among the slowest growth of financial institution assets between 1900 and 1913, relative to GNP, because they were already well along the path to industrialization by that late in the period.

Time-Series Evidence for Two Universal Banking Countries: Germany and Italy

The cross-country or small-panel results do help in determining the relationship between growth and financial development, but the relatively small number of sufficiently developed countries at the time limits the explanatory power of these exercises. Moreover, simple cross-country or even small-panel studies cannot explain the large variation in finance and growth that may be observed within countries over longer periods. Time-series evidence on the relationship between economic growth and financial development can help. In addition, the literature so far has done little to assess the role of particular segments of the financial system. Replacing total financial assets with the volume of commercial banking assets allows some determination of the relationship between banking sector development specifically and real

Table 8.5. *Economic factors in financial development, 1900–1913*

	FI/GNP 1900		FI/GNP growth (1900–1913)		
	(1)	(2)	(1)	(2)	(3)
Real GDP per	37.7*		–0.26*		
capita 1880	15.3		0.09		
Industrial development		0.07*			
1880		0.04			
Industrial development		–0.00002			
1880 squared		0.00002			
Real GDP per				0.23*	
capita 1900				0.11	
Real GDP per capita					13.0
growth 1880–1900					8.7
Constant	–204.9*	52.5*	2.2*	2.1*	–0.03
	115.2	18.9	0.65	0.85	0.13
P(F)	0.03	0.22	0.01	0.04	0.17
Number of Observations	19	19	18	18	10

Note: Regressions use Huber/biweight limited influence estimation; standard errors are in italics.
* denotes statistical significance at the 10 percent level.
Source: Author's original analysis based on GDP data from Maddison (1995) and Mitchell (1983).

economic growth. If certain types of financial systems promote faster growth than others, then the coefficients of financial development should be larger for countries with that sort of system. The necessary data are available for two countries – Germany and Italy – and the results are illuminating.

By traditional accounts, universal banking systems contributed significantly to industrial development in Germany and Italy; whether the banks played an unusually major role by virtue of their organization as universal banks is less certain. The goal, then, is to quantify the links between financial and real growth and determine how it is connected with the onset of universal banking. Chapters 3 and 4 demonstrated little impact of the Italian and German universal banks on the behavior and outcomes of industrial firms in those countries. But the fact that the universal banks hardly influenced industrial firms overall does not imply that the rapid growth of the universal banking sector had no effect on the progress of industrialization. It could well be that financial development spurred real sectors of the economy, and that the universal banks represented such a catalyst for industrial growth.[69]

---

[69] Similar analysis could reveal interesting results for the less-clearly universal systems, but additional data must be gathered to ensure comparability. Such work is underway.

In the context of the German industrialization, the time-series methodology set out earlier in this chapter demonstrates little in the way of a finance-growth nexus. Bank capital mobilization likely requires several years to produce results in the real economy, and contemporaneous relationships therefore probably represent the simultaneous effects of other influences on both bank assets and economic growth. The expansion of the German financial system is impressive, yet it did not clearly precede that of the real economy overall (Table 8.6). Contemporaneous correlations between GNP per capita and financial assets as a share of GNP are high (97 percent), but no systematic relationship emerges between lagged and current values of these variables, regardless of direction of causation. Regressions of NNP per capita, using both logged levels and annual growth rates, indicate statistically insignificant effects of bank liabilities (either in logged levels or logged levels as a share of GNP) out to five lags.[70] The relationship is especially weak using the Cochrane-Orcutt or Hildreth-Lu estimators to correct for serially correlated errors. Hypothetically, it is more plausible that the effects would appear after two or more years; the first lag may simply continue to reflect contemporaneous influences. The fifth lag of bank assets – a more plausible period of time for financial institutions to make an impact on the economy – does not relate significantly to growth.[71] The permanent effect of bank assets, measured as the sum of the estimated coefficients, is also quite small (0.19).

Statistical evidence for Italy is a bit sparse, but at least provisional patterns emerge. Because the activities of banks require time to produce results in the real economy, contemporaneous relationships probably represent the simultaneous effects of other influences on both bank assets and economic growth. The expansion of the Italian financial system is impressive; however, it did not clearly precede that of the economy overall.[72] Contemporaneous correlations between GNP per capita and financial assets as a share of GNP are high (88 percent). Regressions of NNP per capita, using logged levels, first differences, and annual growth rates, indicate statistically insignificant effects of bank liabilities at most estimated lags

---

[70] The table reports several different estimators and lag structures, but none yields robust positive relationships between GNP growth and financial assets.

[71] The coefficient estimate is positive, but the significance of the estimate is very weak (t-statistic of 0.77).

[72] Using national aggregates for output per capita disguises the significant regional variation in levels of industrial development. Although it is obvious that levels of the ratio would be higher in more developed areas compared to less-developed regions, it is not clear that growth rates would show a corresponding gap.

Table 8.6. *Estimated annual growth rates, Germany and Italy, 1895–1913*

Variable	Units of underlying variable	Germany	Italy
Capital formation	millions constant marks (Germany) or lire (Italy)	0.028** 4.660 [0.535]	0.071** 6.622 [0.704]
Gross national product (Italy) or Net national product (Germany)	millions constant marks (Germany) or lire (Italy)	0.025** 23.646 [0.969]	0.029** 23.661 [0.969]
Capital formation per capita	millions constant marks (Germany) or lire (Italy)/ thousands at mid-year	0.014* 2.341 [0.199]	0.065** 5.876 [0.651]
Gross national product (Italy) or Net national product (Germany) per capita	millions constant marks (Germany) or lire (Italy)/ thousands at mid-year	0.011** 10.539 [0.859]	0.021** 17.343 [0.943]
Population	thousands at mid-year	0.014** 121.359 [0.999]	0.008** 57.520 [0.995]
Price index	wholesale prices, 1913=100	0.017** 9.094 [0.819]	0.013** 6.529 [0.698]
Assets of all commercial banks	millions constant	0.065** 26.636 [0.975]	0.065** 11.963 [0.888]
Assets of largest commercial banks	millions constant	0.066** 20.545 [0.959]	0.151** 15.929 [0.934]
Assets of all commercial banks/GNP (Italy) or NNP (Germany)		0.035** 10.781 [0.865]	0.036** 7.252 [0.741]
Assets of all commercial banks/capital formation		0.037** 5.979 [0.659]	−0.006 −0.524 [−0.042]
Assets of all commercial banks per capita	millions constant/ thousands at mid-year	0.051** 21.474 [0.962]	0.058** 10.678 [0.863]

Notes: Growth rates are estimated as the coefficient in an OLS regression of the log of the given variable on a constant and a time trend. T-statistics are in italics below coefficient estimates, and R-squared statistics are given in brackets. ** and * indicate statistical significance at better than 1 and 5 percent, respectively.

Sources: Author's analysis based on data from Mitchell (1992) (GNP, NNP, population), Deutsche Bundesbank (1976) (German bank figures), Credito Italiano (1912) and Cotula et al. (1996) (Italian bank figures).

(Table 8.7).[73] Significant positive effects of bank assets on GNP per capita emerge only at the first lag and only using logged levels. As in the German case, it is more plausible theoretically that the effects would appear after two or more years, and the fifth lag of bank assets seems more plausible. In contrast to the German case, Italian bank assets do seem to provide some impetus to real growth.[74] The permanent effect of bank assets, measured as the sum of the estimated coefficients, is also greater in Italy (0.3) than in Germany. The statistical relationship is relatively weak, however, so there is not an overwhelmingly clear causal effect.[75]

The findings for Italy and Germany underscore a difficulty in the traditional story of continental European industrialization, and possibly other countries with similar financial systems and industrialization experiences, namely the late appearance of large-scale, universal banking relative to the growth of industry. The problem is twofold: that the biggest growth of the banking sectors followed several bursts of industrial growth, and that, in any case, a consistent causal relationship between real and bank-related financial growth is difficult to establish. The problem is more severe for Germany, where industrialization bloomed a bit earlier, than it is for Italy. Thus, the evidence casts some doubt on the traditional presumption that the universal banks played the most significant role in spurring real GNP growth by linking private savers with productive uses for their funds and thereby mobilizing large sums of financial capital.[76] To be sure, financial systems provide a vital input for industrial development, but its importance is difficult to measure or predict. In fact, financial institutions' influence appears to be largely one of quality rather than quantity. While these findings

---

[73] Economists have debated the causal relationship between financial and real economic growth for decades, and the most recent research seems to favor the financial-to-real direction of causation. This issue is beyond the scope of the current investigation. See the review of recent work by Ross Levine (1998) and the further details in Fohlin (1999a). One might also test for a relationship between the two series using cointegration tests, although these procedures have little power in the relatively small samples used here. Not surprisingly, in the current series (1895–1913) augmented Dickey-Fuller tests all fail to reject the null hypotheses on the existence of a unit root. Similarly, the null hypothesis that bank assets and real output per capita are not cointegrated cannot be rejected. In particular, all test statistics fall far below 5.91 – the critical value of the augmented Dickey-Fuller statistic at the 10 percent significance level with the minimum twenty-five observations.

[74] The fifth lag of banking assets has a positive coefficient estimate, and the significance of the estimate is moderately strong (t-statistic of 1.82).

[75] Cochrane-Orcutt or Hildreth-Lu estimators correct for serially correlated errors, and those results are particularly weak.

[76] See Burhop (2006) finds that joint-stock banks propelled growth from 1850 to 1880 but not thereafter.

Table 8.7. *Bank assets and economic growth, 1895–1913*

Variable	Germany		Italy	
	differences	logged levels	differences	logged levels
(Bank assets/GNP)$_{t-1}$	−0.00	0.06	0.01	0.24**
	0.01	*0.40*	*0.01*	*3.90*
(Bank assets/GNP)$_{t-2}$	−0.01	−0.01	−0.01**	−0.12
	0.01	*−0.08*	*0.01*	*−1.85*
(Bank assets/GNP)$_{t-3}$	−0.01	0.11	0.00	0.08
	0.01	*0.67*	*0.01*	*1.29*
(Bank assets/GNP)$_{t-4}$	−0.02	−0.09	0.00	0.02
	0.01	*−0.55*	*0.00*	*0.37*
(Bank assets/GNP)$_{t-5}$	–	0.12	–	0.08
		0.77		*1.82*
Intercept	0.00*	−4.08**	0.00**	−4.32**
	0.00	*−31.19*	*0.00*	*−23.13*
Adjusted R^2	0.06	−0.09	0.31	0.70
P-value of F-statistic	0.37	0.58	0.12	0.01
Durbin-Watson statistic	2.18	2.02	1.99	2.06
Rho		0.50		0.60
N	14	13	14	13
Correlation (real GNP/ cap, bank assets/GNP)	0.93		0.88	

Notes: The dependent variable is real NNP (Germany) or GNP (Italy) per thousand capita, using logged levels or first differences. Independent variables are also measured in logged levels or first differences, according to column headings. Bank assets are divided by NNP for Germany. Logged level regressions use a Hildreth-Lu estimator to correct for serially correlated residuals, and reported DW statistics for these regressions are corrected. T-statistics are in italics below coefficient estimates, and R-squared statistics are given in brackets. * and ** indicate statistical significance at better than 5 percent and 1 percent (two-sided tests), respectively.

Sources: Author's analysis based on data from Mitchell (1992) (GNP, NNP), Maddison (1995) (population), Credito Italiano (1912) (Italian bank figures), Deutsche Bundesbank (1976) (German bank figures).

may seem disappointing, the upshot of the results is actually encouraging: Qualitative factors may contribute even more to industrial growth than do quantitative ones, and industry can thrive even with modest facilities to mobilize finance.

CONCLUSION

Throughout this chapter, the discussion has focused on types of financial systems, development of financial systems, and the impact of both on real economic growth. The preceding analysis considers and rejects several hypotheses for the causes of growth. In particular, neither various attributes of financial systems – bank-based versus market-based, branching versus unit, universal versus specialized – nor legal traditions in themselves can explain the different experiences across countries over the last 100 years or more. In fact, although the set of industrialized (and industrializing) countries at the end of the nineteenth century exhibited a diversity of overall financial system types, rates of financial development, and legal orientation, for most of the twentieth century, long-run growth rates turn out to be remarkably similar. One central conclusion to draw from this study, therefore, is that the development of a financial system must surely be important for economic growth, but the type of financial system that develops is far less so. This conclusion runs counter to received wisdom about the history of financial and economic development and to debates over the advantages and disadvantages of various types of systems.

The chapter results suggest further that whatever "causes" economic growth must have occurred a long time ago, at least in this set of countries that had established economic, financial, and political systems prior to World War I. Moreover, many of the factors underscored in current research (regulation, branch banking, universality, market orientation) cannot constitute singular causes of growth, as they did not even precede the earliest industrialization experiences. Likewise, legal factors typically fell into place at varying points in the nineteenth century, some earlier than others, and therefore cannot explain the growth experience of the earliest industrial period. The findings here also indicate that past economic development plays some role in financial growth. The wealthier among these pre–World War I industrial nations tended to deepen their financial base more than those less well off. In other words, financial and real development went hand in hand in that period of rapid industrial growth.

The historical evidence in this chapter therefore puts modern-period research into a new perspective, making it much less surprising that economic growth in the past few decades hinges little, if at all, on financial and legal system design. It also bolsters the idea of a feedback mechanism by which financial and real growth spur each other on.

If none of these legal or financial system design theories can explain why some countries grew faster than others, what is the reason for different growth outcomes? The important factor may lie in the fact of having a financial system that is strong and legally protected, regardless of the form of that system. For financial systems, it seems most important that there be some means for allocating investment, whether through banks or other intermediaries or through stock markets, however thin, and that this investment apparatus is supported with a legal structure powerful enough to enforce contracts and ensure that debts are repaid in due course. Undoubtedly other more transient or idiosyncratic factors, such as political climates and regulatory regimes, have made an impact at least in the short run. But over the long run, having a system that works is more important than having a particular type of system.

9

What Is Important for Long-Term Growth?

This book has brought together a wide array of evidence – from the level of individual firms to the broadest possible international comparison – to offer a new synthesis of financial system design and industrial development. What causes financial systems to develop as they do, and how does the pattern of financial development influence real economic outcomes? Both parts of the book shed new light on these questions.

By taking a close look at the emergence of corporate finance systems in five economies, the first set of chapters provides new insights into the details of financial systems. Each of the countries examined in these chapters began the process of large-scale industrialization at some point in the nineteenth century – early on in the case of the United Kingdom, mid-century for Germany and the United States, and toward the end for Italy and Japan. The microeconomic view that predominates in these four chapters permits a fine-grained portrait of the range of political, economic, legal, and even cultural factors that have played into these five financial systems.

By the end of the nineteenth century, all of these countries created complex financial systems, with differentiated institutions serving the needs of most anyone in need of financial intermediation: from savings banks and credit cooperatives to commercial banks and trust companies; from merchant and investment banks to universal banks to investment banking arms of commercial banks; and from specialized commodity markets to national and international financial markets (Chapter 2). The design of these systems varied across the five countries, but all gathered resources from investors, grew rapidly, and mobilized enormous amounts of capital toward productive ends. All of these countries also created a national-level financial regulatory system, with central banks providing some degree of lender-of-last resort facilities and – for better or for worse – monetary policy.

Despite their considerable differences in culture, society, legal systems, and political processes, all five countries created well-functioning systems for corporate finance by the late nineteenth century. Mostly in the 1850s to 1870s, these countries (and many others not studied here) formalized, standardized, and liberalized incorporation and liability systems. Within a decade or two thereafter, businesses and entrepreneurs in all five countries turned to corporations to grow and diversify, financing an unprecedented scale of operations. The acceleration of incorporation in most places during the last years of the nineteenth and into the twentieth century spurred rapid advancement in the corporate financial sector and of the securities markets.

For businesses in this period, banks often served as one of the most important sources of outside capital, whether for short-term trade credit or longer-term investment finance. Thus, industrial development usually proceeded hand in hand with the growth of commercial banking. As these five economies evolved and industrialized, the organization of the banking industries, and of the banks themselves, changed in step (Chapter 3). The largest banks grew larger, and densely networked, nationwide banks almost always emerged. Only in the United States did regulatory restrictions prevent this natural progression, and even there, a few banking giants appeared in the important trading centers.

The five countries did create disparate types of commercial banks, in some cases becoming true universal banks, in other cases not. In at least two cases, the distinction is hard to see: Japanese commercial banks are usually considered universal at this time, but they underwrote very little equity. The U.S. banks – at least some of them – remained specialized on the surface but participated actively in industrial securities (particularly equity) through affiliates or other indirect means. The British banks used deposit funding by far the most out of these five countries, but deposit usage does not otherwise vary at all by the universality of banking services. Indeed, in the other four countries, deposits began as a minor part of banks' funding sources in the mid-nineteenth century; but by World War I (and even more thereafter), deposits took on the leading role. For all five countries, it was World War I that brought the most marked increase in the deposit business.

For all the variation in these banking systems, bank behavior was more similar than different, particularly among the European and Japanese banks. The limits on branching clearly influenced the financial structure of American banks, mostly because of the greater idiosyncratic risks they faced. The banks in these countries also profited at similar rates, despite all their differences. Profitability (ROA) declined almost monotonically over the late nineteenth and early twentieth centuries, falling from the 2-to-3 percent range in the 1880s and early 1890s to around 1 percent or below in the early 1920s. Most notably, bank profitability did not differ systematically with banking system type.

If commercial banks differed in their financial structure and scope of activities, they varied even more in their responses to changing needs in industrial finance and their engagement in corporate governance. The new system of corporate firms that emerged over the last half of the nineteenth century began to loosen the ties between families and the firms they started. Where management of company business grew more distinct from the ultimate ownership of the revenue streams created by the company, an increasing need for new modes of corporate governance emerged. The increasing use of securities exchanges to trade the claims of corporations often meant the increased dispersion of ownership among these firms; the process created a new need for oversight mechanisms to protect the interests of shareholders, particularly those with small stakes and limited voting power. Each of the countries studied here developed its own version of corporate governance, and banks played different roles in each (Chapter 4). Direct stakeholding in nonfinancial firms over extended periods seemingly arose in the United States, but mainly through private investment banks or sometimes commercial banks' securities affiliates. The largest Italian universal bank took sometimes substantial equity stakes, but the German and Japanese universal banks did far less of it. In other words, "relationship banking" in this era did not typically involve direct equity ownership. Moreover, the little extant evidence on proxy voting suggests that the German banks held an unusual, if not unique, position in their apparently avid use of proxy votes stemming from the deposit of customers' shares and the virtually automatic transfer of voting rights.

Relationships via interlocking directorates did become widespread in some countries, but only quite late in the industrialization process, as corporate boards became increasingly formalized and prevalent. Bankers appeared on boards in Germany, Italy, and the United States, but often via multiple supervisory board mandates, not only by the positioning of bank directors on company supervisory boards. In Japan and the United Kingdom, by contrast, bankers took board positions only occasionally. Overall, it proves difficult to divide the five countries into only two categories of corporate governance practices, particularly not ones that coincide with banking types.

Given the variety of corporate governance practices, it comes as no surprise that no significant or definitive role for formal bank relationships appears in the countries examined here (Chapter 5). Even where banks played the greatest role in formal governance, they exerted little measurable influence on the behavior and performance of industrial firms. In both cases, important links appear among stock markets, ownership dispersion, and bank relationships – connections that suggest fundamental revisions to common views of bank relationships and their role in the promotion of industrial development. In all of these cases, capital market finance played a significant, even critical, role in financing corporate firms in the later stages of industrialization. In the European and Japanese cases, bank finance entered to a lesser extent than did internal sources. In the United States, by contrast, debt played a relatively large role. The difference may have stemmed from the extreme level of concentration in the U.S. investment banking industry – the apparent domination of a core group of individuals over access to equity capital – and possibly from inefficient and poorly integrated capital markets

Overall, then, the comparison of these five banking systems dramatizes the wide variety in systems that arose in countries that were, in economic terms, more similar to one another than they were to many other, far less developed economies of the time. Developing their own approaches to the problem of capital mobilization, they created banking institutions that on the surface looked different from each other but that performed, in broad terms, similar functions and did so in a similar manner. The American experience – particularly in contrast to the German and British ones – surely suggests that the factors that shape corporate finance and governance systems are myriad and complex, making it difficult to boil the longer history down to a very tidy story about a small number of types or categories of financial systems. Herein lies the difficulty of such approaches as the "varieties of capitalism" or the "law and finance" literatures, with the focus on binary outcomes.

This problem of categorizing systems creates the starting point for the second part of the book. Having studied the five exemplar systems at a detailed, micro level, the analysis widens the lens to seek out general patterns of financial development among the full set of early industrial economies over the past 150 years. The first of these chapters (Chapter 6) examines the design and development of national financial systems. This broad-scale analysis underscores the results of the country studies and the difficulty of identifying particular countries with well-defined, overarching categories of financial system: Most systems mixed various characteristics, fitting poorly into narrow categories.

Banking systems turn out to be particularly difficult to pin down into categories, because numerous institutions emerged in any given country, often providing similar services in different ways to varying clientele. For example, in many economies undergoing industrialization in the mid- to late nineteenth century, a small number of large-scale universal banks appeared simultaneously with a much larger number of more specialized banks. Even in the classic universal-banking countries, such as Germany, a variety of more narrowly defined financial institutions operated alongside the big banks. Likewise, nationwide branching appeared and flourished in virtually all countries outside of the United States between the 1890s and World War I, regardless of the type or structure of commercial banks. Even in the highly-restrictive U.S. regulatory environment, a few states – notably California – supported branch banking prior to World War I. In some countries, multiple branching systems coexisted, serving different segments of the population and industry. Indeed, there has been no link between the design of financial institutions and the extent of branching, which emerged as a tool for geographic and financial diversification as well as a mode of competition.

Relationship-banking practices do relate a bit more systematically with financial system types. It is more common to see banks taking corporate ownership and control rights in universal systems, and those relationship practices are less evident in places like the United States and United Kingdom, where specialized banking has traditionally prevailed. Still, the analysis highlights cases in which universal banks pursued limited relationships as well as cases in which specialized banks maintained active relationships with industrial firms. The two institutional features clearly existed separately from each other – as they did in Japan at different points in its history, and as they continue to do as well today.

Of particular interest for today's policy makers, the long-term view of financial system development reveals that the link between universal banking and limited securities markets, to the extent that it even exists currently, is a post–World War II phenomenon. Most industrialized economies maintained important securities markets in the prewar era, and some of the largest and most active markets of the time were embedded in at least partially universal systems, such as France and Germany.

Banking structure exhibits considerable path-dependency, or path reversion, over the past 100 to 150 years. Countries with universal banks in the 1850s or 1870s kept those banking structures up to the Great Depression and – even if they regulated them away for a few decades in the middle of the twentieth century – almost all have universal banking institutions today. As the twenty-first century progresses, financial conglomerates have emerged in most industrialized countries. Combining an array of products and services under one umbrella organization, conglomerates look like universal banks on a larger scale. This increased scale, however, tends to disintegrate the connections among the units in the organization, undermining the scope economies that constituted the key theoretical benefit of universality. Thus, formerly specialized systems are becoming ostensibly more universal, while traditional universal banks are less classically so.

This observation brings us to the next problem: examining what sorts of institutional factors – economic, political, and legal – determine, or at least influence, what type of financial systems emerge and how they evolve over time. To answer this question, the analysis (Chapter 7) worked to identify the factors that led some countries to take on certain sets of institutions while others turned to a different type of system. Naturally, after arguing that financial systems are not easily categorized, this quantitative exploration requires us to temporarily suspend that skepticism and implement as clean a measure of system structure as possible. The study uncovers several patterns in the development of financial systems and helps disentangle the various forces involved. Economic factors have the greatest and most consistent power in predicting the type of banking system that subsequently developed among the pre–World War I industrial nations; it also factors into the strength of financial system development. In particular, moderately industrialized countries of the time depended more on financial institutions to mobilize capital than did the most and least advanced economies.

Whether these tests of financial system development address the so-called Gerschenkron hypothesis is open to debate, but the results do seem supportive of his general idea that the timing of industrialization influences the nature of financial institutions that develop. At the same time, however, the "economic backwardness" line of reasoning cannot explain the emergence of very broad and active securities markets within such differing systems as England, France, Germany, and the United States in the late nineteenth and early twentieth centuries. In this area of the financial system, independent of financial institution typology, the demand for financial capital to fund large-scale projects, and the driving force of investors and entrepreneurs on the two sides of that equation dictated the liberalization of incorporation. Once the free-incorporation dam broke, and investors could use securitization to diversify away the idiosyncratic risk of these projects, the equilibrating power of globalization propelled the development of markets around the world, especially for investments that could be understood internationally, such as infrastructure and standardized or commodity-like products. In this gilded age, liberal thinking on markets prevailed sufficiently broadly that markets developed across the political spectrum.

Political systems do partially relate over the long term to further market development. For example, levels of state centralization in the nineteenth century relate strongly to measures of present-day market orientation – itself a path-dependent process. At the same time, quantifiable political factors, such as government centralization, provide very little power in explaining banking system design or overall growth of financial assets in the economy. Two related facts make it difficult to identify political determinants of financial development. First, national political characteristics vary a great deal across countries and over time. Second, political forces that seem to influence financial development do not relate uniformly with the overall political system in place. Thus, when we try to categorize political systems, as in the "varieties of capitalism" literature, we cannot find a political system type that consistently impedes or encourages broader financial development.

In contrast to political centralization, which is admittedly hard to measure accurately, legal traditions correlate highly with both market orientation and banking institution design (but not with government centralization). Analytically, it is convenient that legal systems fall more easily into well-defined categories, and that countries tend to stick to one legal type permanently, because there is little concern that a country might be miscategorized. It seems highly likely, however, that legal system categories coincide with other important influences on financial systems, that countries adopt from colonizing powers, adapt from neighbors or trading partners, or that evolve out of innate cultural and social beliefs. So, legal tradition itself may exert little influence on the financial system and does not provide a useful lever of financial development. Once again, the devil is in the details: We need to identify specific laws and regulations that support financial development in the most successful cases and then assess whether they can be imported regardless of legal tradition.

The analysis of financial system development reveals the difficulty of pinpointing simple causal explanations. Instead, economic, political, and legal factors most likely work together, and some combination of the rather distinct theories is required to explain the shape of financial systems at their origins and their trajectories over the past century and a half. Undoubtedly, as the case study chapters very clearly illustrate, idiosyncratic factors – particular regulations, specific events, unique mixes of natural resources and human capital, perhaps even national culture – also matter for explaining the emergence and persistence of systematic characteristics.

These findings lead next to the question of consequences: Do differences in financial system design impact real economic growth? The short answer, delivered in Chapter 8, is "no." Neither various attributes of financial systems – bank-based versus market-based, branching versus unit, universal versus specialized – nor legal traditions in themselves can explain the different experiences across countries over the last 150 years or more. In fact, although the set of industrialized (and industrializing) countries at the end of the nineteenth century exhibited a diversity of overall financial system types, rates of financial development, and legal orientation, for most of the twentieth century, long-run growth rates turn out to be remarkably similar. This conclusion runs counter to received wisdom about the history of financial and economic development and to debates over the advantages and disadvantages of various types of systems.

The findings here also indicate that past economic development plays some role in financial growth. The wealthier among these pre–World War I industrial nations tended to deepen their financial base more than those less well off. In other words, financial and real development went hand in hand in that period of rapid industrial growth. The results thereby bolster the idea of a feedback mechanism by which financial and real growth spur each other on.

If none of these legal or financial system design theories can explain why some countries grew faster than others, what is the reason for different growth outcomes? The important factor may lay in the fact of having a financial system that is strong and legally protected, regardless of the form of that system. One central conclusion to draw from this study, therefore, is that the development of a financial system must surely be important for economic growth, but the type of financial system that develops is far less so.

As promised in the introductory chapter, these results yield three key conclusions about financial development and growth. First, history matters – it influences future institutions for a long time – but it does so in idiosyncratic fashion. Second, financial development and economic growth work in a feedback mechanism that provides mutual reinforcement, at least when the system works well. Finally, there is no one-size-fits-all financial system that will ensure that a country reaches the optimal growth path.

These conclusions cut both ways. On the one hand, we cannot give a set prescription for increasing growth rates by setting up specific kinds of institutions. But the good news is that we do not need to: Allowing the financial system to evolve in response to emergent needs, resisting the urge to hinder capital markets while safeguarding systemic stability, and supporting financial development with legal protections for investors is the best a national financial policy can hope to do.

References

Acemoglu, D. and S. Johnson (2005) "Unbundling Institutions," *Journal of Political Economy*, Vol. 113, No. 5: 949–995.

Acemoglu, D., S. Johnson, and J. Robinson (2004) "Institutions as the Fundamental Cause of Long Run Growth," NBER working paper 10481.

Aldcroft, Derek H. (1964) "The Entrepreneur and the British Economy, 1870–1914," *Economic History Review*, Vol. 17, No. 1: 113–114.

Allen, F. (1992) "Stock Markets and Resource Allocation," in *Capital Markets and Financial Intermediation* (81–108), eds. C. Mayer and X. Vives. Cambridge: Cambridge University Press.

Allen, Franklin and Douglas Gale (2000) *Comparing Financial Systems*. Cambridge, MA: MIT Press.

Amatori, F. and Andrea Colli (2007) "European Corporations: Ownership, Governance, Strategies and Structures. A Review of Five Countries: United Kingdom, Germany, France, Italy and Spain," in *The European Enterprise. Historical Investigation into a Future Species*, ed. Harm Schroeter, Springer Verlag.

Anan'ich, Boris (1999) "State Power and Finance in Russia, 1802–1917: The Credit Office of the Finance Ministry and Governmental Control Over Credit Institutions," in *The State, the Financial System and Economic Modernization* (210–223), eds. Richard Sylla, Richard Tilly, and Gabriel Tortella. Cambridge: Cambridge University Press.

Anderson, B. L. and P. L. Cottrell (1974) *Money and Banking in England: The Development of the Banking System, 1694–1914*. Newton Abbot: David & Charles.

Ang, James (2008) "A Survey of Recent Developments in the Literature of Finance and Growth," *Journal of Economic Surveys*, Vol. 22, No. 3: 536–576.

Aoki, Masahiko (1988) *Information, Incentives, and Bargaining in the Japanese Economy*. New York: Cambridge University Press.

——— (1994) "Monitoring Characteristics of the Main Bank System: An Analytical and Developmental View," in *The Japanese Main Bank System: Its Relevancy for Developing and Transforming Economies*, eds. Aoki, Masahiko and Hugh Patrick. New York: Oxford University Press.

Arellano, M. and S. Bond (1991) "Some Tests of the Specification for Panel Data: Monte Carlo Evidence and an Application to Employment Equations," *Review of Economic Studies*, Vol. 58, No. 2: 277–297.

References

Arestis, Philip, Panicos O. Demetriades, and Kul B. Luintel (2001) "Financial Development and Economic Growth: The Role of Stock Markets," *Journal of Money, Credit and Banking*, Vol. 33, No. 1: 16–41.

Auerbach, W. (1969) *Das Actienwesen*. Frankfurt: Ferdinand Keip Verlag.

Augello, Massimo M. and Marco E. L. Guidi (2002) "La scienza economica in Parlamento 1861–1922," *Franco Angeli Editore*: 317–330.

Bagehot, Walter (1873) *Lombard Street: A Description of the Money Market*. London: Henry S. King and Co.

Baia Curioni, Stefano (1995) "Regolazione e Competizione. Storia del mercato azionario in Italia (1808–1938)," *il Mulino*, Bologna.

Baliga, S. and B. Polak (2004) "The Emergence and Persistence of the Anglo-Saxon and German Financial Systems," *Review of Financial Studies*, Vol. 17, No. 1: 129–163.

Bank of Japan (1966) "Meiji ikoh honpou shuyo keizai tokei," *Hundred-Year Statistics of the Japanese Economy: Statistics Department*. The Bank of Japan (July).

Barnett, George E. (1911) *State Banks and Trust Companies since the Passage of the National-Bank Act*. Washington: Government Printing Office.

Barone, G. (1972) "Sviluppo Capitalistico e Politica Finanziaria in Italia," *Studi Storici* a13: 568–599.

Barro, Robert J. (1991) "Economic Growth in a Cross Section of Countries," *The Quarterly Journal of Economics*, Vol. 106, No. 2: 407–443.

Baskin, J. (1988) "The Development of Corporate Financial Markets in Britain and the United States, 1600–1914: Overcoming Asymmetric Information," *Business History Review*, Vol. 62, No. 2: 199–237.

Baskin, J. and P. J. Miranti, Jr. (1997) *A History of Corporate Finance*. New York: Cambridge University Press.

Bava, U. (1926) *I quattro maggiori istituti italiani di credito*. Doctoral Dissertation, Université de Lausanne. Genova: Editrice Soc. An. Valugani & C.

Becht, Marco, Patrick Bolton, and Alisa Röell (2002) "Corporate Governance and Control," NBER Working Paper No. 9371.

Becht, Marco and J. Bradford DeLong (2005) "Why Has There Been So Little Block Holding in America?" in *A History of Corporate Governance around the World: Family Business Groups to Professional Managers* (NBER series) (613–666), ed. R. Morck. Chicago: University of Chicago Press.

Beck, Thorsten (2008) "The Econometrics of Finance and Growth," Policy Research Working Paper Series, Paper 4608, The World Bank, April 1.

Beck, T., A. Demirguc-Kunt, L. Laeven, and R. Levine (2004) "Finance, Firm Size, and Growth," NBER Working Paper No. 10983, December.

Beck, Thorsten, Asli Demirgüç-Kunt, and Ross Levine (2000) "A New Database on Financial Development and Structure," *World Bank Economic Review*, Vol. 14: 597–605.

Beck, T., R. Levine, and N. Loayza (2000) "Financial Intermediation and Growth: Causality and Causes" *Journal of Monetary Economics*, Vol. 46, No. 1: 31–77.

Beck, Thorsten and Ross Levine (2002) "Industry Growth and Capital Allocation: Does Having a Market- or Bank-Based System Matter?" *Journal of Financial Economics*, Vol. 64, No. 2: 147–180.

Berkowitz, D., K. Pistor, and J. F. Richard (2003) "Economic Development, Legality and the Transplant Effect," *European Economic Review*, Vol. 47, No. 1: 165–195.

Besley, T. and T. Persson (2009) "Repression or Civil War?" *American Economic Review*, Vol. 99, No. 2: 292–297.

Bhide, A. (1993) "The Hidden Costs of Stock Market Liquidity," *Journal of Financial Economics*, Vol. 34: 31–51.

Board of Governors of the Federal Reserve System (1959) *All Bank Statistics: United States 1896–1955*. Washington, DC: Library of Congress.

Bodenhorn, Howard (2000) *A History of Banking in Antebellum America: Financial Markets and Economic Development in an Era of Nation-Building*. New York: Cambridge University Press.

(2003) *State Banking in Early America: A New Economic History*. New York: Oxford University Press.

Boot, A. W. A. and A. V. Thakor (1997a) "Banking Scope and Financial Innovation," *The Review of Financial Studies*, Vol. 10, No. 4: 1099–1131.

(1997b) "Financial System Architecture," *The Review of Financial Studies*, Vol. 10, No. 3: 693–733.

Boot, A., A. V. Thakor, and G. Udell (1991) "Credible Commitments, Contract Enforcement Problems and Banks: Intermediation as Credibility Assurance," *Journal of Banking and Finance*, Vol. 15, No. 3: 605–632.

Borchardt, K. (1963) "Zur Frage des Kapitalmangels in der Ersten Hälfte des 19. Jahrhunderts in Deutschland," *Jahrbuch für Nationalökonomie und Statistik*, Band 173, 401–421.

Bordo, M. and P. Rousseau (2006) "Legal-Political Factors and the Historical Evolution of the Finance-Growth Link," *European Review of Economic History*, Vol. 10, No. 3: 421–444.

Bordo, Michael (1997) "Regulation and Bank Stability: Canada and the United States, 1870–1980," in *Reforming Financial Systems: Historical Implications for Policy* (65–84), eds. Gerard Capiro, Jr. and Dimitri Vitas. Cambridge: Cambridge University Press.

Bordo, Michael D., Angela Redish, and Hugh Rockoff (1995) "A Comparison of the U.S. and Canadian Banking System in the 20th Century," in *Anglo-American Financial System: Institutions and Markets in the Twentieth Century* (11–40), eds. Michael D. Bordo and Richard E. Sylla. New York: New York University Press.

Bosenick, A. (1912) *Neudeutsche Gemischte Bankwirtschaft*. Berlin: J. Schweitzer Verlag.

Bossaerts, Peter and Caroline Fohlin (2000) "Has the Cross-Section of Average Returns Always Been the Same? Evidence from Germany, 1881–1913," Social Science Working Paper No. 1084, California Institute of Technology.

Bösselmann, K. (1939) *Die Entwicklung des Deutschen Aktienwesens im 19. Jahrhundert*. Berlin: W. de Gruyter.

Botticelli, P. (1997) "British Capitalism and the Three Industrial Revolutions," in *Creating Modern Capitalism: How Entrepreneurs, Companies, and Countries Triumphed in Three Industrial Revolutions* (49–93), ed. Thomas K. McCraw. Cambridge, MA: Harvard University Press.

Bovykin, V. I. and B. V. Anan' ich (1991) "The Role of International Factors in the Formation of the Banking System in Russia," in *International Banking, 1870–1914* (130–158), eds. R. Cameron and V. I. Bovykin. New York: Oxford University Press.

Boyd, J. H. and B. D. Smith (1996) "The Co-evolution of the Real and Financial Sectors in the Growth Process," *The World Bank Economic Review*, Vol. 10, No. 2: 371–396.

(1997) "Capital Market Imperfections, International Credit Markets, and Nonconvergence," *Journal of Economic Theory*, Vol. 73, No. 2: 335–364.

(1998) "The Evolution of Debt and Equity Markets in Economic Development," *Economic Theory*, Vol. 12, No. 3: 519–560.

Braggion, F. and L. Moore (2010) "The Economic Benefits of Political Connections in Late Victorian Britain," Working Paper, Tilburg University.

Braggion, Fabio (2005) "Credit Market Constraints and Financial Networks in Late Victorian Britain," Working Paper, Northwestern University.

Brandies, Louis (1914) *Other People's Money and How the Bankers Use It.* Boston: Bedford Books of St. Martin Press.

Brockhage, B. (1910) "Zur Entwicklung des Preuss-Deutschen Kapitalexports," *Schmollers Jahrbuch*, Heft 148.

Brown Jr., W., J. Mulherin, and M. Weidenmier (2008) "Competing with the New York Stock Exchange," *The Quarterly Journal of Economics*, Vol. 123, No. 4: 1679–1719.

Buchwald, B. (1909) *Die Technik Des Bankbetriebs*, 5th ed. Berlin: Springer Verlag.

Buckle, Mike and John Thompson (1995) *The UK Financial System: Theory and Practice*, 2nd ed. Manchester: Manchester University Press.

Bundesbank (1976) *Deutsches Geld und Bankwesen in Zahlen.* Frankfurt: Bundesbank.

Burhop, C. (2006) "Did Banks Cause the German Industrialization?" *Explorations in Economic History*, Vol. 43, No. 1: 39–63.

Burhop, C. and S. Gelman (2008) "Taxation, Regulation and the Information Efficiency of the Berlin Stock Exchange, 1892–1913," *European Review of Economic History*, Vol. 12: 39–66.

Cairncross, Alec (1953) *Home and Foreign Investment, 1870–1913; Studies in Capital Accumulation.* Cambridge: Cambridge University Press.

Calomiris, C. (1995) "The Costs of Rejecting Universal Banking: American Finance in the German Mirror, 1870–1914," in *Coordination and Information* (257–322), eds. N. Lamoreaux and D. Ra. Chicago: University of Chicago Press.

Calomiris, Charles (2000) *U.S. Bank Deregulation in Historical Perspective.* New York: Cambridge University Press.

Calomiris, Charles and Carlos Ramirez (1996) "Financing the American Corporation: The Changing Menu of Financial Relationships," in *The American Corporation Today* (128–186), ed. Carl Kaysen. New York: Oxford University Press.

Cameron, R. (1972) "Introduction," in *Banking and Economic Development* (3–25), ed. R. Cameron. New York: Oxford University Press,

Cameron, Rondo (1967) "England, 1750–1844," in *Banking in the Early Stages of Industrialization. A Study of Comparative Economic History* (15–59), ed. Rondo Cameron et al. New York: Oxford University Press.

Capie, Forrest (1988) "Structure and Performance in British Banking 1870–1939," in *Money and Power: Essays in Honour of L.S. Pressnell* (73–102), eds. P. L. Cottrell and Donald E. Moggridge. Hampshire: Macmillan Press.

(1995a) "Commercial Banking in Britain between the Wars," in *Banking, Currency, and Finance in Europe between the Wars* (395–413), ed. Charles H. Feinstein. New York: Oxford University Press.

(1995b) "Prudent and Stable (but Inefficient?): Commercial Banks in Britain, 1890–1940," in *Anglo-American Financial Systems: Institutions and Markets in the Twentieth Century* (41–64), eds. Michael D. Bordo and Richard Sylla. Burr Ridge, IL: Irwin Professional Publishing.

(1999) "Banking in Europe in the Nineteenth Century: The Role of the Central Bank," in *The State, the Financial System, and Economic Modernization* (118–133), eds. Richard Sylla, Richard Tilly, and Gabriel Tortella. Cambridge: Cambridge University Press.

(2001) "The Origins and Development of Stable Fiscal and Monetary Institutions in England," in *Transferring Wealth and Power from the Old to the New World: Monetary and Fiscal Institutions in the 17th through the 19th Century* (19–58), eds. Michael D. Bordo and Roberto Cortés-Conde. New York: Cambridge University Press.

Capie, Forrest and Michael Collins (1992) *Have the Banks Failed British Industry? An Historical Survey, 1870–1990.* London: Institute of Economic Affairs.

Capie, Forrest and Alan Webber (1985) *A Monetary History of the United Kingdom, 1870–1982.* London: Allen & Unwin.

Carlin, W. and C. Mayer (2003) "Finance, Investment, and Growth," *Journal of Financial Economics*, Vol. 69, No. 1: 191–236.

Carosso, Vincent P. (1970) *Investment Banking in America.* Cambridge, MA: Harvard University Press.

(1987) *The Morgans: Private International Bankers, 1854–1913.* Cambridge, MA: Harvard University Press.

Caselli, F., G. Esquivel, and F. Lefort (1996) "Reopening the Convergence Debate: A New Look at Cross-Country Growth Empirics," *Journal of Economic Growth*, Vol. 1, No. 3: 363–389.

Cassis, Youssef (1987) *La city de Londres, 1870–1914.* Paris: Belin.

(1990) "British Finance: Success and Controversy," in *Capitalism in a Mature Economy. Financial Institutions, Capital Exports and British Industry, 1870–1939* (1–22), eds. Youssef Cassis and Jean-Jacques van Helten. Aldershot: Edward Elgar.

ed. (1992) *Finance and Financiers in European History, 1880–1960.* Cambridge: Cambridge University Press.

(1994) *City Bankers, 1890–1914.* English trans. Cambridge: Cambridge University Press.

Chakraborty, S. and R. Ray (2006) "Bank-Based versus Market-Based Financial Systems: A Growth-Theoretic Analysis," *Journal of Monetary Economics*, Vol. 53, No. 2: 329–350.

Chakraborty, Shankha and Tridip Ray (2007) "The development and structure of financial systems," *Journal of Economic Dynamics and Control*, Vol. 31: 2920–2956.

Champ, Bruce and Scott Freeman (1994) *Modeling Monetary Economies.* New York: J. Wiley.

Chandler Jr., A. D. (1977) *The Visible Hand: The Managerial Revolution in American Business.* Cambridge, MA: The Belknap Press of Harvard University Press.

Chandler, Alfred D. (1990) *Scale and Scope: The Dynamics of Industrial Capitalism.* Cambridge, MA: The Belknap Press of Harvard University Press.

Charkham, Jonathan P. (1994) *Keeping Good Company: A Study of Corporate Governance in Five Countries.* Oxford: Clarendon Press.

Cheffins, Brian (2008) *Corporate Ownership and Control: British Business Transformed.* New York: Oxford.

Christopoulos, Dimitris K. and Efthymios G. Tsionas (2004) "Financial Development and Economic Growth: Evidence from Panel Unit Root and Cointegration Tests," *Journal of Development Economics*, Vol. 73, No. 1: 55–74.

Clough, S. (1964) *The Economic History of Modern Italy.* New York: Columbia University Press.

Cohen, J. (1977) *Finance and Industrialization in Italy, 1894–1914.* New York: Arno Press.

Cole, Rebel A. (1998) "The Importance of Relationships to the Availability of Credit." *Journal of Banking and Finance*, Vol. 22, No. 6–8: 959–977.

Collins, Michael (1991) *Banks and Industrial Finance in Britain: 1800–1939.* Hampshire: Macmillan Press.

   (1994) "The Growth of the Firm in the Domestic Banking Sector," in *Business Enterprise in Modern Britain. From the Eighteenth to the Twentieth Century* (263–286), eds. Maurice W. Kirby and Mary B. Rose. London: Routledge.

   (1998) "English Bank Development within a European Context, 1870–1939," *The Economic History Review*, Vol. 51, No. 1: 1–24.

Collins, Michael and Mae Baker (1999a) "English Industrial Distress before 1914 and the Response of the Banks," *European Review of Economic History*, Vol. 3, No. 1: 1–24.

   (1999b) "Financial Crises and Structural Change in English Commercial Bank Assets, 1860–1913," *Explorations in Economic History*, Vol. 36, No. 6: 428–444.

   (1999c) "The Durability of Transaction Banking Practices in the Provision of Finance to the Business Sector by British Banks," *Entreprises et Histoire*, Vol. 22: 78–92.

   (2001) "Sectoral Differences in English Bank Asset Structures and the Impact of Mergers, 1860–1913," *Business History*, Vol. 43, No. 4: 1–28.

   (2004) *Commercial Banks and Industrial Finance in England and Wales, 1860–1939.* New York: Oxford University Press.

Collins, Michael and Forest Capie (1996) "Industrial Lending by English Commercial Banks, 1860s–1914: Why Did Banks Refuse Loans?" *Business History*, Vol. 38, No. 1: 26–44.

   (1999) "Banks, Industry and Finance, 1880–1914," *Business History* Vol. 41, No. 1: 37–62.

Comptroller of the Currency (various years) *Annual Report.*

Conant, Charles A. (1910) *Banking System of Mexico.* U.S. National Monetary Commission.

Confalonieri, Antonio (1974) *Banca e Industria in Italia.* Milan: Banca Commerciale Italiana.

   (1975) *Banca e Industria in Italia dalla Crisi del 1907 all'Agosto 1914.* Vol. I. Milan: Banca Commerciale Italiana.

   (1982) *Banca e Industria in Italia dalla Crisi del 1907 all'Agosto 1914.* Vol. II Milan: Banca Commerciale Italiana.

Cottrell, P. L. (1980) *Industrial Finance, 1830–1914: Finance and Organization of English Manufacturing Industry.* New York: Methuen.

   (1985) *Investment Banking in England, 1856–1881: A Case Study of the International Financial Society.* New York: Garland.

(1991) "Great Britain," in *International Banking 1870-1914* (25-47), eds. Rondo Cameron and V. I. Bovykin. New York: Oxford University Press.

(1992) "The Domestic Commercial Banks and the City of London, 1970-1939," in *Finance and Financiers in European History, 1880-1960* (39-62), ed. Youssef Cassis. Cambridge: Cambridge University Press.

(1994) "The Historical Development of Modern Banking within the United Kingdom," in *Handbook on the History of European Banks* (1137-1161), ed. European Association for Banking History E.V. Aldershot: Edward Elgar.

(2004) "Domestic Finance, 1860-1914," in *The Cambridge Economic History of Modern Britain. Volume II: Economic Maturity, 1860-1939* (253-279), eds. Roderick Floud and Paul Johnson. Cambridge: Cambridge University Press.

Cottrell, P. L. and D. Moggridge, eds. (1988) *Money and Power: Essays in Honour of L. S. Pressnell.* Hampshire: Macmillan Press.

Cottrell, P. L. and Lucy Newton (1999) "Banking Linearization in England and Wales, 1826-1844," in *The State, the Financial System and Economic Modernization* (75-117), eds. Richard Sylla, Richard Tilly, and Gabriel Tortella Casares. Cambridge: Cambridge University Press.

Cotula, F., R. Iacobini, and Banca d'Italia (1996) *I bilanci delle aziende di credito, 1890-1936.* Vol. III della series Statistische storiche, Roma: Laterza, Bari.

Credito Italiano (1912) *Notizie Statistiche sulle Principali Societa Italiane per Azioni*, Rome: Stampato per il Credito Italiano dalla Casa editr. italiana di C. d Luigi.

Da Rin, M. (1993) "German *Kreditbanken* 1850-1914: An Informational Approach." Stanford University mimeo.

Däbritz, W. (1931) *Gründung und Anfänge der Disconto-Gesellschaft Berlin.* Leipzig: Verlag Von Duncker & Humblot.

Dahrendorf, Ralf (1967) *Society and Democracy in Germany.* New York & London: W. W. Norton & Company.

Daniel, K. and S. Titman (1997) "Evidence on the Characteristics of Cross Sectional Variation in Stock Returns," *Journal of Finance*, Vol. 52, No. 1: 1-33.

Davis, Gerald and Henrich R. Grieve (1997) "Corporate Elite Networks and Governance Changes in the 1980s," *The American Journal of Sociology*, Vol. 103, No. 1: 1-37.

Davis, Gerald and Mark S. Mizruchi (1999) "The Money Center Cannot Hold: Commercial Banks in the US System of Corporate Governance," *Administrative Science Quarterly*, Vol. 44, No. 2: 215-239.

Davis, J. L., E. F. Fama, and K. R. French (2000) "Characteristics, Covariances, and Average Returns: 1929 to 1997," *Journal of Finance*, Vol. 55, No. 1: 389-406.

Davis, L. and R. A. Huttenback (1986) *Mammon and the Pursuit of Empire: The Political Economy of British Imperialism, 1860-1912.* New York: Cambridge University Press.

Davis, Lance E. (1966) "The Capital Markets and Industrial Concentration: The U.S. and the U.K., a Comparative Study," *Economic History Review*, Vol. 19: 255-272.

Davis, Lance E. and Robert Gallman (2001) *Evolving Financial Markets and International Capital Flows: Britain, the Americas, and Australia, 1865-1914.* New York: Cambridge University Press.

De Long, J. Bradford (1988) "Productivity Growth, Convergence and Welfare: Comment," *American Economic Review* Vol. 78, No. 5: 1138-1154.

(1991) "Did J. P. Morgan's Men Add Value? An Economist's Perspective on Financial Capitalism," in *Inside the Business Enterprise: Historical Perspectives on the Use of*

Information (205–250), ed. Peter Temin. Chicago: University of Chicago Press for NBER.

(1992) "J. P. Morgan and His Money Trust," *Wilson Quarterly*, Vol. 16, No. 4: 16–30.

De Mattia, R. (a cura di) (1967) *I bilanci degli istituti di emissione italiani 1845–1936*. Roma: Banca d'Italia.

De Vries, Johann (1994) "Netherlands," in *Handbook on the History of European Banks* (719–790), ed. Manfred Pohl and Sabine Freitag (European Association for Banking History). Aldershot: Edward Elgar Publishing.

Deidda, Luca and B. Fattouh (2005) "Concentration in the Banking Industry and Economic Growth," *Macroeconomic Dynamics*, Vol. 9, No. 2: 198–219.

Demirguc-Kunt, Asli and Vojislav Maksimovic (1998) "Law, Finance, and Firm Growth," *The Journal of Finance*, Vol. 53, No. 6: 2107–2137.

(2002) "Funding growth in bank-based and market-based financial systems: evidence from firm-level data," *Journal of Financial Economics*, Vol. 65: 337–363.

Deutsche Bundesbank (1976) *Deutsches Geld- und Bankwesen in Zahlen 1876–1975*. Frankfurt: Fritz Knapp Verlag.

Der Deutsche Ökonomist (various volumes). Berlin.

Dewatripont, M. and E. Maskin (1990) "Contract Renegotiation in Models of Asymmetric Information," *European Economic Review*, Vol. 34, No. 2–3: 311–321.

(1995) "Credit and Efficiency in Centralized and Decentralized Economies," *Review of Economic Studies*, Vol. 62, No. 4: 541–555.

Diamond, D. (1984) "Financial Intermediation and Delegated Monitoring," *Review of Economic Studies*, Vol. 51, No. 3: 393–414.

(1991) "Monitoring and Reputation: The Choice between Bank Loans and Directly Placed Debt," *Journal of Political Economy*, Vol. 99, No. 4: 689–721.

Diaper, Stefanie (1990) "The Sperling Combine and the Shipbuilding Industry. Merchant Banking and Industrial Finance in the 1920s," in *Capitalism in a Mature Economy. Financial Institutions, Capital Exports and British Industry, 1870–1939* (71–94), eds. Youssef Cassis and Jean-Jacques van Helten. Aldershot: Edward Elgar.

Dietl, Helmut (1998) *Capital Markets and Corporate Governance in Japan, Germany and the United States: Organizational Response to Market Inefficiencies*. New York: Routledge.

Dimson, E., P. Marsh, and M. Staunton (2002) *Triumph of the Optimists: 101 Years of Global Investment Returns*. Princeton, NJ: Princeton University Press

Dintenfass, Michael (1999) "Converging Accounts, Misleading Metaphors and Persistent Doubts. Reflections on the Historiography of Britain's 'Decline,'" in *The British Industrial Decline* (7–26), eds. Jean-Pierre Dormois and Michael Dintenfass. London: Routledge.

Djankov, S., C. McLiesh, and A. Shleifer (2007) "Private Credit in 129 countries," *Journal of Financial Economics*, Vol. 84: 299–329.

Donaubauer, K. A. (1988) *Privatbankiers und Bankenkonzentration in Deutschland von der Mitte des 19. Jahrhunderts bis 1932*. Frankfurt am Main: Fritz Knapp Verlag.

Donges, J. and P. Tillman (2001) "Challenges for the Global Financial System," in *New Directions in Global Economic Governance: Managing Globalisation in the Twenty-First Century* (33–44), eds. J. J. Kirton and G. M. von Furstenberg. Aldershot: Ashgate.

Dooley, Peter C. (1969) "The Interlocking Directorate," *The American Economic Review*, Vol. 59, No. 3: 314–323.

Dritsas, Margarita (1994a) "La structure du système bancaire commercial grec 1840–1980," in *Handbook on the History of European Banks* (491–530), eds. M. Pohl and S. Freitag. European Association for Banking History E.V. Aldershot: Edward Elgar.

(1994b) "Networks of Bankers and Industrialists in Greece in the Interwar Period," in *Universal Banking in the Twentieth Century: Finance, Industry and the State in North and Central Europe* (229–245), eds. A. Teichova, T. Gourvish, and A. Pogány. London: Aldershot.

Dumke, R. (1976) *The Political Economy of German Economic Unification: Tariffs, Trade and Politics of the Zollverein Era*. Ph.D. Dissertation, University of Wisconsin, Madison.

Edelstein, Michael (1982) *Overseas Investment in the Age of Imperialism: The United Kingdom, 1850–1914*. New York: Columbia University Press.

(1994) "Foreign Investment and Accumulation, 1860–1914," in *The Economic History of Britain since 1700: 1860–1939*. Vol 2 (173–196), eds. Roderick Floud and Deidre N. McCloskey. Cambridge: Cambridge University Press.

(2004) "Foreign Investment, Accumulation and Empire, 1860–1914," in *The Cambridge Economic History of Modern Britain. Volume II: Economic Maturity, 1860–1939* (190–226), eds. Roderick Floud and Paul Johnson. Cambridge: Cambridge University Press.

Edwards, A. and K. Fischer (1994) *Banks, Finance, and Investment in Germany*. New York: Cambridge University Press.

Edwards, George T. (1987) *The Role of Banks in Economic Development*. London: Macmillan Press.

Edwards, J., and S. Ogilvie (1996) "Universal Banks and German Industrialization: a Reappraisal," *Economic History Review*, Vol. 49, No. 3: 427–446.

Ehrlich, Edna E. (1960) *The Role of Banking in Japan's Economic Development* (unpublished dissertation). New School for Social Research.

Eistert, E. (1970) "Die Beeinflussung des Wirtschaftswachstums in Deutschland von 1883–1913 durch das Banksystem." Berlin.

Elsas, Ralf and Jan Pieter Krahnen (2003a) "Universal Banks and Relationships with Firms." *Center for Financial Studies*, Number 2003/20.

(2003b) "Universal Banks and Relationships with Firms," in *The German Financial System* (197–232), eds. J. P. Krahnen and R. Schmidt. New York: Oxford University Press.

Fama, E. F. and K. R. French (1993) "Common Risk Factors in the Returns on Stocks and Bonds," *Journal of Financial Economics*, Vol. 33, No. 1: 3–56.

(1996) "Multifactor Explanations of Asset Pricing Anomalies," *Journal of Finance*, Vol. 51, No. 1: 55–84.

Favarra, Giovanni (2006) "An Empirical Reassessment of the Relationship between Finance and Growth." University of Lausanne. Switzerland.

Fazzari, S., R. G. Hubbard, and B. Petersen (1988) "Investment and Finance Reconsidered," *Brookings Papers on Economic Activity*, 141–95.

Fear, Jeffrey (2004) *Organizing Control: From August Thyssen to Heinrich Dinkelbach*. Cambridge, MA: Harvard University Press.

Fear, Jeffrey and Christopher Kobrak (2006) "Diverging Paths: Accounting for Corporate Governance in America and Germany," *Business History Review*, Vol. 80: 1–48.

Federico, G. and G. Toniolo (1992) "Italy," in *Patterns of European Industrialization: The Nineteenth Century* (197–217), eds. R. Sylla and G. Toniolo. New York: Routledge.

Feinstein, Charles (1972) *National Income, Expenditure and Output of the United Kingdom, 1855-1965*. Cambridge: Cambridge University Press.

Feldman, Gerald (1998) *Hugo Stinnes: Biographie eines Industriellen*. Munich: Beck.

Fenoaltea, S. (1973) "Le Ferrovie e lo Sviluppo Industriale Italiano," in *Lo Sviluppo Economico Italiano 1861-1940* (157–186), ed. G. Toniolo. Bari: Laterza.

　　(1983) "Railways and the Development of the Italian Economy to 1913," in *Railways and the Economic Growth of Western Europe* (49–120), ed. P. O'Brien. London: Macmillan.

Fischer, K. (1990) "Hausbankbeziehungen als Instrument der Bindung zwischen Banken und Unternehmen: eine theoretische und empirische Analyse." Doctoral Dissertation, University of Bonn.

Flavin, M. (1991) "The Joint Consumption/Asset Demand Decision: A Case Study in Robust Estimation." Working Paper No. 3802, NBER.

Fohlin, C. (1994) "Financial Intermediation, Investment, and Industrial Development: Universal Banking in Germany and Italy from Unification to World War I." Dissertation, University of California Berkeley.

　　(1997a) "The Universal Banks and the Mobilization of Capital in Imperial Germany," in *Finance & the Making of Modern Capitalism*, eds. P. Cottrell, G. Feldman, and J. Reis. Aldershot: Scolar Press.

　　(1997b) "Universal Banking Networks in Pre-War Germany: New Evidence from Company Financial Data," *Research in Economics*, Vol. 51, No. 3: 201–225.

　　(1997c) "Bank Securities Holdings and Industrial Finance before World War I: Britain and Germany Compared," *Business and Economic History*, Vol. 26: 463–475.

　　(1998a) "*Fiduciari* and Firm Liquidity Constraints: The Italian Experience with German-Style Universal Banking," *Explorations in Economic History*, Vol. 35: 83–107.

　　(1998b) "Relationship Banking, Liquidity, and Investment in the German Industrialization," *The Journal of Finance*, Vol. 53: 1737–1758.

　　(1999a) "Capital Mobilization and Utilisation in Latecomer Economies: Germany and Italy Compared," *European Review of Economic History*, Vol. 2: 139–174.

　　(1999b) "The Rise of Interlocking Directorates in Imperial Germany," *Economic History Review*, Vol. 52, No. 2: 307–333.

　　(1999c) "Universal Banking in Pre-World War I Germany: Model or Myth?" *Explorations in Economic History*, Vol. 36: 305–343.

　　(2000) "Economic, Political, and Legal Factors in Financial System Development: International Patterns in Historical Perspective." Social Science Working Paper No. 1089, California Institute of Technology.

　　(2001a) "A Comprehensive Panel Database for 400 German Stock Companies, 1895–1913." Caltech, mimeo.

　　(2001b) "The Balancing Act of German Universal Banks and English Deposit Banks, 1880-1913," *Business History*, Vol. 43: 1–24.

　　(2002a) "Corporate Capital Structure and the Influence of Universal Banks in Pre-World War I Germany," *Jahrbuch für Wirtschaftsgeschichte*, Vol. 2: 113–134.

(2002b) "Regulation, Taxation, and the Development of the German Universal Banking System," *European Review of Economic History*, Vol. 6: 221–254.

(2005) "The History of Corporate Ownership and Control in Germany," in *A History of Corporate Governance around the World: Family Business Groups to Professional Managers* (223–277), ed. R. Morck. Chicago: University of Chicago Press.

(2006) "Banking Industry Structure, Competition, and Performance: Does Universality Matter?" Social Science Working Paper No. 1078, California Institute of Technology.

(2007a) *"Finance Capitalism and Germany's Rise to Industrial Power.* New York: Cambridge University Press.

(2007b) "Does Civil Law Tradition (or Universal Banking) Crowd out Securities Markets? Pre-World War I Germany as Counter-Example," *Enterprise & Society*, Vol. 8: 602–641.

(2009) "Competition in American Commercial Banking, 1888–1925." Johns Hopkins University mimeo.

(2010) "Asymmetric Information, Market Power, and the Underpricing of New Stock Issues in Germany, 1882–1892," *Journal of Economic History*, Vol. 70, No. 3: 630–656.

Fohlin, C. and Steffen Reinhold (2010) "Pricing Anomalies in the Berlin Stock Exchange, 1904–1910," *Cliometrica*, Vol. 4: 75–96.

Fohlin, C., and T. Gehrig, (2010) "Liquidity and Competition in Unregulated Markets: The NYSE before the SEC." Johns Hopkins University, Mimeo.

Frankel, Allen B. and John D. Montgomery (1991) "Financial Structure: An International Perspective," *Brookings Paper on Economic Activity*, Vol. 1: 257–310.

Frankl, Jennifer (1999) "An Analysis of Japanese Corporate Structure, 1915–1937," *Journal of Economic History*, Vol. 59, No. 4: 997–1015

Franks, J., C. Mayer, and S. Rossi (2005) "Spending Less Time with the Family: The Decline of Family Ownership in the United Kingdom," in *A History of Corporate Governance Around the World* (581–607), ed. R. Morck. Chicago: University of Chicago Press, 581–607.

Franks, J. R., C. P. Mayer, and H. Miyajima (2009) "Equity Markets and Institutions: The Case of Japan," *Working Paper*, London Business School.

Franks, Julian and Colin Mayer (1997) "Corporate Ownership and Control in the UK, Germany, and France," *Morgan Stanley Journal of Applied Corporate Finance*, Vol. 9, No. 4: 30–45.

Franks, Julian, Colin Mayer, and Johannes Wagner (2006) "The Origins of German Corporation – Finance Ownership and Control," *Review of Finance*, Vol. 10, No. 4: 537–585.

Freixas, Xavier and Jean-Charles Rochet (1998) "Fair Pricing of Deposit Insurance. Is It Possible? Yes. Is It Desirable? No," *Research in Economics*, Vol. 52, No. 3: 217–232.

Fremdling, R. (1975) *Eisenbahnen und Deutsches Wirtschaftswachstum, 1840–1879.* Dortmund: Gesellschaft für Westfälische Wirtschaftgeschichte.

(1983) *Productivity in the Economies of Europe.* Klett-Cotta: Speyer.

Fujino, Shozaburo and Juro Teranishi (2000) *Nihon Kin'yu no Suryo Bunskei* (Quantitative Analysis of Financial Development in Japan). Tokyo: Keizai Shimposha.

Gale, Douglas and Martin Hellwig (1985) "Incentive-Compatible Debt Contracts: The One Period Problem," *Review of Economic Studies*, Vol. 52: 647–663.

Garbade, K. and W. Silber (1978) "Technology, Communications, and the Performance of the Financial Markets: 1840–1975," *Journal of Finance*, No. 3: 819–832.

Gaytan, A. and R. Ranciere (2006) *Banks, Liquidity and Economic Growth*. Working Paper.

Gehrig, T. and C. Fohlin (2006) "Trading Costs in Early Securities Markets: The Case of the Berlin Stock Exchange, 1880–1910," *Review of Finance*, Vol. 10: 585–610.

Gerschenkron, A. (1955) "Notes on the Rate of Industrial Growth in Italy 1861–1913," *Journal of Economic History*, Vol. 14: 473–499.

(1962) *Economic Backwardness in Historical Perspective*. Cambridge, MA: Harvard University Press.

(1968) "The Modernisation of Entrepreneurship," in *Continuity in History and Other Essays* (128–139). Cambridge, MA: Belknap Press of Harvard University Press.

(1970) *Europe in the Russian Mirror: Four Lectures in Economic History*. London: Cambridge University Press.

Gilbert, Alton (1996) "A Comparison of Proposals to Restructure the US Financial System," in *Stability in the Financial System* (214–241), ed. D. Papadimitriou. New York: St. Martin's Press.

Glagau, O. (1876) *Der Börsen- und Gründungs-Schwindel in Berlin*. Leipzig: Verlag von Paul Frohberg.

Goldsmith, R. (1969) *Financial Structure and Development*. New Haven, CT: Yale University Press.

(1972) *The Development of Financial Institutions During the Post-War Period*. New Haven, CT: Yale University, Economic Growth Center.

(1983) *The Financial Development of Japan, 1868–1977*. New Haven, CT: Yale University Press.

Good, David (1973) "Backwardness and the Role of Banking in Nineteenth-Century European Industrialization," *The Journal of Economic History*, Vol. 33: 845–850.

Goodhart, C. A. E. (1972) *The Business of Banking, 1891–1914*. London: Weidenfeld & Nicolson.

Gourvish, T. R. and R. G. Wilson (1994) *The Brewing Industry 1830–1980*. London: Cambridge University Press.

Greasley, David and Les Oxley (1999) "Competitiveness and Growth. New Perspectives on the Late Victorian and Edwardian Economy," in *The British Industrial Decline* (65–84), eds. Jean-Pierre Dormois and Michael Dintenfass. London: Routledge.

Greenbaum, Stuart I., George Kanatas, and Itzhak Venezia (1989) "Equilibrium Loan Pricing under the Bank-Client Relationship," *Journal of Banking and Finance*, Vol. 13: 221–235.

Greenwood, J. and B. D. Smith (1997) "Financial Markets in Development, and the Development of Financial Markets," *Journal of Economic Dynamics and Control*, Vol. 21: 145–181.

Guinnane, T. (1993) "Cooperatives as Information Machines: The Lending Practices of German Agricultural Credit Cooperatives, 1883–1914." Working Paper, Yale University.

Gurley, J. and E. Shaw (1960) *Money in a Theory of Finance*. Washington, DC: Brookings.

Haber, Stephen (1998) "The Efficiency Consequences of Institutional Change: Financial Market Regulation and Industrial Productivity Growth in Brazil, 1866–1934," *Estudos Econômicos*, Vol. 28, No. 3: 379–420.

Haber, S. and N. Mauer (2002) "Institutional Change and Economic Growth? Banks, Financial Markets, and Mexican Industrialization, 1878–1913," in *The Mexican Economy, 1870–1930: Essays on the Economic History of Institutions, Revolution, and Growth* (23–49), eds. Jeffrey L. Bortz and Stephen Haber. Palo Alto, CA: Stanford University Press.

Hadley, E. (1970) *Antitrust in Japan*. Princeton, NJ; Princeton University Press.

Hamao, Yasushi, Takeo Hoshi, and Tetsuji Okazaki (2009) "Listing Policy and Development of the Tokyo Stock Exchange in the Pre-War Period," in *Financial Sector Development in the Pacific Rim* (51–94), eds. Ito Takatoshi and Andrew Rose. East Asia Seminar on Economics, Volume 18, National Bureau of Economic Research.

Hannah, Leslie (1976) *The Rise of the Corporate Economy. The British Experience.* Baltimore: Johns Hopkins University Press.

Hansen, Svend Aage (1982) "The Transformation of Bank Structures in the Industrial Period: the Case of Denmark," *Journal of European Economic History*, Vol. 3: 575–603.

Harley, C. Knick (1991) "Substitution for Prerequisites: Endogenous Institutions and Comparative Economic History," in *Patterns of European Industrialization* (29–44), eds. Richard Sylla and Gianni Toniolo. London and New York: Routledge.

Harris, Milton and Artur Raviv (1991) "The Theory of Capital Structure," *Journal of Finance*, Vol. 46: 297–355.

Hawawini, G. and D. Keim (1998) "The Cross-Section of Common Stock Returns: A Review of the Evidence and Some New Findings." Working Paper, INSEAD and Wharton School.

Hellwig, M. (1991) "Banking, Financial Intermediation and Corporate Finance," in *European Financial Integration* (35–63) eds. A. Giovannini and C. Mayer. New York: Cambridge University Press.

(1998) "Banks, Markets, and the Allocation of Risks," *Journal of Institutional and Theoretical Economics*, Vol. 154: 328–351.

(1997) "Unternehmensfinanzierung, Unternehmenskontrolle und Ressourcenalloka-tion: Was leistet das Finanzsystem?" Sonderforschungsbereich 504 Publications 97–02, Sonderforschungsbereich 504, Universität Mannheim & Sonderforschun-gsbereich 504, University of Mannheim.

Herrigel, G. (1996) *Industrial Constructions: The Sources of German Industrial Power.* London: Cambridge University Press.

Hertner, Peter (1994) *Handbook on the History of European Banks* (1137–1161). European Association for Banking History E.V. Aldershot: Edward Elgar.

Heyn, U. (1981 [1969]) *Private Banking and Industrialization: The Case of Frankfurt am Main 1825–75.* New York: Arno Press.

Hilferding, R. (1910) *Das Finanzkapital*, Vienna: Wiener Volksbuchhandlung (English translation [*Finance Capital*] ed. Tom Bottomore, Boston: Routledge and Kegan Paul, 1981).

Hirschmeier, Johannes and Tsunehiko Yui (1975) *The Development of Japanese Business 1600–1973*. Cambridge, MA: Harvard University Press.

Hoffman, Walter (1965) *Das Wachstum der Deutschen Wirtshaft seit der Mitte ds 19. Jahrhunderts.* New York: Springer-Verlag.

Horn, N. (1979) "Aktienrechtliche Unternehmensorganisation in der Hochindustrialisierung (1860–1920)," In *Recht und Entwicking der Großunternehmen im 19. und frühen 20. Jahrhundert* (123–189), eds. N. Horn and J. Kocka. Göttingen: Vandenhoeck & Ruprecht.

Horn, N. and J. Kocka, eds. (1979) *Recht und Entwicklung der Großunternehmen im 19. und frühen 20. Jahrhundert.* Göttingen: Vandenhoeck & Ruprecht.

Hoshi, T., A. Kashyap, and D. Scharfstein (1991) "Corporate Structure, Liquidity, and Investment," *Quarterly Journal of Economics*, Vol. 106, No. 1: 33–60.

Hoshi, Takeo and Anil Kashyap (2001) *Corporate Financing and Governance in Japan: The Road to the Future.* Cambridge, MA: MIT Press.

(2004) "Japan's Financial Crisis and Economic Stagnation," *The Journal of Economic Perspectives*, Vol. 18: 3–26.

Hüffer, Wilm (2002) *Theodizee der Freiheit: Hegels Philosophie des Geschichtlichen Denkens.* Hamburg: Felix Meiner.

Huber, P. J. (1973) "Robust Regression: Asymptotics, Conjectures, and Monte Carlo," *Annals of Statistics*, Vol. 1: 799–821.

(1977) "Robust Methods of Estimation of Regression Coefficients," *Mathematische Operationsforschung Statist. Ser. Statist.* Vol. 8: 41–53.

Hubner, O. (1968 [1853]) *Die Banken.* Band II, Frankfurt: Sauer und Auvermann Verlag.

Imuta, Toshimitsu (1976) *Meiji ki kabushiki kaisha bunseki josetsu* (English Trans.: Introduction to the Analysis of Meiji-Era Corporations). Tokyo: Hosei University Press.

James, C. (1987) "Some Evidence on the Uniqueness of Bank Loans," *Journal of Financial Economics*, Vol. 16: 217–236.

Jayaratne, J. and P. E. Strahan (1996) "The Finance-Growth Nexus: Evidence from Bank Branch Deregulation," *The Quarterly Journal of Economics*, Vol. 111: 639–670.

Jeidels, Otto (1905) *Das Verhältnis der Deutschen Groβbanken zur Industrie.* Leipzig: Duncker und Humblot.

Jensen, Michael C. and William H. Meckling, "Theory of the Firm: Managerial Behavior, Agency Costs and Ownership Structure," *Journal of Financial Economics*, Vol. 3, No. 4: 305–360.

Johansen, Hans Christian (1991) "Banking and Finance in the Danish Economy," in *International Banking, 1870–1914* (159–173), eds. Rondo Cameron and V. I. Bovykin. Oxford: Oxford University Press.

(1994) "Danish Banking History," In *Handbook on the History of European Banks* (1137–1161), eds. M. Pohl and S. Freitag. European Association for Banking History E.V. Aldershot: Edward Elgar.

Jonker, Joost. (1991) "Sinecures or Sinews of Power? Interlocking directorship and bank-industry relations in the Netherlands, 1910–1940," in *Economic and Social History in the Netherlands.* Vol. 3 (119–132), ed. J. L. van Zanden.

Kazuo, S. (1966) "The Early History of the Zaibatsu," *The Developing Economies*, Vol. 4: 535–566.

Kennedy, William P. (1987) *Industry Structure, Capital Markets, and the Origin of British Economic Decline.* Cambridge: Cambridge University Press.

(1992) "Historical Patterns of Finance in Great Britain: A Long-Run View," in *Finance and the Enterprise*, eds. V. Zamagni. London: Academic Press.

Kennedy, William P. and Rachel Britton (1985) "Portfolioverhalten und Wirtschaftliche Entwicklung im späten 19. Jahrhundert. Ein Vergleich zwischen Großbritannien und Deutschland. Hypothesen und Spekulationen," in *Beiträge zur Quantitativen Vergleichenden Unternehmensgeschichte* (45–93), ed. Richard Tilly. Stuttgart: Klett-Cotta.

Kindleberger, Charles Poor (1993) *A Financial History of Western Europe.* New York: Oxford University Press.

King, R. G. and R. Levine (1993) "Finance and Growth: Schumpeter Might Be Right," *The Quarterly Journal of Economics*, Vol. 108: 717–737.

Kirby, M. W. (1981) *The Decline of British Economic Power since 1870.* London: Allen & Unwin.

Klebaner, Benjamin J. (1990) "The Impact of Consolidation and Safety-Net Support on Canadian, US, and UK Banks: 1983–1992," *Journal of Banking & Finance*, Vol. 23: 537.

Kocka, J. (1978) "Entrepreneurs and Managers in German Industrialization," in *The Cambridge Economic History of Europe*, vol. VII, part I (492–589), eds. P. Mathias and M. M. Postan. New York: Cambridge University Press.

Kocka, J. and H. Siegrist (1979) "Die Hundert Größten Deutschen Industrieunternehmen im Späten 19. und Frühen 20. Jahrhundert," in *Recht und Entwicklung der Großunternehmen im 19. und Frühen 20. Jahrhundert* (55–122), eds. N. Horn and J. Kocka. Göttingen: Vandenhoeck und Ruprecht.

Kotz, David M. (1978) *Bank Control of Large Corporations in the United States.* Los Angeles: University of California Press.

Krengel, J. (1980) "Zur Berechnung von Wachstumswirkungen Konjunkturell Bedingter Nachfrageschwankungen Nachgelagerter Industrien auf die Produktionsentwicklung der Deutschen Roheisenindustrie Während der Jahre 1871–1882," in *Historische Konjunkturforschung* (186–207), eds. W. Schröder and R. Spree. Stuttgart: Klett-Cotta.

Kroszner, Randall (1998) "Interest-Group Competition and the Organization of Congress: Theory and Evidence from Financial Services' Political Action Committees," *The American Economic Review*, Vol. 88: 1163–1187.

Kroszner, R. and R. Rajan (1994) "Is the Glass Steagall Act Justified? A Study of the US Experience with Universal Banking before 1933," *American Economic Review*, Vol. 84: 810–832.

(1997) "Organizational Structure and Credibility: Evidence from Commercial Bank Securities Activities before the Glass-Steagall Act," *Journal of Monetary Economics*, Vol. 39: 475–516.

Kroszner, R. and P. Strahan (2001) "Bankers on Boards: Monitoring, Conflicts of Interest, and Lender Liability," *Journal of Financial Economics*, Vol. 62, no. 3: 415–452.

Kugler, M. and K. Nuesser (1998) "Manufacturing Growth and Financial Development: Evidence from OECD Countries," *Review of Economics and Statistics*, Vol. 80, No. 4: 638–646.

Kurgan-van Hentenryk, G. (1995) "Commercial Banks in Belgium, 1935–90," in *The Evolution of Financial Institutions* (47–63), eds. Y. Cassis, G. D. Feldman, U. Olsson.

Kuustera, Antti (1994) "The Finnish Banking System in Broad Outline from the 1860s to the mid 1980s," in *Handbook on the History of European Banks* (135–184). European Association for Banking History E.V. Aldershot: Edward Elgar.

La Porta, R., F. Lopez-De-Silanes, and A. Shleifer (1999) "Corporate Ownership around the World," *The Journal of Finance*, Vol. 54: 471–517.

La Porta, R., F. Lopez-De-Silanes, A. Shleifer, and R. W. Vishny (1997) "Legal Determinants of External Finance," *The Journal of Finance*, Vol. 52: 1131–1150.

(1998) "Law and Finance," *Journal of Political Economy*, Vol. 106: 1113–1155.

Lamoreaux, Naomi R. (1991) "Bank Mergers in Late Nineteenth-Century New England: The Contingent Nature of Structural Change," *The Journal of Economic History*, Vol. 51, No. 3: 537–557.

Lamoreaux, N. (1994) *Insider Lending: Banks, Personal Connections and Economic Development in Industrial New England*. Cambridge: Cambridge University Press.

Lanaro, S. (1979) *Nazione e Lavoro*, Padova: Marsilio.

Landes, Davis S. (1965) "Technological Change and Development in Western Europe, 1750–1914," in *The Cambridge Economic History of Europe, vol. VI: The Industrial Revolution and After: Incomes, Population and Technological Change* (I) (274–601), eds. H. J. Habakkuk and M. Postan. Cambridge: Cambridge University Press.

Lange, Even (1994) "The Norwegian System of Banking Institutions," in *Handbook on the History of European Banks* (791–830). European Association for Banking History E.V. Aldershot: Edward Elgar.

Lansburgh, A. (1909) *Das Deutsche Bankwesen*. Berlin Charlottenburg: Bank Verlag.

Larsson, Mats. (1995) "Overcoming Institutional Barriers: Financial Networks in Sweden, 1910–90," in *The Evolution of Financial Institutions and Markets in Twentieth Century Europe* (122–142), eds. Y. Cassis, G. D. Feldman, and U. Olsson. Aldershot: EABA and Scholar Press.

Lavington, F. E. (1921). *The English Capital Market*. London: Methuen.

Levine, R. (2002) "Bank-Based or Market-Based Financial Systems: Which Is Better?" *Journal of Financial Intermediation*, Vol. 11: 398–428.

Levine, R., N. Loayza, and T. Beck (2000) "Financial Intermediation and Growth: Causality and Causes," *Journal of Monetary Economics*, Vol. 46: 31–77.

Levine, Ross (1991) "Stock Markets, Growth, and Tax Policy," *Journal of Finance*, Vol. 46: 1445–1465.

(1997) "Financial Development and Economic Growth: Views and Agenda," *Journal of Economic Literature*, Vol. 35: 688–726.

(1998) "The Legal Environment, Banks, and Long-Run Economic Growth," *Journal of Money, Credit and Banking*, Vol. 30: 596–613.

Levine, Ross and Sara Zervos (1998) "Stock Markets, Banks, and Economic Growth," *The American Economic Review*, Vol. 88: 537–558.

Lindert, P. H. and J. G. Williamson (2003) "Does Globalization Make the World More Unequal?", in *Globalization in Historical Perspective* (NBER Series) (227–276), eds. Peter H. Lindert and Jeffrey G. Williamson. Chicago: University of Chicago Press.

Loeb, E. (1902) "Das Institut des Aufsichtsrat," *Jahrbuch für National-Ökonomie*, Vol. 2, No. 23, 1–28.

Loewenstein, A. (1912) *Geschichte des Württembergischen Kreditbankwesens und Seiner Beziehungen zu Handel und Industrie*. Tübingen: Verlag von J. C. B. Mohr.

Lotz, W. (1976 [1888]) *Geschichte und Kritik des Deutschen Bankgesetzes von 1875*. Leipzig: Duncker und Humblot.

Maddison, Angus (1995) *Monitoring the World Economy 1820–1992*. Paris: Organisation for Economic Co-operation and Development.

Madhavan, Ananth (2000) "Market Microstructure: A Survey," SSRN Working Paper Series. ITG, Inc.

Manning, Mark J. (2003) "Finance Causes Growth: Can We Be So Sure?" *Contributions to Macroeconomics*, Vol. 3, No. 1, article 12.

Maschke, E. (1966) "Deutsche Kartelle des 15. Jahrhunderts," in *Festschrift zum 65. Geburtstag von Friedrich Lütge* (74–87), eds. Willhelm Abel and Willi Alfred Boelcke. Stuttgart: Gustav Fischer.

(1969) "Outline of the History of German Cartels from 1873 to 1914," in *Essays in European Economic History, 1789–1914* (226–258), eds. F. Crouzet, W. Chaloner, and W. Stern. London: Edward Arnold.

Mattoo, Aaditya, Marcelo Olarreaga, and Kamal Saggi (2004) "Mode of Foreign Entry, Technology Transfer, and FDI Policy," *Journal of Development Economics*, Vol. 75, No. 1: 95–111.

Mayer, C. (1988) "New Issues in Corporate Finance," *European Economic Review*, Vol. 32: 1167–1188.

McCloskey, D. N. (1970) "Did Victorian Britain Fail?" *The Economic History Review*, Vol. 23, No. 3: 446–459.

(1999) "1066 and a Wave of Gadgets. The Achievements of British Growth," in *The British Industrial Decline* (27–44), eds. Jean-Pierre Dormois and Michael Dintenfass. London: Routledge.

McCraw, T. (1997) *Creating Modern Capitalism: How Entrepreneurs, Companies, and Countries Triumphed in Three Industrial Revolutions*. Cambridge, MA: Harvard University Press.

Merton, Robert C. and Zvi Bodie (1995) "A Conceptual Framework for Analyzing the Financial Environment," in *The Global Financial System: A Functional Perspective* (3–32), eds. Dwight Crane et al. Cambridge, MA: Harvard Business School Press.

(2005) "Design of Financial Systems: Towards a Synthesis of Function and Structure," *Journal Of Investment Management*, Vol. 3, No. 1: 1–23.

Michie, R. C. (1986) "The London and New York Stock Exchanges, 1850–1914." *The Journal of Economic History*, Vol. 46: 171–187.

(1990) "The Stock Exchange and the British Economy, 1870–1939," in *Capitalism in a Mature Economy. Financial Institutions, Capital Exports and British Industry, 1870–1939* (95–114), eds. Youssef Cassis and Jean-Jacques van Helten. Aldershot: Edward Elgar.

(1999) *The London Stock Exchange. A History*. Oxford: Oxford University Press.

Mitchell, B. R. (1983) *International Historical Statistics: The Americas and Australasia*. Detroit, MI: Gale Research Company.

(1992) *International Historical Statistics: Europe 1750–1988*. 3rd ed. New York: Stockton Press.

Miwa, Yoshiro and Mark J. Ramseyer (1999). "The Value of Prominent Directors: Lessons in Corporate Governance from Transitional Japan," Working Paper. University of Tokyo.

(2000) "Corporate Governance in Transitional Economies: Lessons from the Prewar Japanese Cotton Textile Industry," *Journal of Legal Studies*, Vol. 29, No. 1: 171–203.

(2002a) "The Value of Prominent Directors: Corporate Governance and Bank Access in Transitional Japan," *Journal of Legal Studies* vol. 31: 273–301.

(2002b) "Banks and Economic Growth: Implications from Japanese History," *Journal of Law & Economics*, University of Chicago Press, vol. 45: 127–164.

(2004) "Directed Credit? The Loan Market in High-Growth Japan," *Journal of Economics & Management Strategy*, Vol. 13, No. 1: 171–205.

Miyajima, Hideaki, Yusuke Omi, and Nao Saito (2003) "Corporate Governance and Performance in Twentieth Century Japan," *Business and Economic History* On-Line. https://h-net.org/~business/bhcweb/publications/BEHonline/2003/Miyajimaomi-saito.pdf

Modigliani, Franco and M. H. Miller (1958). "The Cost of Capital, Corporation Finance, and the Theory of Investment," *American Economic Review*, Vol. 48: 261–297.

Morck, Randall and Masao Nakamura (2005) "A Frog in a Well Knows Nothing of the Ocean: A History of Corporate Ownership in Japan," in *A History of Corporate Governance around the World: Family Business Groups to Professional Managers* (367–459), ed. R. Morck. Chicago: University of Chicago Press.

Motschmann, G. (1915) *Das Depositengeschäft der Berliner Großbanken.* Leipzig: Verlag von Duncker und Humblot.

Moussa, Hassouna and Jiro Obata (2009) "The Rise of the Current Banking System in Japan, 1868–1936." Tsukuba Economics Working Papers 2009–011, Economics, Graduate School of Humanities and Social Sciences, University of Tsukuba.

Mulherin, J. H., J. M. Netter, and J. A. Overdahl (1991) "Prices Are Property: The Organization of Financial Exchanges from a Trading Cost Perspective," *Journal of Law and Economics*, Vol. 34: 591–644.

Musacchio, Aldo (2008) "Do Legal Origins Have Persistent Effects over Time? A Look at Law and Finance around the World c. 1900." Working Paper. Harvard Business School.

Myers, S. and N. Majluf (1984) "Corporate Financing and Investment Decisions When Firms Have Information That Investors Do Not Have," *Journal of Financial Economics*, Vol. 13: 187–221.

Narayanan, M. P. (1985) "Managerial Incentives for Short-Term Results," *Journal of Finance* Vol. 40, No. 5: 1469–1484.

Navin, Thomas R. and Marian V. Sears (1955) "The Rise of a Market for Industrial Securities, 1887–1902," *The Business History Review*, Vol. 29, No. 2: 105–138.

Neal, Larry (1971) "Trust Companies and Financial Innovation, 1897–1914," *Business History Review*, Vol. 45, No. 1: 35–51.

Neuberger, H. (1977 [1974]) *German Banks and German Economic Growth from Unification to World War I.* New York: Arno Press.

Neuberger, H. and H. Stokes (1974) "German Banks and German Growth 1883–1913: An Empirical View," *Journal of Economic History*, Vol. 34: 710–731.

Nevin, Edward and E. W. Davis (1970) *The London Clearing Banks.* London: Elek Books.

Obstfeld, M. (1994) "Risk-Taking, Global Diversification, and Growth," *The American Economic Review*, Vol. 84: 1310–1329.

Obst, G. (1924) *Das Bankgeschäft.* 8th edition. Stuttgart: C. E. Pöschel.

Okazaki, T. (1993). "Senkanki no Kin'yu Kozo Henka to Kin'yu Kiki (The change of the financial structure and financial crisis during the wartime)," *Keiza Kenkyu*, Vol. 44: 300–310.

(1994) "Japanese Firm under Planned Economy," *Journal of Japanese and International Economies*, Vol. 7: 175–203.

(1999) *The Japanese Economic System and Its Historical Origins*. Oxford University Press.

(2001) "The Role of Holding Companies in Pre-War Japanese Economic Development: Rethinking Zaibatsu in Perspectives of Corporate Governance," *Social Science Japan Journal*, Vol. 4: 243–268.

Okazaki, Tetsuji and Masahiro Okuno-Fujiwara, eds. (1999) *The Japanese Economic System and Its Historical Origins*. New York: Oxford University Press.

Ollerenshaw, Philip (1987) *Banking in Nineteenth-Century Ireland: The Belfast Banks 1825–1914*. Manchester: Manchester University Press.

O'Rourke, Kevin (2001) "Globalization and Inequality: Historical Trends," *Annual World Bank Conference on Development Economics* (2001/2): 39–67.

Pagano, M. and P. Volpin (2005) "The Political Economy of Corporate Governance," *American Economic Review*, Vol. 95, No. 4: 1005–1030.

Papadimitriou, Dimitri (1996) "Stability in the US Financial System," in *Stability in the Financial System*, ed. D. Papadimitriou. New York: St. Martin's Press.

Passow, R. (1906) "Die Bedeutung des Aufsichtsrats für die Aktiengesellschaft," in *Thünen-Archiv*, vol. 1, no. 5, ed. R. Ehrenberg. Jena: Verlag von Gustav Fischer.

(1922) *Die Aktiengesellschaft. Eine Wirtschaftswissenschaftliche Studie*. Jena: G. Fischer.

Persson, Torsten and Guido Tabellini (2009) "Democratic Capital: The Nexus of Political and Economic Change," *American Economic Journal: Macroeconomics*, Vol. 1, No. 2: 88–126.

Plessis, Alain (1994) "The History of Bans in France," in *Handbook on the History of European Banks* (185–298). European Association for Banking History E.V. Aldershot: Edward Elgar.

Pohl, M. (1982) *Konzentration im Deutschen Bankwesen, 1848–1980*. Frankfurt: Fritz Knapp.

Pollard, Sidney and Dieter Ziegler (1992) "Banking and Industrialization: Rondo Cameron Twenty Years On," in *Finance and Financiers in European History, 1880–1960* (17–38), ed. Y. Cassis. New York: Cambridge University Press.

(1865) *Preussische Statistik*. Berlin.

Poschinger, H. V. (1971 [1879]) *Bankwesen und Bankpolitik in Preussen*. Glashütten im Taunus: Verlag Detlev Auvermann.

Pritchett, Lant (1997) "Divergence, Big Time," *The Journal of Economic Perspectives*, Vol. 11: 3–17.

Prowse, Stephen (1994) "Corporate Governance in an International Perspective: A Survey of Corporate Control Mechanisms among Large Firms in the United States, the United Kingdom, Japan and Germany." *BIS Economic Papers*, No. 41.

Quah, Danny (1993) "Empirical Cross Section Dynamics in Economic Growth," *European Economic Review*, Vol. 37, No. 2–3: 426–434.

Rajan, R. G. and L. Zingales (1998) "Financial Dependence and Growth," *American Economic Review*, Vol. 88: 559–586.

(1999) *The Politics of Financial Development*. Working paper. University of Chicago and NBER.

(2000) *The Great Reversals: The Politics of Financial Development in the 20th Century*. OECD Working Papers Vol. 8, No. 84.

(2003) "The Great Reversals: The Politics of Financial Development in the Twentieth Century," *Journal of Financial Economics*, Vol. 69: 5–50.

Rajan, Raghuram (1992) "Insiders and Outsiders: The Choice between Informed and Arm's Length Debt," *Journal of Finance*, Vol. 47: 1367–1400.

Ramakrishnan, R. and A. Thakor (1984) "Information Reliability and a Theory of Financial Information," *The Review of Economic Studies*, Vol. 51: 415–432.

Ramirez, Carlos D. (1999) "Did Glass-Steagall Increase the Cost of External Finance for Corporate Investment? Evidence from Bank and Insurance Company Affiliations," *The Journal of Economic History*, Vol. 59, No. 2: 372–396.

Reden, F. von (1848) *Zeitschrift des Vereins für Deutsche Statistik*, 2. Jahrgang, Berlin: F. Schneider und Companie.

Reis, J. (1994) *Handbook on the History of European Banks*. European Association for Banking History E.V. Aldershot: Edward Elgar.

(2000) "Bank Structures, Gerschenkron, and Portugal (Pre-1914)," in *The Origins of National Financial Systems: Alexander Gerschenkron Reconsidered* (182–204), eds. Douglas James Forsyth and Daniel Verdier. New York: Routledge.

Riesser, Jakob (1910) *Die Deutschen Großbanken und ihre Konzentration*. Jena: Verlag von Gustav Fischer. (English translation: *The German Great Banks and their Concentration*. Published by The National Monetary Commission. Washington: Government Printing Office, 1911.)

Rioja, Felix and Valev Neven (2004) "Does One Size Fit All? A Reexamination of the Finance and Growth Relationship," *Journal of Development Economics*, Vol. 74, No. 2: 429–447.

Riva, Angelo (2004) "The Competition between the Genoa and Milan Stock Exchanges before 1914: A View from Industrial Economics," Working Paper, University of Genoa.

(2005) "Competition Entre Places Financieres: Les Bourses De Milan Et De Genes A L'epoque Giolittienne, 1894–1913," PhD Dissertation, University of Orleans and University of Genoa.

(2009) "Le strutture sociali della regolazione delle Borse italiane nel XIX secolo," in *Credito e nazione in Francia e in Italia da fine '800 a fine '900* (359–387), eds. G. Conti, O. Feiertag, and R. Scatamacchia. Pisa: Edizioni Plus – Pisa University Press.

Robertson, R. M. (1968) *The Comptroller and Bank Supervision: A Historical Appraisal*. Washington, DC: Office of Comptroller of the Currency.

Robinson, J. (1952) "The Generalization of the General Theory," in *The Rate of Interest and Other Essays* (67–146). London: Macmillian.

Roe, M. (1993) "Some Differences in Corporate Structure in Germany, Japan and America," *Yale Law Journal*, Vol. 102: 1927–2003.

Rose, Mary B. (1994) "The Family Firm in British Business, 1780–1914," in *Business Enterprise in Modern Britain. From the Eighteenth to the Twentieth Century* (263–286), eds. Maurice W. Kirby and Mary B. Rose. London: Routledge.

(1999) "Networks, Values and Business: The Evolution of British Family Firms from the Eighteenth to the Twentieth Century," *Entreprises et Histoire*, Vol. 22: 16–30.

Ross, Duncan M. (1990) "The Clearing Banks and Industry – New Perspectives on the Inter-War Years," in *Capitalism in a Mature Economy. Financial Institutions, Capital*

Exports and British Industry, 1870–1939 (52–70), eds. Youssef Cassis and Jean-Jacques van Helten. Aldershot: Edward Elgar.

Rousseau, Peter (2003) "Historical perspectives on financial development and economic growth," *Federal Reserve Bank of St. Louis Review* (July): 81–106.

Rousseau, Peter and Richard Sylla (2003) "Financial Systems, Economic Growth, and Globalization," in *Globalization in Historical Perspective* (373–416), eds. Michael D. Bordo, Alan M. Taylor, and Jeffrey G. Williamson. Chicago: University of Chicago Press.

Rousseau, Peter L. and Paul Wachtel (1998) "Financial Intermediation and Economic Performance: Historical Evidence from Five Industrialized Countries," *Journal of Money, Credit and Banking*, Vol. 30: 657–678.

Rubinstein, M. (1981) "A Discrete-Time Synthesis of Financial Theory," *Research in Finance*, Vol. 3, No. 53: 53–102.

Sannucci, V. (1989) "The Establishment of a Central Bank: Italy in the 19th Century," in *A European Central Bank?* (244–289), eds. M. DeCecco and A. Giovannini. Cambridge: Cambridge University Press.

Sassi, Salvatore (1986) *La vita di una banca attraverso i suoi bilanci. Il Banco di Roma dal 1880 al 1933*. Bologna: il Mulino.

Sattler, H. (1977 [1890]) *Die Effektenbanken*. Vaduz, Liechtenstein: Topos Verlag.

Sayers, Richard Sidney (1952) *Banking in the British Commonwealth*. Oxford: Clarendon.

——— (1957) *Lloyds Bank in the History of English Banking*. Oxford: Clarendon Press.

Schneider, U. H. (1984) "Die Entwicklung des Bankenaufsichtsrechts," in *Standortbestimmung. Entwicklungslinien der deutschen Kreditwirtschaft* (83–111), ed. Deutscher Sparkassen- und Giroverband. Stuttgart: Deutscher Sparkassenverlag.

Schönitz, H. (1912) *Der Kleingewerbliche Kredit in Deutschland*. Karlsruhe: G. Braunsche Hofbuchdruckerei und Verlag.

Schultz, K. and B. Weingast (2003) "The Democratic Advantage: Institutional Foundations of Financial Power in International Competition," *International Organization*, Vol. 57: 3–42.

Schumacher, H. (1911) "Ursachen und Wirkungen der Konzentration im Deutschen Bankwesen," in *Weltwirtschaftliche Studien* (170–208). Leipzig: Veit.

Schumpeter, J. (1912) *Theorie der wirtschaftlichen Entwicklung*. Leipzig: Duncker & Humblot.

——— (1930) *Theory of Economic Development*. Cambridge, MA: Harvard University Press.

——— (1939) *Business Cycles*. New York: McGraw-Hill.

Sheppard, D. K. (1971) *The Growth and Role of UK Financial Institutions, 1880–1962*. London: Methuen.

Shleifer, Andrei and Robert W. Vishny (1997) "A Survey of Corporate Governance," *The Journal of Finance*, Vol. LII, No. 2: 737–783.

Shibagaki, K. (1966) "The Early History of the Zaibatsu," *The Developing Economies*, Vol. 4: 1973.

Simon, Miguel Cantillo (1998) "The Rise and Fall of Bank Control in the United States: 1890–1939," *American Economic Review*, Vol. 88, no. 5: 1077–1093.

Sirri, E. and P. Tufano (1995) "The Economics of Pooling," in *The Global Financial System: A Functional Perspective*, eds. D. Crane et al. Cambridge, MA: Harvard Business School Press.

Sombart, Werner (1903) *Die Deutsche Volkswirtschaft im Neunzehnten Jahrhundert.* Berlin: Georg Bondi.

(1909 and 1913). *Die Deutsche Volkswirtschaft im Neunzehnten Jahrhundert.* 2nd and 3rd editions. Berlin: Georg Bondi.

Spence, Michael (1973) "Job Market Signaling," *Quarterly Journal of Economics*, Vol. 87, No. 3: 355–374.

Statistisches Amt der Stadt Frankfurt a.m. 1903, 1906.

Statistisches Bundesamt Wiesbaden (1972) *Bevölkerung und Wirtschaft 1872–1972*, Stuttgart: W. Kohlhammer.

Statistisches Reichsamt (various years) *Statistik des Deutschen Reichs*, Berlin.

(various years) *Statistisches Jahrbuch für das Deutsche Reich*, Berlin.

Staub, H. (1900) *Kommentar zum Handelsgesetzbuch*, 6th edition. Berlin: W. de Gruyter.

Stein, Jeremy C. (1989) "Efficient Capital Markets, Inefficient Firms: A Model of Myopic Corporate Behavior," *Quarterly Journal of Economics*, Vol. 104: 655–669.

Stiglitz, J. E. and A. Weiss (1981) "Credit Rationing in Markets with Imperfect Information," *American Economic Review*, Vol. 71: 393–410.

Story, Jonathan and Ingo Walter (1997) *Political Economy of Financial Integration in Europe.* Cambridge, MA: MIT Press.

Stulz, Rene M. and Rohan Williamson (2003) "Culture, Openness, and Finance," *Journal of Financial Economics*, Vol. 70, No. 3: 313–349.

Sylla, R. E. (1982) "Monetary Innovation in America," *The Journal of Economic History*, Vol. 42: 21–30.

(1991) "The Role of Banks," in *Patterns of European Industrialization* (45–63), eds. Richard Sylla and Gianni Toniolo. London and New York: Routledge.

(1996) "The 1930s Financial Reforms in Historical Perspective," in *Stability in the Financial System* (13–25), ed. D. Papadimitriou. New York: St. Martin's Press.

(1999) "Shaping the US Financial System, 1690–1913: The Dominant Role of Public Finance," in *The State, the Financial System and Economic Modernization* (249–270), eds. Richard Sylla, Richard Tilly, and Gabriw Tortella. Cambridge: Cambridge University Press.

(2006) "Schumpeter Redux: A Review of Raghuram G. Rajan and Luigi Zingales's *Saving Capitalism from the Capitalists*," *Journal of Economic Literature*, Vol. 44: 391–404.

Tadesse, Solomon A. (2002) "Financial Architecture and Economic Performance: International Evidence," *Journal of Financial Intermediation*, Vol. 11, No. 4: 429–454.

Tamaki, Norio (1995) *Japanese Banking: A History, 1859–1959.* Cambridge: Cambridge University Press.

Teichova, Alice (1994) "Banking in Austria," in *Handbook on the History of European Banks* (1137–1161). European Association for Banking History E.V. Aldershot: Edward Elgar.

Teranisi, Juro (2000) "The Fall of the Tsisho Economic System," in *Finance, Governance, and Competitiveness in Japan* (43–63), eds. Masahiko Aoki and Gary R. Saxonhouse. Oxford: Oxford University Press.

Thakor, A. V. (1996a) "Capital Requirements, Monetary Policy, and Aggregate Bank Lending: Theory and Empirical Evidence," *Journal of Finance*, Vol. 51: 279–324.

(1996b) "The Design of Financial Systems: An Overview," *Journal of Banking & Finance*, Vol. 20: 917–948.

Thomas, Samuel Evelyn (1931) *British Banks & the Finance of Industry*. London: P.S. King & Son, Ltd.

Thomas, William Arthur (1973) *The Provincial Stock Exchanges*. London: Cass.

Thompson, F. (1963) *English Landed Society in the Nineteenth Century*. London: Routledge and Kegan Paul.

Tilly, R. (1965) "Germany (1815–1870)," in *Banking in the Early Stages of Industrialization* (151–82), ed. R. Cameron. London: Oxford University Press.

(1986) "German Banking, 1850–1914: Development Assistance for the Strong," *Journal of European Economic History*, Vol. 15: 113–151.

(1966) *Financial Institutions and Industrialization in the Rhineland, 1815–1870*. Madison: University of Wisconsin Press.

(1994a) "German Banks and Foreign Investment in Central and Eastern Europe before 1939," in *Economic Transformations in East and Central Europe* (201–230), ed. D. Good. New York: Routledge.

(1994b) "Banks and Industry: Lessons from History," Paper presented at European Economic Integration as a Challenge to Industry and Government. Münster, Germany.

(1995) "The Berlin Securities Exchange in national context: actors, rules and reforms to 1914," Working paper, University of Munster, Germany.

Tirole, J. (1988) *The Theory of Industrial Organization*. Cambridge, MA: MIT Press.

Tobin, J. (1969) "A General Equilibrium Approach to Monetary Theory," *Journal of Money, Credit, and Banking*, Vol. 1: 15–29.

Toniolo, G. (1977) "Effective Protection and Industrial Growth: The Case of Italian Engineering," *Journal of European Economic History*, Vol. 6: 659–673.

(1990) *An Economic History of Liberal Italy, 1850–1918*. London: Routledge.

Toniolo, Gianni, Leandro Conte, and Giovanni Vecchi (2003) "Monetary Union, Institutions and Financial Market Integration: Italy, 1862–1905," *Explorations in Economic History*, Vol. 40, No. 4: 443–461.

Tornell, A., F. Westermann, and L. Martinez (2004) "NAFTA and Mexico's Less-than-Stellar Performance," NBER Working Paper 10289.

Tortella, Gabriel (1994) "Optimal Contracts and Competitive Markets with Costly State Verification," *Journal of Economic Theory*, Vol. 21: 265–293.

Townsend, R. (1979). "Optimal Contracts and Competitive Markets with Costly State Verification." *Journal of Economic Theory* 21: 265–293.

Trebilcock, C. (1981) *The Industrialization of the Continental Powers 1780–1914*. New York: Longman.

Trew, Alex William (2006) "Finance and Growth: A Critical Survey," *The Economic Record*, Vol. 82, No. 259: 481–490.

Triner, Gail (2000–2001) private communication, e-mail.

Tronci, A. (1891) *Le operazioni e la materia di Borsa*. L. Roux, Torino-Roma.

U.S. Bureau of the Census (1960) *Historical Statistics of the United States, Colonial Times to 1957*. Washington, DC: Government Printing Office.

U.S. Congress. House of Representatives. Committee on Banking and Currency (1913) *Money trust investigation. (Pujo Committee hearings) Investigation of financial and monetary conditions in the United States under House resolutions nos.429 and 504, before a subcommittee of the Committee on Banking and Currency*. Washington, DC: Government Printing Office.

U.S. National Monetary Commission: Withers, Hartley & Palgrave, R. H. Inglis (1910) *The National Banking System*.

Verdier, Daniel (1997) "The Political Origins of Banking Structures," *Policy History Newsletter*, 2 pp. 1-6.

———— (2002) "Explaining Cross-National Variations in Universal Banking in 19th-Century Europe, North America and Australasia," in *The Origins of National Financial Systems: Alexander Gerschenkron Reconsidered* (23–42), eds. Douglas Forsyth and Daniel Verdier. London: Routledge.

Verlag für Börsen- und Finanzliteratur A.-G. (various years) *Saling's Börsen-jahrbuch*, Leipzig.

Volpi, Alessandro (2002) "Breve storia del Mercato Finanziario Italiano dal 1861 ad oggi," Carocci Editore.

von Falkenhausen, Bernhard Freiherr (1966) "Das Bankenstimmrecht im Neuen Aktienrecht," *Die Aktiengesellschaft*, Vol. 11, No. 3: 69–79.

———— (1967) *Verfassungsrechtliche Grenzen der Mehrheitsherrschaft nach dem Recht der Kapitalgesellshaften (AG und GmbH)*. Karlsruhe: C. F. Müller.

von Thadden, E. L. (1995) "Long-Term Contracts, Short-Term Investment and Monitoring." *Review of Economic Studies*, Vol. 62: 557–575.

Wagenblass, H. (1973) *Der Eisenbahnnau und das Wachstum der Deutschen Eisen- und Maschinenbauindustrie, 1835 bis 1860*. Stuttgart: Gustav Fischer.

Wagon, E. (1903) *Die Finanzielle Entwicklung Deutscher Aktiengesellschaften von 1870–1900*. Jena: Verlag von Gustav Fischer.

Walker, Francis (1876) *The Wages Question: A Treatise on Wages and the Wage Class*. New York: Holt.

Wallich, Paul (1905) *Die Konzentration im deutschen Bankwesen*. Stuttgart: Union deutsche Verlagsgesellschaft.

Warburg, P. M. (1910) *The Discount System in Europe, 61st Congress, 2nd session Senate Document 402*. National Monetary Commission. Washington, DC: Government Printing Office.

Watson, Katherine (1995) "The New Issue Market as a Source of Finance for the U.K. Brewing and Iron and Steel Industries, 1870–1913," in *The Evolution of Financial Institutions and Markets in Twentieth-Century Europe* (209–248), eds. Youssef Cassis et al. London: Scolar Press.

———— (1996) "Banks and Industrial Finance: The Experience of Brewers, 1880–1913," *The Economic History Review*, Vol. 49, No. 1: 58–81.

———— (1999) "Funding Enterprise: The Finance of British Industry during the Nineteenth Century," *Entreprises et Histoire*, Vol. 22: 31–54.

Watson, M (2002) "Britain's Financial System: A Help or a Hindrance to the 'New Economy'?" *New Economy*, Vol. 9, No. 3: 171–176.

Webb, D. (1992) "Two-Period Financial Contracts with Private Information and Costly State Verification," *The Quarterly Journal of Economics* (August): 1113–1123.

Webb, S. (1980) "Tariffs, Cartels, Technology, and Growth in the German Steel Industry," *Journal of Economic History*, Vol. 40, No. 3: 309–330.

Weber, A. (1915) *Depositenbanken und Spekulationsbanken*. 2nd edition. Leipzig: Duncker & Humblot.

Wellhöner, Volker (1989) *Großbanken und Großindustrie im Kaiserreich*. Göttingen: Vandenhoek-Ruprecht.

Whale, P. Barrett (1930) *Joint-Stock Banking in Germany*. London: Macmillan and Company.

White, E. N. (1986) "Before the Glass-Steagall Act: An Analysis of the Investment Banking Activities of National Banks," *Explorations in Economic History*, Vol. 23: 33–55.

White, Eugene Nelson (1983) *The Regulation and Reform of the American Banking System, 1900–1929*. Princeton, NJ: Princeton University Press.

White, H. (1980) "A Heteroskedastic-Consistent Covariance Matrix Estimator and a Direct Test of Heteroskedasticity," *Econometrica*, Vol. 48, No. 4: 817–829.

Wilson, P. (1994) "Public Ownership, Delegated Project Selection and Corporate Financial Policy," Working Paper. Indiana University.

Wirth, M. (1883) *Handbuch des Bankwesens*. 3rd edition, Cologne: Verlag der M. DuMont-Schauberg'schen Buchhandlung.

World Bank (1989) *World Development Report*.

Zamagni, Vera (1993) *The Economic History of Italy 1860–1990*. London: Oxford University Press.

Ziegler, D. (1993) "Zentralbankpolitische Steinzeit? Preußische Bank und Bank of England im Vergleich," *Geschichte und Gesellschaft*, Vol. 19, 475–505.

Index

acceptance credit, 19, 65
Acemoglu, D., 172, 177, 191
agricultural credit union, 21
Aktiengesellschaften. See joint-stock company
Aldcroft, D., 17
Allen, F., 7, 16, 151, 169, 200, 201
Amatori, F., 87
Anderson, B., 50
Ang, J., 204
Arellano, M., 209
Arestis, P., 208
asymmetric information, 1, 8, 113, 151, 169
   costs, 3
   mitigating problems, 2
   relationship to capital structure, 113
Augello, M., 34

Bagehot, W., 73
Baia-Curioni, S., 34, 35, 36, 37, 38, 39,
   40, 41
Baker, M., 60, 86, 98, 99
Baliga, S., 200
Banca Commerciale Italiana (Italy), 23, 37,
   56, 68, 78, 80, 92, 93, 106, 107, 108, 120,
   121, 123
Banca d'Italia. *See* central bank
Banca Generale (Italy), 37, 92
Banco di Roma (Italy), 92, 108
bank amalgamation, 50
bank attachment. *See* banking relationships
Bank Decree of 1890 (Japan), 69
Bank Holding Act of 1956 (US), 89
Bank Holding Company Act (1956) (US),
   142, 158
Bank of England. *See* central bank
   monopoly, 18

Bank of Japan. *See* central bank
Banking Act of 1826 (UK), 18
banking concentration, 4, 142
banking crises and failures. *See* banking
   panic
banking industry, organization of, 48–58,
   See also commercial banks:industrial
   organization
banking panic, 74
banking partnerships (United Kingdom), 18
banking relationships, 4, 5, 29, 84, 99, 102, 106,
   110, 143, 158–59, *See also* relationship
   banking
   comparison with arms-length banking, 144
Barnett, G., 51, 52, 63, 64, 74
Barone, G., 24
Barro, R.J., 204, 205
Baskin, J., 43
Bava, U., 56, 67
Becht, M., 88, 100, 134
Beck, T., 191, 204, 207, 208, 209
Berkowitz, D., 191, 204
Berlin Stock Exchange, 45
Besley, T., 166, 171, 172, 174
Bhide, A., 151
bills of exchange, 60, 65, 67, 115
bimetallic standard, 23
Bodenhorn, H., 135
Bodie, Z., 201
Bond, S., 70, 209
Boot, A., 151
Boot, A. W. A., 169, 200
Bordo, M., 205
Botticelli, P., 17
Boyd, J. H., 7
Braggion, F., 97, 129, 130

branching, 146–48
  commercial banking, 51
  Germany, 54
  international comparisons, 159
  Italy, 56
  Japan, 57
  networks, 48
  regulations (United States), 49, 52, 71
  United Kingdom, 50, 147
  United States, 51, 52, 75
Brandeis, L., 132
Britton, R., 6
Burhop, C., 32

Calomiris, C., 6, 51, 53, 62, 74, 88, 100, 131, 146, 148, 160
Capie, F., 8, 18, 19, 30, 51, 60, 72, 73, 74, 79, 98, 129, 170
capital markets. *See* stock exchanges
capital mobilization, 15, 49, 71, 76, 97, 216
capital structure (corporate), 2, 113, 114–16, 134
  in Italy, 120
  in Japan, 124–25
  in United Kingdom, 128
  in United States, 131–32
capital structure of banks, 59
  Germany, 66
  Japan, 70, 80, 124
  United Kingdom, 61, 72
  United States, 65
Carlin, W., 191
Carosso, V. P., 63, 64, 87, 89, 99, 100, 131, 132, 133
cartelization, 101
Caselli, F., 206
cash-asset ratio (banks), 71
Cassis, Y., 61, 97, 98
central bank, 76
  Banca d'Italia, 23
  Bank of England, 16, 18, 49, 77
  Bank of Japan, 25, 42
  Federal Reserve Bank (US), 27
  lender of last resort, 77
  Reichsbank (Germany), 20, 77, 170
Chakraborty, S., 200
Champ, B., 71
Chandler Act of 1938 (US), 89
Chandler, A. D., 3, 6, 89, 131
Cheffins, B., 87, 128
Christopoulos, D. K., 208
Clarkham, J. P., 89

Clayton Act of 1914 (US), 100, 133
Clough, S., 23
Code of Commerce of 1882 (Italy), 34, 36
Cohen, J., 22, 23, 24, 106, 123
Colli, A., 87
Collins, M., 8, 18, 30, 50, 51, 60, 85, 86, 98, 129
Comit. *See* Banca Commerciale Italiana (Italy)
commercial banks
  branching. *See* branching
  business methods, 59–71
  competition, 71–81
  concentration, 56, 58, *See* banking concentration
  in Germany, 20, 22, 90
  in Italy, 23, 67
  in Japan, 25, 57
  in United Kingdom, 18, 49, 51, 59, 61, 87, 97
  in United States, 28, 51, 62, 63, 65, 70
  industrial organization, 48–58
  performance, 71–81
  profit rate, 71, 81
Commercial Code (Japan), 41
Companies Act of 1862 (UK), 61
Companies Act of 1948 (UK), 87
concentration (banks), of. *See also* banking concentration
Confalonieri, A., 24, 37, 40, 56, 92, 93, 108
conflicts of interest (between debt and equity holders), 2, 4, 40, 112, 134
Consolidated Stock Exchange (U.S.), 44, 45
continuous market (stock exchange), 44
corporate performance (growth, profits), 117–20
  in Italy, 123–24
  in United Kingdom, 114
  in United States, 132–34
Cottrell, P., 31, 49, 50, 51, 60, 61, 62, 98, 128, 129
Cotula, F., 67, 217
creative destruction, Schumpeterian, 118
creative destruction, theory of.
  See Schumpeter, J.
Creditgenossenschaften (German cooperative credit societies), 21
Credito Italiano (Italy), 23, 56, 67, 68, 78, 80, 92, 93
Credito Mobiliare (Italy), 23, 37, 92
cross-country growth models. *See* economic growth, long run

Dahrendorf, R., 169
Davis, E., 50

Davis, L., 30, 31, 50, 85, 86, 135
debentures, 31, 86
debt-equity ratio, 103, 107, 115, 120
Deidda, L., 202
DeLong, J. B., 63, 88, 100, 133, 134, 204
DeMattia, R., 37
Demetriades, P. O., 208
Demirguc-Kunt, A., 207
Deutsche Bank (Germany), 54, 56
Dewatripont, M., 4, 7
Diamond, D., 2, 7, 151
Diaper, S., 61
Dietl, H., 7, 150, 164, 166, 171, 173, 176
Dimson, E., 30
Dintenfass, M., 17
dividends, 80, 118, 119, 123, 127
Djankov, S., 172
Donaubauer, K. A., 55

economic growth, long run, 192–97, 214
    Germany and Italy, 219
    international comparisons, 204–07
    relationship to financial development, 204
    time series evidence, 210
economies of scope (banking), 4, 146
Edelstein, M., 30
Edwards, G., 8
Edwards, J., 111
Ehrlich, E. E., 58
Elsas, R., 143, 144
equity stakeholding, 96, 110
Esquivel, G., 206
external finance. *See* capital structure

Fattouh, 202
Favarra, G., 209
Fear, J., 119, 202
Federal Reserve Bank. *See* central bank
Federico, G., 22, 24
Feldman, G., 101
Fenoaltea, S., 24
financial market microstructure, 29, 34, 39, 61
financial markets. *See* stock exchanges
financial statements, 72
financial structure, measures of, 177–87
financial system, development, 16–28
financing constraints, 116, 120–23,
    See liquidity constraints
First National Bank of New York (US), 99
Fohlin, C., 20, 21, 24, 32, 33, 40, 45, 46, 51,
    54, 55, 56, 66, 67, 72, 75, 77, 90, 101, 103,
    104, 107, 113, 114, 115, 116, 117, 118,

    119, 120, 123, 142, 143, 146, 147, 149,
    150, 170, 173, 189, 218
Frankl, J., 94, 127
Franks, J., 91, 96, 128
free bank (United States), 27
Freeman, S., 71
Freixas, X., 1
Fremdling, R., 20
futures contract, 32, 41

Gale, D., 2, 151, 169, 200, 201
Garbade, K., 38
Gaytan, A., 199
Gehrig, T., 33, 46
Gelman, S., 32, 33
Genoa Stock Exchange (Italy), 35, 38, 39, 40,
    See also stock exchanges
Gerschenkron, A., 5, 6, 7, 22, 23, 24, 67, 96,
    140, 143, 151, 166, 167, 168, 169, 173,
    174, 175, 176, 183, 188, 200, 227
    hypothesis on financial structure and
        growth, 166, 167–70
    hypothesis, empirical evidence on, 175–76,
        178, 179–83
Glass-Steagall Act (1933) (US), 62, 89, 140,
    142, 158
Goldman Sachs, 63
Goldsmith, R., 19, 22, 25, 26, 28, 42, 56, 58,
    65, 69, 70, 87, 91, 177, 180, 182, 184, 198,
    212, 214
Good, D., 175
Goodhart, C. A. E., 60, 61, 85
Gourvish, T. R., 128
Greasley, D., 17
great banks (Germany). *See* universal
    banks:Germany
Greenbaum, S., 4
Greenwood, J., 7
Großβanken. *See universal banks:Germany*
Guidi, M., 34
Guinnane, T., 21, 29

Hadley, E., 94
Hannah, L., 16, 128
Harley, C. K., 167
Harris, M., 2, 29
Hellwig, M., 2, 200, 201
Herrigel, G., 169
Heyn, U., 19
Hirschmeier, 94
Hoffman, W., 73, 111
honsha (Japan), 94, 109

Horn, N., 170
Hoshi, T., 26, 41, 42, 70, 81, 94, 150
house banking. *See* banking relationships
Hüffer, W., 91
Huttenback, R.A., 86
Hypothec (Kangyo) Bank (Japan), 26
Hypothekenbanken. See joint-stock mortgage bank (Germany)

Imuta, T., 124
incorporated banks (United Kingdom). *See* commercial banks
industrialization, 3, 15, 16–28, 140, 166
European spread of, 19
Germany, 21, 101
Italy, 22
Japan, 24
United Kingdom, 16
United States, 26, 62, 90
initial public offering, 89
United Kingdom, 18
interest-bearing mortgage bond, 21
interlocking directorates, 89, 96–110, 111, 126, 133, 160, 224
investment banks
in Germany, 66
in United Kingdom, 87
in United States, 63, 87
Investment Company Act of 1940 (US), 89
Italian Commercial Code of 1865, 34, 35

Japanese Commercial Code, amendment to (1908), 41
Jayaratne, J., 206
Jeidels, O., 5, 6, 143
Jensen, M., 2
Johnson, S., 172, 177, 191
joint–stock bank. *See* commercial banks
joint-stock commercial-investment bank. *See* universal banks: Germany
joint-stock company, 149
Germany, 20
Japan, 41
United Kingdom, 18, 30
joint-stock credit bank (Germany), 65, *See also* universal banks:Germany
joint-stock mortgage bank (Germany), 21, 115

Kanatas, G., 4
Kashyap, A., 26, 41, 42, 70, 81, 94, 110, 150
keiretsu (Japan), 150
Kennedy, W. P., 6, 8, 73, 128, 170

Kindleberger, C. P., 98
King, R. G., 5, 204, 205
Kingdom of Italy
unification, 23
Kirby, M., 16
Klebaner, B., 27, 28, 51
Knickerbocker Trust Company, 28
Kobrak, C., 202
Kocka, J., 170
Kotz, D. M., 88, 89, 99, 100, 132
Krahnen, J. P., 143, 144
Kroszner, R., 144, 147
Kugler, M., 208, 209
Kuhn, Loeb & Co, 63

La Porta, R., 9, 166, 171, 172, 173, 176, 191, 201, 202, 206
Laeven, L., 207
Lamoreaux, N., 29, 64, 112
Lanaro, S., 24
Landes, D., 17
Landschaften. See agricultural credit union
Lansburgh, A., 21
Lavington, F., 5
law and finance, 170–72
empirical evidence, 174–75, 176–77
Lefort, F., 206
legal origins, 170–72
empirical evidence, 178, 183
Lehman Brothers, 63
leverage
banks, 124
corporations, 116
Levine, R., 5, 11, 96, 150, 151, 157, 165, 177, 182, 184, 185, 191, 192, 200, 201, 202, 204, 205, 206, 207, 208, 209, 214, 218
Limited Liability Law of 1856 (UK), 50
Lindert, P. H., 196
liquidity constraints, 117–23
Lloyds Bank (UK), 97, 98
Loayza, N., 191, 208, 209
Loewenstein, A., 19
London and Westminster Bank, 49
London Stock Exchange (UK), 29, 30, 31, 41, 60, 129
Lopez-de Silanes, F., 9, 201
Lotz, W., 20
Luintel, K. B., 208

Maddison, A., 10, 178, 180, 193, 194, 195, 196, 197, 198, 219
Madhavan, A., 33

Majluf, N., 2
Maksimovic, V., 207
Manning, 206
market power, relationship to size of banks, 54
Marsh, P., 30
Martinez, L., 200
Maskin, E., 4, 7
maturity transformation, 19, 71, 73, 79
    maturity risk, 71
Mayer, C., 5, 91, 96, 128, 191, 206
McCloskey, D., 17
McCraw, T., 130, 131
McLiesh, C., 172
Meckling, W., 2
Merton, R. C., 201
Michie, R., 18, 30, 31, 43, 44, 45, 61, 128
Midland Bank (United Kingdom), 51, 97
Milan Stock Exchange (Italy), 34, 39
Miller, M., 2
Mitchell, B. R., 178, 180, 212, 214, 217
Mitsui Bank (Japan), 25, 57, 94
Miwa, Y., 94, 95, 96, 109, 124, 125, 126, 127
Miyajima, H., 96, 126
Modigliani, F., 2
monetary policy, Giolitti era (Italy), 38
Moore, L., 97, 99, 129
moral hazard, 5, 7, 112, 151, 200
Morck, R., 94, 95
Morgan, J. P., 63, 88, 90, 99, 100, 132, 133
mortgage bank (Japan), 26
Moussa, H., 69, 80
Mulherin, J., 44, 45
Musacchio, A., 30, 211
Myers, S., 2

Nakamura, M., 94, 95, 150
Narayanan, M., 4
National Bank Act of 1863 (US), 27
National Bank Act of 1876 (Japan), 25
National Bank Decree of 1872 (Japan), 80
National Banking Act of 1864 (US), 52, 62
National Provincial Bank (UK), 98
Navin, T. R., 131
Neal, L., 30, 31, 63
Neuberger, H., 19
Nevin, E., 50
New York Stock Exchange, 42, 43, 44, 45
    joint-account arbitrage, 45
    listing requirements, 43
    membership, cost of, 44
Nuesser, K., 208, 209
NYSE. *See* New York Stock Exchange

O'Rourke, K., 196
Obata, J., 69, 80
Obstfeld, M., 200
off-balance sheet operation, 61, 74
    Germany, 20
    Japan, 96
Ogilvie, S., 111
Okazaki, T., 41, 95, 109, 124, 127
Okuno, M., 95, 249
Ollerenshaw, P., 60
Oxley, L., 17

Pagano, M., 171, 174, 176
Passow, R., 91
pecking order. *See* capital structure
Persson, T., 166, 171, 172, 174, 191
Pfandbriefe. *See* interest-bearing mortgage
    bond
Pistor, K., 191
Pohl, M., 55
Polak, B., 200
political systems, relationship to growth,
    173–74
    empirical evidence, 176, 179, 183
preferred stock, 88
price setting in securities markets
    bank intervention in, 29
Pritchett, L., 196
proxy shareholding. *See* proxy voting
proxy voting, 84, 91, 96, 104, 108, 110, 111,
    117, 143, 144, 145, 154, 158, 159, 224
    Germany, 91–92
Public Utility Holding Act of 1935 (US), 89
Pujo Committee (US), 88, 100
pyramid-style holding company (Japan).
    See zaibatsu (Japan)

Quah, D., 206
qualitative asset transformation (QAT), 1

Rajan, R., 7, 161, 173, 177, 178
Rajan, R. G., 141, 161, 166, 173, 189, 191, 192,
    200, 201, 205
Ramakrishnan, R., 200
Ramirez, C. D., 62, 88, 100, 132, 133, 134
Ramseyer, M., 94, 95, 96, 109, 124, 125, 126, 127
Ranciere, R., 199
Raviv, A., 2
Ray, R., 200
Reichsbank. *See* central bank
Reinhold, S., 33
relationship banking. *See* banking relationships

return on assets (ROA), 72, 74, 77, 79, 81, 82, 119, 126, 223
return on Equity (ROE), 74
Richard, J. F., 191
Riesser, J., 3, 6, 20, 143
Rioja, 207
risk profile. *See* qualitative asset transformation (QAT)
Riva, A., 35, 36, 37, 38, 39, 40
Robertson, R. M., 52
Robinson, J., 191
Rochet, J., 1
Rose, M. B., 128
Ross, D. M., 98, 218
Rossi, S., 128
Rousseau, P., 205, 210, 213
Rubinstein, M., 97

Sannucci, V., 23
Sardinian Commercial Code of 1842 (Italy), 34
savings banks
  in Germany, 21
  in Japan, 26
  in US, 27
Sayers, R., 50
Schleifer, A., 9
Schönitz, H., 21
Schultz, K., 173
Schumpeter, J., 199, 204
Sears, M. V., 131
Second Empire (Germany, *Kaiserreich*)), 20
securitization. *See* maturity transformation
Sheppard, D.K., 19, 67, 73
Shibagaki, K., 58
Shleifer, A., 172, 201
short-term coverage ratio (banks), 71
Simon, M. C., 100, 101, 133
Sirri, E., 200
Smith, B. D., 7
Società Bancaria Italiana (Italy), 92
Sombart, W., 3
Sparkassen. *See* savings banks:in Germany
specialization of banking services, 11, 76
  United Kingdom, 60
  United States, 28, 62
Standard Oil Company, 88, 130
Staunton, M., 30
Stein, J., 4
Stock Exchange Act of 1874 (Japan), 41
Stock Exchange Act of 1878 (Japan), 41
Stock exchange law (Act no. 272) (Italy), 39

Stock exchange law of 1896 (Germany), 32
  1908 amendment to, 53,
stock exchanges, 7, 28, 29, 35, 46, 104
  barriers to entry, 37
  capital markets (United Kingdom), 29
  Germany, 32, 33
  Italy, 34, 36
  Japan, 41
  microstructure, 29
  Milan and Genoa, competition between, 38
  off-exchange trading, 44
  relationship to financial structure, 150–51
  technological innovations. *See* telegraph
  United Kingdom, 18
  United States, 43
stock exchanges, regulation of
  Germany, 32
  Japan, 41
  United Kingdom, 31
  United States, 45
stock returns, 33, 103, 118, 119, 126, 205, 243
Story, J., 7
Strahan, P., 144, 206
Sylla, R., 27, 89, 99, 131, 132, 161, 167, 205, 210, 213

Tadesse, S. A., 202
Tamaki, N., 41, 42, 57, 58, 69, 80
telegraph, 37
  atlantic cable, 44
Thakor, A. V., 5, 7, 151, 169, 200
Thirteenth National Bank (Japan), 95
Thompson, F., 97, 99
Thyssen, August, 119
Tilly, R., 6, 19, 86, 170
Tokyo Stock Exchange, 42
Toniolo, G., 22, 24, 35, 37, 38
Tornell, A., 200
Townsend, R., 2
Trew, A. W., 204
trust (financial institution), 28
  United States, 52, 63, 88
Tsionas, E. G., 208
Tufano, P., 200

unit banking, 49, 208
  in Germany, 54, 76, 147
  in Japan, 57
  in United States, 52, 160

United States Steel, 88, 99, 130
universal banks, 3, 48, 75, 112, 141–42, 156
  activities, 59
  board seats, importance, 6, 96, 98, 100, 102,
    107, 111, 145
  comparison with specialized banks, 142
  efficient scale, 48, 58
  financial markets, tradeoff, 7, 8
  Germany, 6, 10, 20, 21, 32, 54, 56, 65, 75, 77,
    90, 140
  Italy, 6, 10, 23, 56, 67, 68, 78, 92, 107
  Japan, 69, 93, 109
  measuring importance, 59
  relationship to arms-length systems, 5, 6,
    139
  resistance to, 8
  stock exchange involvement in, 40
  United Kingdom, 8, 10, 18, 61, 85
  United States, 10, 53, 62, 63

Valev, N., 207
varieties of capitalism, 8
Venezia, I., 4
Verdier, D., 20, 59, 166, 173, 174, 176, 177, 178,
  179, 183, 184, 185
Vishny, R.W., 9, 201
Volpi, A., 35, 36, 40
Volpin, P., 171, 174, 176
von Falkenhausen, B. F., 91
von Thadden, E., 4, 7
voting trust, use of, 88

Wachtel, P., 210
Wagner, J., 91
Walker, F., 27
Wallich, P., 6
Walter, I., 7
Warburg, P. M., 77
Watson, K., 31, 60, 98, 128, 129, 219
Watson, M., 16, 18
Webber, A., 19, 72, 73
Weber, A., 74, 77
Weingast, B., 173
Wellhöner, V., 101, 102
Westermann, F., 200
Whale, P., 3, 6, 21
White, E.N., 51, 52, 62, 63, 64
Williamson, J. G., 196, 204
Wilson, P., 7
Wilson, R. G., 128

Yamaguchi, K., 96, 110
Yankee houses, 63
Yokohama Specie Bank (Japan), 26
Yui, 94

zaibatsu (Japan), 93, 94, 95, 96, 109, 124, 125,
  126, 129, 150
Zamagni, V., 23
Zervos, S., 157, 165, 184, 185, 204, 205, 206, 208
Ziegler, D., 73, 170
Zingales, L., 141, 161, 166, 173, 177, 178, 189,
  191, 192, 202, 205, 206, 207

1999, Caroline Fohlin, Johns Hopkins University. *Mobilizing Money: How the World's Richest Nations Financed Industrial Growth*

2000, J. Bradford De Long, University of California, Berkeley. *A Quantitative Account of Globalization*

2001, Barry Eichengreen, University of California, Berkeley. *International Capital Markets in the 20th Century*

2002, Masanao Aoki, University of California, Los Angeles, and Hiroshi Yoshikawa, University of Tokyo. *Reconstructing Macroeconomics: A Perspective from Statistical Physics and Combinatorial Stochastic Processes*

Printed in the United States
By Bookmasters